SOUL
STEPS

Cathryn L. Taylor, MA, MFT, LADC

ISBN-13: 978-1719496100
ISBN-10: 1719496102

PRINTED BOOKS BY CATHRYN

Cathryn's bestselling *The Inner Child Workbook*— (Available at Barnes and Noble, amazon.com)

Life Beyond Confusion and Fear

… an overview of the four stages of addiction and recovery…

Maximized

… a shamanic tale about a road trip with her dog named Max…

Which Lifetime Is This Anyway?

… a metaphysical bible for multidimensional healing…

Soul Steps

… an innovative 90-day Program integrating body, mind, heart, and Soul … and introducing "conscious aerobic exercise."

Share the Gift

Introducing Cathryn's *Seven-layer Healing Process* featuring her signature "Interactive Tapping™". This Process <u>is</u> applied to Attracting Intimate Relationships; Attracting Abundance; Attracting Right Livelihood and Developing Reciprocal Partnerships with Inner Child Work and EFT.

Beyond Compassion

… a program which teaches you how to *"Access your Point of Power in Response to Loss …* "(Inspired by the author's personal losses)

Accept Who You Are! Get What You Want!

… a seven-layer healing formula that takes you into self-acceptance and depicts the connection between this acceptance and the ability to attract all that you desire. Includes a 30-day EFT/Inner Child video program!

All books are available through Cathryn's website-
www.EFTForYourInnerChild.com

In addition, her YouTube channel, which can be accessed at: https://www.youtube.com/user/ctinnerchildwork, has over 100 Educational videos demonstrating her unique style of energy therapy she calls, Interactive Tapping™ Also you can tune into Cathryn's Internet-based Radio show on EFT Radio called, EFT for Your Inner Child and Soul, and on BBM Radio entitled, EFT for Spiritual Fitness.

DEDICATION

This book is dedicated to the following men and women—
special Angels who run on this earth.

I call them my Angels because they are part of **my** Healing Team—
called into **my** inner world—the world of the unseen.

Maya Angelou—for holding the vibration of a Crone like a Queen;

Hal Zina Bennett—for connecting me with the spirit of Wolf;

Dr. Wayne W. Dyer—for his power of intention;

Melissa Etheridge—for putting verse and song to Why I Run!

Shelly Farley—for believing in the value of this work;

Dr. Jason Fredericks—for instilling the confidence to succeed;

Esther and Jerry Hicks—for mainstreaming the *Teachings of Abraham*

Lynn Grabhorn—for combining Recovery with Abraham' Teachings

Shirley MacLaine—for going out on a limb; **Dan Millman**—for being
a peaceful warrior; **Tina Turner**—for being Tina Turner;

Oprah Winfrey—for her willingness to make public what most choose
to hide.

Most of those above do not know my name.

But my heart has been touched and my path inspired by their presence
on this earth. For this I am grateful.

Special Acknowledgments

I want to thank my brother, **John Taylor,** for his support and encouragement with this project; **Cathy, Pierre, Mikal, Taylor and Thomas Allan Cremas,** for enveloping me in their hearts; **Laurel King,** for her continued friendship and feedback; **Darlene Turner** for her touch of the Divine; **Dahna Fox** for inspiration and friendship; **Arthur Anczarski**—my Soul's other half—for helping me retrieve my heart, expand my mind, and learn to revere my body; **Deanna Petron** and **Karen Maskell,** for their editorial wizardry; **Jennifer Forrest,** for running the trails with me. **Jodi Taylor,** my sister-in-law, a true *soul-stepper* who embodies the essence of *Taylor-Strong.* And last but not least, my mother, **Gladys Taylor,** who will always be my one special angel.

In addition—I have now completed four marathons—one in each of the four corners of my world. As I accomplished this task I anchored the essence of the elements from each of these directions into the essence of my body, mind, heart, and Soul. By doing so I honored the physical, mental, emotional and spiritual dimensions of my being. I learned how to simultaneously step from the heart of my Soul into the four corners of all I have ever been.

I did not do this alone. I want to thank… My God-child, **Lillian Berger,** for holding the heart of my Soul; for crowning me Crone at Grandma's Marathon as I anchored in the spiritual essence of the **North** and for running me to the finish line in San Francisco as I claimed the fluidity offered from the emotionally-infused direction of the **West.**

My niece, **Michelle Tabor,** for gathering my weary one and running her across the finish line at Grandma's.

My friend and co-worker, **Nancy Kaley,** for so much more, but most specifically, for being at the end of the New York marathon and helping me honor the direction of the **East** as I re-programmed the DNA of my mind and belief systems.

My niece, **Cathy Cremas** and my god-child, **Thomas Allan Cremas,** for combining their first 5k with my fourth marathon in New Orleans where we not only paid tribute to the physical body of Mother Earth by participating in this fund-raising event for the survivors of Hurricane Katrina but also paid tribute to the direction of the **South** which holds the essence of the physical body and houses the energy of the inner children. Having completed my tribute to the four directions, I then set my sights on participating in the Breast Cancer 3-day 60-mile event in 2008 as a way to celebrate my sixtieth year on this planet. Between now and then...only God and Mother Earth know! And so it is...and so it is...June 9th, 2006

WHAT OTHERS SAY ABOUT THIS WORK

The best part about working this program was getting to know myself on all levels...I was able to understand my past challenges and why I react to certain situations the way I do. I have been able to apply what I learned to all of my relationships with my husband to my children to my co-workers and friends...

Michelle, Airline Stewardess

Cathryn's program has had a profound effect on the way I respond to myself. In the past, compulsive behaviors, self-deprecating thoughts and my relationship with my body kept me stuck, numb and negative. In this program, I learned how to re-direct my energy to daily workouts, self-acceptance, and physical health.

Nancy, Addictions Counselor

I have achieved more in these past several months than I could have possibly imagined. I truly can hardly believe the shifts in my life and consciousness—it is so amazing. If it wasn't for this program I know I'd still be caught up in a lot of old patterns that have been holding me back for so long. I will be able to utilize these tools throughout my life, as new lessons emerge.

Christy, Massage Therapist

I began working with Cathryn in December of 2003 on inner child issues, as I was a very insecure and angry 45-year old man. After about a year and a half, our work moved onto spirituality. Since then I am 35 pounds lighter and have integrated spirituality into a personalized workout routine, I no longer need external validation and feel accepted and accomplished.

Bruce, Sales, and Marketing Manager

We are extremely grateful for this program and for Cathryn. This powerful regimen, combined with Cathryn's honesty and intuition, has given us the opportunity to re-develop our relationship from its core. Individually we have each learned to step into our own power, healed old patterns and used conscious exercise to reconnect to our own intuition. As a couple, we have developed more compassion for each other and our children. There is not one area of our lives which has not been touched by this work.

Jennifer and Douglas, Health and Wellness Educator and Software Consultant

BEFORE YOU READ

I INVITE YOU TO PARTICIPATE IN THIS FIRST ACTIVITY

Imagine you are writing your life story—the book about your life. Now think for a moment…what would you call it and which individuals would you honor in your dedication?

Before you answer, take a moment to consider the following… Whom do you admire? What individuals have touched you—inspired you—protected you—assisted you?

Responding to the above helps you begin to construct your own Healing Team just as each of the men and women acknowledged in the dedication have, at different times in my life, inspired and mentored me in the unseen. They are not aware of this, but when I am on my daily run or walk I talk to them as if they are right by my side. I ask for guidance. I listen. I emulate. I mimic. If I am in a situation and am confused about how to most effectively proceed, I pretend they give me direction and guidance. It is for this reason I was inspired to dedicate my book to them. Each has his or her special place on my healing team. I have others on my Healing Team, as well. There are Angels, relatives, and power animals. There are spiritual figures and characters from books, movies, and plays.

It became apparent to me a long time ago that we grow and expand by following the example of others…by acting as if we are those that we admire…by practicing the traits of those beings who inspire, protect, and challenge. We may know them—we may not. They may be real or exist in our imagination…but their essence touches our lives. We model ourselves after them. We season our personality with their traits and create the recipe for our own unique character. Drawing from those we admire augments the cookbook from which we can draw. It expands the possibilities available to us from our own personal smorgasbord of choices that can dictate, moment-to-moment, the person we want and choose to be.

Once you have given this sufficient thought—record your responses in some manner so that later you can add these pages to the special journal you ill be using as you work the exercises in your Soul Steps program.

AUDIO OVERVIEWS
FOR THE KINDLE FORMAT

A Personal Welcome Audio .....

A word about the components of the program ...

Recording your progress ...

And so the process begins ...

Overview of Month One!

THE ESSENCE OF "CONSCIOUS-AEROBIC EXERCISE"

It has been said we have all been all things.

If this is indeed true...

> *...then our Higher Power must hold the blueprint for true mastery... and our Higher Self must hold the key.*

If this is indeed true...

> *...then for every memory of abandonment, our Higher Power must hold a blueprint of union; for every incident of abuse, there must be a memory of empowerment and safety. Every expression of rebellion can, therefore, be softened by remembering how to speak our truth without fear.*

If this is indeed true...

> *...the time has come for us to remember...to consciously bring forth the aspects of our Higher Self who hold the seeds for our abundance, grace, energetic and illumined physical forms, fulfilled relationships, and a livelihood which expresses our highest good.*

If this is indeed true...

> *It is time to remember and give birth to our ever-evolving future self.*

Your Soul Steps Program invites you to use *conscious-aerobic exercise* as a way to remember. The structure transforms you—each day building on the next—helping you to remember—to invent—to reclaim—to realign—until the day arrives when you simultaneously step from the heart of your Soul into the four corners of all you have ever been.

Contents

THE PREFACE

Introduction

SOUL STEPS INVITES you to step into your future self. It suggests that deep within every cell a spark of your Soul awaits ignition. When you awaken your body, mind, and heart through the activity of aerobic exercise you vibrationally connect with that spark and bring into alignment all four dimensions of your being. If you infuse that alignment with deliberate thought and intention you create the platform needed to attract all you desire and deserve. It is that simple. When the body is in motion it activates each cell to receive every intention—conscious or unconscious—your mind, heart, and Soul transmits. It brings to the surface any voice or wound which does not resonate with that higher desire and makes it available for resolution and transformation.

Presented as Twelve Modules this program inspires you on a day-to-day basis to not only ignite those sparks of mastery but also provides a way to keep the flame burning at the intensity needed to guarantee success in whatever you pursue. Module by Module you are assisted in identifying the strengths and challenges which support your success. The structure itself wards off the threat of your becoming overwhelmed and makes your inner work manageable and systematic. It is this very structure which allows your infant self to relax and trust...gives your toddler within something against which to separate...your shameful and guilt-ridden self a way to forgive and move into compassion. The three days of ceremony before and after your twelve-week regimen bookends your process and ritualizes its benefits thus honoring not only *your* body, mind, heart, and Soul but the body, mind, heart and Soul of Mother Earth as well.

As you begin this process you'll find you will draw from previous experiences. If you currently exercise you have perhaps felt that expansive moment in your aerobic activity when your body releases a rush of endorphins and you feel the exaltation of pure ecstasy. It is a moment of total harmonious commitment to the activity at hand as you merge into the elements and animal instincts of Mother Earth. It is as if you are running with the wind…dancing on the wings of the Angels. It is as though you are galloping like a stallion, leaping with the grace of a deer…as if you possess the focus of a lion as it chases its prey… or you are transposed into any animal essence which appeals and speaks to you. No matter how you personally experience that moment, there is some invisible boundary which dissolves and allows you to melt into absolute alignment with the Universe…and when you are aligned with the Universe you are stepping from the heart of your Soul and are connected with all the Souls of the Universe.

The first time I was conscious of this universal connection was in 2003 at the Twin Cities, Susan G. Komen, *Race for the Cure,* breast cancer event. I remember this experience very distinctly.

> *As my running partner and I waited for the run to start I said a sacred prayer and consciously connected my heart and mind to my Higher Guidance and Universal Consciousness. The run progressed. The endorphins began to flow. I became aware of the pitter-patter of feet hitting the pavement. Suddenly I heard this parallel echo. I realized there was another event going on right above us—in the next dimension. This group of spirits—those who were being honored on this plane were running—in celebration and appreciation—right along with us. This parallel event was simultaneously taking place just on the other side of my immediate awareness. I could feel the energy—the enthusiasm—the appreci-ation—the reciprocation.*

It was awesome; heartfelt, tearful, and profound to realize that when we participate in fund-raising events such as this, that those who we honor join us and match our efforts with their own.

I consciously began to connect to that universal oneness and my higher guidance every time I worked out. Magic occurred. I experienced pure, unadulterated joy—and a sense of complete mastery. Anything I envisioned or contemplated during my workout time manifested more precisely in my life. I came to understand the power of this bio-chemically infused, peak, spiritual moment, and thus the concept of "conscious aerobic exercise" was conceived.

Conscious-aerobic exercise occurs when you optimize on the time spent exercising by using this 30–45 minutes or more a day to simultaneously commune with your Angels, say your prayers, and with deliberate intent, invite issues which need to be addressed to be made known. In the presence of your Masters, Teachers, Angels and Loved Ones you can receive guidance and assistance on transforming any adversity and be given direction on how to most effectively proceed. Often my guidance would even nudge me in certain directions with respect to my exercise regimen or my food plan. They would bring just the right person into my life who would introduce me to a new approach, tool or supplement.

One such example was when I was introduced to the overall effectiveness of *rebounding*, a form of exercise which involves a gentle bouncing on a small trampoline; the necessity of a good water filter system and the need for supplementation. Resources for the products I have found useful are included in the last pages of this manual. Rebounding as a form of exercise is covered in more detail under the section entitled: Program Commitments.

I encourage you to do your own research and find supplemental programs which speak to you. In this day and age when our environment and food sources are so compromised it is essential to support our bodies through appropriate supplementation; proper hydration and an effective cellular and aerobic exercise regimen.

Your Soul Step *"Conscious Aerobic Exercise"* Program outlined in the following pages is a distillation of my discoveries and experiences.

It has been three years in the writing but a lifetime in the making. The structure itself has been integrative and empowering. Over time I came to realize, that when my *well-fueled* body was in motion, I was aligned with Spirit, had set my intention for clarity and became quiet enough to listen—I was escorted to the other side of any issue successfully.

I hope it offers you the same. I hope this format inspires you to step into your future self and view your world from the eyes of your Soul—for when we have the courage to do so—every step is filled with passion and every mile with magic.

Cathryn Taylor, Valentine's Day, 2006

Overview

THE STRUCTURE OF your Soul Step Program outlined in the following pages allows you to design a viable, day-by-day plan. It assists you in weaving your physical and professional goals with the spiritual aspirations inspired by your Higher Power and higher guidance.

Within the privacy of your own home and with enhanced support via phone you will:

1. Identify antiquated belief systems.
2. Resolve the emotional challenges of abandonment, inability to set boundaries, fear of guilt or sense of shame.
3. Be encouraged to examine your issues of self-consciousness, passivity or rebellion and your struggle with bringing forth that which you sense you were put here to share.

The regimen provides you with a way to be held accountable daily and supported weekly. The format is designed to act as a midwife, of sorts, assisting you in giving birth to the future you. It welcomes the scared, lonely and tired parts within to be seen, comforted and healed. It provides the day-to-day structure needed to come home to your body in a way never before known, to connect with Mother Earth in sacred ceremony and to embrace your Higher Power with renewed faith and undying trust.

The Promise of Conscious Aerobic Exercise

Many of us go to church on Sundays or do our meditations behind closed doors but, for the rest of the day, divert our energies to getting by—pretty much forgetting about our bodies and sometimes even our spiritual pursuit. We may engage in the activity of exercise but only in conjunction with a distraction such as watching television or listening to the radio or a tape. The goal is not to be consciously connected to the physical activity but rather to distract or entertain the rational mind long enough to complete this act of physical discipline. Surely, this approach is better than no approach. Your body does benefit and your physical health reaps the rewards of such sacrifice.

When you commit to a specific goal, this program helps you infuse that goal with a more holistic intention— taking that goal beyond the physical achievement to one which incorporates not only your body but your mind, heart, and Soul as well.

This program is built on the premise that every time you show up for your workout your body offers you the opportunity to exercise in a more holistic way. In this day and age, when many of us are attempting to operate in a unified and integrated manner, we can weave the components of physical exercise, emotional well-being, and spiritual pursuit together through the commitment to a regular regimen of *Conscious Aerobic Exercise.*

If you are conscious of your exercise and simultaneously use that time to consciously connect to your Higher Power while being open to allowing your unresolved emotions to emerge, you can experience your workout as so much more than just stretching and taxing your muscles. The mere act of extended exercise escorts you through the aches and pains experienced as you challenge your body to move from one level of fitness to another.

On a meta-level, a parallel process is taking place. From an emotional, mental and spiritual perspective, extended exercise mimics the process occurring when we wash a load of dirty laundry. No matter how soiled we feel when we begin our exercise routine, we are always assured that, if we endure aerobically, we will be spun back into that vibration of joy. The wash cycle, lasting for about the first 30 minutes, loosens the issues—the dirt of our life. The rinse cycle cleanses these issues and prepares our internal garment for the vibrational shift. The spin cycle realigns our energies and alters our electromagnetic field.

Remember: The weave and integration of the physical, emotional, mental and spiritual intentions pave the way for you to not only experience but to also sustain joy. They provide you with the opportunity—every time you show up for your workout—to step into the vibration of joy. It is this vibration which holds the capacity to heal.

A Bird's Eye View Of The Weave

My introduction to exercising with my higher guidance began on the morning of my 54th birthday when I sat down for my daily meditation. Turning 54 was a milestone. I asked my Higher Teachers how I could best use the upcoming year as a platform for the rest of my life.

In the next several days three events co-mingled to inspire me to train for my first marathon. I chose Grandma's Marathon scheduled in Duluth, Minnesota on Summer Solstice. I had never before exercised with such spiritual and deliberate intent. At the beginning of each training session, I blended this physical goal with my spiritual pursuit and the wisdom and guidance of my Higher Power.

Changes were abundant. The discipline of exercise gave my body the chance needed to realign itself. Sensitivities and allergies, which had developed in response to the hormonal changes of menopause, balanced themselves out. Muscles remembered what it meant to be fit.

Changes were not only in the physical realm; I had set the intention for all parts of me to cross that finish line—not just my body. I revisited old belief systems determining which ones remained useful and which ones needed to be replaced or discarded. I invited the inner children who had unexpressed feelings to make those feelings known so I could heal and revere them.

The more I ran and trained the more integrated I became. Being caught in the constant flow of movement enabled me to go into an altered state of consciousness for an extended period of time. The insights and connections which evolved during these workouts were amazing and began to filter into my day-to-day life as I became more and more anchored into my physical form. What is just as amazing to me is how my own body, via the commitment I made to an exercise regimen, not only gave me the opportunity to experience the vibrational frequency of joy but when I failed to retain that frequency, it provided me with a surefire way to step back into that vibration. I have come to understand our bodies never let us down. They also never lie.

Pain And Joy—Opposite Sides Of The Same Coin

If you can embrace pain while at the same time daring to feel joy, you acquire the opportunity to sustain the healing, vibrational frequency of joy. To more fully embody joy, you must be willing to embrace your pain. The two emotions exist on the same frequency— they are just at opposite ends of the spectrum…the more depth to your pain, the more depth to your joy. The deeper your fear, the deeper your faith when you come back into the light. The richness of your pain becomes the fertilizer by which your joy can be nourished.

I integrated my spiritual practice into each workout by deliberately setting my intention to do so and by asking what needed to be cleared. Resistances and blocks which emerged during the pursuit of this endeavor were addressed and guidance on resolution received. The hours of training provided the arena in which I could process my inner blocks. One by one they cleared and I found myself able to sustain more joy.

Our ability to feel joy is not built on emotions alone. Our bodies have an even greater gift for us.

No matter how we feel when we begin an extended session of physical exertion we are guaranteed, after 30 to 45 minutes of aerobic exercise, a biochemical release in our brains which provides a renewed sense of well-being. This biochemical element is the release of endorphins. Endorphins are the body's natural pain-killer.

I soon came to realize no matter what mood I was in when I began my workout—if I just stayed with it—I ended up being able to step back into the vibration of joy. My commitment to my physical workouts which resulted in the release of the endorphins combined with the infusion of spiritual intent and willingness to run to and through my emotions of that day WAS JOY!

Remember: No matter what you determine to be your physical goal, no matter how you define aerobic exercise for yourself, if you approach it holistically, your commitment will not only enhance your ability to seek joy but will also pave the road for you to sustain it.

The Role Of Your Body

A unique component offered in this program is the opportunity to integrate the healing of your psychological issues and spiritual challenges into a daily regimen of exercise. Why exercise and why the focus on the body? The advantage, as well as the difficulty, in working with our body is that our bodies do not lie. They are constantly sending us messages providing clues to the issues we need to heal in order to become whole. They send us messages through our allergic reactions to ingestants and toxins in our day-to-day environment. They send us messages through our ailments and addictions; through our weight loss and our weight gain. They are constantly providing us with the information we need to decode the memories of our past so the traumas they store can once and for all be resolved. Unfortunately, we cannot understand our body's messages if we do not understand the language our body speaks.

Before we continue it may help to have some understanding of how our body stores pain. The psyche experiences traumas. These traumas can be a result of neglect, sexual or physical abuse or mental cruelty through shame and belittlement. In response to these traumas, irrespective of their origin, the system goes into shock. If the response to these traumas is not processed and emotionally released, we either dissociate from the emotion of the event or bury recall of the event, thus banishing the memory deep into the unconscious mind. The stress of these traumas, however, gets recorded in the electrical systems of our bodies and the body and mind collude in keeping us stuck.

The end result is that maladaptive habits develop which prohibit us from living the life we want and deserve to live. For instance, the scent of tobacco or your reaction to sugar can trigger the memory of a past trauma and your body responds to the stress in the same electrical manner in which it responded at the time of the actual event. Your body actually re-experiences the event every time the same associated stimulus is encountered, thus giving you a daily opportunity to relive, confront and resolve the residual stress related to your past trauma.

These reactions can also get stored in the electrical systems of our etheric bodies and be carried from one lifetime to the next. For example, a Soul wound which is stored in the physical body may be detected when you find yourself reacting with a "fight or flight" response to a relatively common every-day event. Your body is simply responding physiologically to a Soul wound of which your personality has no conscious awareness. If you are interested in this line of thinking it is covered in more detail in a later section.

If you have participated in traditional counseling you may have witnessed how the therapeutic relationship can provide the tools needed to communicate with the experiences of your past. A therapist can help you connect your body sensations to the events that originally occurred. Processing the emotions of these events is certainly an important step of the resolution. You may have also applied spiritual tools, such as those found in 12-Step programs. This, too, is important. Using prayers and affirmations is vital to overall healing.

Yet, it is as if dealing with our body issues is one of the last frontiers, because in order to heal them we often need to respond to them in a multidimensional manner. We need to not only decipher the emotional triggers but also gain an understanding of the belief systems which accompany and feed those triggers. We need to not only pray and work with these issues in the spiritual realm, we need to also intervene physically and get assistance with our allergies, addictions, and ailments. Bottom line is that we need to intervene in the electrical systems which hold the trauma in the first place.

Perhaps even more important is that we stay aware of the fact that issues with our bodies are the most difficult to resolve simply because they are the most accurate barometer as to how we are anchoring divine light and spiritual intention into our physical forms. They provide us with the most immediate feedback and, if befriended and revered, can offer our most valuable clues for healing. The process of exercise brings these issues to the forefront.

We cannot progress in any exercise regimen without bumping into the issues held in our bodies.

It is for this reason exercise is such a vital component of your Soul Steps Program.

Exercise is a surefire way to trigger the challenges needing to be healed as the very process of exercise invites you to clear the path to your joy.

What You Can Expect

You are being invited to embark on a journey whose structure assists you in moving forward in your growth…invited to confront that which keeps you from humbly standing in your light. Each of us has an aspect or habit which lures us away from the beam of light— tantalizing us with the vibration of the ego-induced "spot-light!" The quest is to discover how that aspect feeds on our fear of abandonment; our challenge with setting and accepting boundaries and limits; our shame and guilt; our productivity versus our procrastination; our self-consciousness versus self-confidence; our rebellion versus our surrender; and our fragmentation versus integration.

This journey brings each of you to the dawning of your new self—a self whose inner mechanics are spiritually-infused, not built on the socialization of the childhood ego which demanded the internal structure give way to societal socialization. Childhood was a time when maladaptive coping mechanisms emerged; dysfunctional patterns were imprinted and you developed your persona accordingly—as a reflection of others. Your sense of self was not an expression of your authentic self. It was built on "should's," needs, and assumptions.

But then you awaken.

Some life event pulls you into remembering. You begin to experience the conflict/tension of being separated from your true self…and that separation throws you onto this unknown journey. Brick by brick you begin to tear down your faulty foundation and begin the process of reconstructing a base which reflects your true destiny and course.

Some of you are just beginning this process. For you, the structure of the program will be welcomed, celebrated—and this manual itself will feel complete—because self-discovery is all new. The structure is new; the accountability with a buddy is new; the process sessions are new, and establishing an exercise program or food plan is new.

Others of you will be mid-stream. You will find the structure familiar, yet refreshing. It will serve to help you remember where you have been—help you re-invent yourself while you revise and redirect where you want to go. You have been on the path before—but have gotten off track—seduced by the field trips of your life which became a detour from your true journey.

Then there are those who have already been there—those of us who are the seasoned ones—we have seen the top of the mountain— have challenged the past, built on the present, and have tasted the fruits of our labors.

We have successes in our life—perhaps many successes—but there is one area of our life which no longer makes sense. It pulls us off course—sometimes becomes stronger than the rest of us— and for those moments we feel as though that is all we are. That exact moment is often filled with shame and a fear of exposure. It is filled with "should" statements—"I *should* know better…, I *should* be beyond this…I *should* not have to deal with this…" There is a dichotomy between the accomplished self and this pathetic, wounded self and we wonder if that experience will ever end.

When we, as the seasoned ones, come up against this self we have come into relationship with what I call the ***cherished saboteur™***. This cherished saboteur™ is the term I coined for the part of us who is so entrenched in our need to do what we need to do to feel safe that we often come to believe it is our true self. Its patterns give rise to our righteous indignation as we defend this saboteur's legitimacy. It's tricky. It can shape-shift, change forms, jump from one area of our lives to another…always leaving us with that one thread in our perfect tapestry that needs reweaving—that one brick in our successful fortress that needs to be replaced.

How does your cherished saboteur™ present itself and how will this program assist you in embracing and thus resolving it?

First of all, as long as we are in body we will have some aspect of our life which is challenging—that challenge provides the backdrop for our growth. We will always have that last 10—15% of our lives which needs work. It is this which keeps us humble—and keeps us forever teachable—always being subject to new growth. The horizon of this 10—15% continually evolves. It is our Higher Power or Soul's way of constantly making the most of this "earthly experiment."

How will this program assist you in that process? It will assist you in changing your relationship to your cherished saboteur. No matter what form it takes, your relationship begins to shift from antagonistic to nurturing. You become a student of this pattern instead of a victim of it. When you embrace this conflict and tension and notice the contrast between feeling good and feeling stuck, you arrive at the threshold of your cherished saboteur™. If, instead of projecting its energy out onto others, and making it about it or them—with the "*if only's*" and the feelings of shame because you aren't good enough— you stay with this tension on a moment-to-moment basis, you claim the opportunity *to separate* from this saboteur. When you can separate from this energy, you can respond to it. You have the opportunity to relate to your cherished saboteur™ as the latest expression of your humanness which is providing the most recent landscape of your growth. When your cherished saboteur™ is viewed in this fashion it becomes workable, manageable and pliable for transformation.

This perspective challenges the age-old myth that at some point we will "get it right…" and will no longer be subject to getting off course. It is similar to the myth of alcoholics who think at some point in their recovery they will have come "far enough" to drink without consequence—but it will never happen. Such is the case with our cherished saboteur™. For as long as we are in the body we will never be free of the backdrop for change. If we choose a spiritual path, evolution and change become our Soul's purpose.

The gift of your Soul Steps Program is that it shows you how the daily structure you create continues to move you down the river no matter what you are doing on the boat itself. It shows you that just by showing up for your day-to-day check-ins and commitments—you progress.

The daily regimen is measurable, concrete. It holds a focus and provides accountability for the day-to-day progress of your goal. If you are working with a partner, the daily check-in with your buddy gives you a touchstone to assess and recommit. The optional, weekly coaching sessions give a context to your struggle; they help flush out the distracters and give a new twist to what is standing in your way. The weekly conference calls umbrella the general themes of your pursuit.

By committing to an exercise program which incorporates your spiritual practice and invites a daily emotional inventory you give form to a daily practice which will extend way beyond this program. It enables you to create a habit of consciousness. Just as your body needs to be exercised throughout your life—so do your emotions and your spiritual pursuit. This program gives you an opportunity to build the habit of that structure and to normalize this day-to-day activity.

From The Essential Wound To The Healing Of The Soul

We have looked at how your body is involved—now let's examine how the psychological element impacts your body biochemically, and how this biochemical reaction either supports your ability to succeed or feeds your addiction to failure and strife.

How It All Begins

It is a scientifically-proven fact that our mind does not know the difference between what is real and what is imagined. What we conceive we achieve.

The movie, *What the Bleep Do We Know?* took the metaphysical and recovery worlds by storm. The movie's storyline weaves a woman's addictive battles, with quirky animation, to depict the impact our thoughts have on every cell of our body. Sprinkled between the real and imaginary scenes are interviews with some of the world's most renowned quantum physicists, spiritualists and alternative healers who substantiate the movie's suggestions with compelling research and extraordinary possibilities.

One significant scene features the work of Dr. Masaru Emoto who discovered that:

> *... Crystals formed in frozen water reveal changes when specific, concentrated thoughts are directed toward them. He found that water from clear springs and water that has been exposed to loving words shows brilliant, complex, and colorful snowflake patterns. In contrast, polluted water, or water exposed to negative thoughts, forms incomplete, asymmetrical patterns with dull colors.*

When you focus positive, loving thoughts on your dreams your mind starts the process of creating them—UNLESS those thoughts get ambushed by your doubts and fears which then create chaos and frustration.

If terror, betrayal, fear of abandonment, or shame are attached to the manifestation of our dreams, those dreams will eventually be annihilated with negativity. If our dreams are based on the values of others instead of our own internal values and desires—we deny the essence of our true self. The manifestation of our dreams is contingent on our being connected to our true self. When we are not connected, we feel a loss—not only of our dreams—but also a loss of our true self!

This loss of our true self evolves when we adapt to other's expectations and become who we think we need to be in hopes of feeling accepted and loved. This loss activates the process of grief. It is involuntary. It is a natural, predictable series of emotional responses encountered any time we experience a loss of any kind. These emotional responses affect the way we think and the manner in which we express our emotions.

What the Bleep Do We Know? offers its audience the latest scientific research supporting the existence of a biochemical component linked to these emotional responses. What you think, feel and say plays such a profound role that you literally can (and unconsciously do) use your thoughts, feelings, and statements to impact your cells.

Athletes know this. Cancer-survivors know this. They have long known the power of positive, deliberate intention and affirmation. They employ these techniques with great success.

What most of us do not keep in mind, on a day-to-day basis, however, is the fact that when our thoughts, feelings, and statements are negative—they produce negative results. Our cells flat-line… become lethargic…and are programmed to energetically attract exactly what we think and envision. If we tell ourselves we are fat, our cells create fat. If we tell ourselves we are a failure, we create situations in which we fail. If we fear getting hurt, we attract hurtful situations. This pattern of negative belief systems, self-negating feelings, and incriminating self-talk begins in childhood in response to the first moment we confront not feeling safe and experience the "essential wound."

A Psychological and Vibrational Perspective

The actual focus of setting one's intention and attracting what is desired began decades ago. However, it actually became "popularized" early this century when an explosion occurred and the laws of the universe, and most specifically the law of attraction, suddenly caught the attention of the masses. An electrical current disseminated as a plethora of information became available to the mainstream in a new way. Workshops offered by Esther Hicks, who brings forth the group of Light Beings called "Abraham", and J.Z. Knight, who channels an entity referred to as "Ramtha,", drew fresh audiences. Movies such as

The Secret and What the Bleep Do We Know? took the world by storm as they revealed the magic of these ancient laws.

A Quick Review of Law of Attraction

We already have covered the fact that universal law simply states that what we think and feel emits a *vibrational* frequency of energy which attracts a *vibrational* match—what we see and feel we create. With the onslaught of the movies mentioned above, this information was delivered cinematically for the first time, and therefore, began to reach those who had not previously found these truths through the written word. These concepts entered the mainstream. People got excited. Lives began to change. There was magic all around as many began to experience the law of attraction first-hand. They manifested those pre-paved parking places; their desired relationships; that divine-right job. Many felt empowered and exuberant.

But for most it was short-lived. The magic began to dampen. Some became frightened and disillusioned. Many assumed they were doing something wrong. They experienced fear—then shame— then anger— then despair. What few realized was that the very act of setting an intention pushed some part of them out of its comfort zone—coming face to face with its doubts and fears. They had not been prepared for the resistance, the backlash, the sabotage.

And for many, this is still true today. They discover these principles, begin practicing them, and then all of a sudden are met with resistance and failure. They begin to fear true mastery. Their wounded inner child takes center stage and begins the process of sabotage. It sabotages the efforts to succeed in an attempt to protect from failure. It sabotages efforts to succeed because, simply, it is terrified of success. And as you have seen, whatever that part of us fears, we attract into our experience.

What we conceive we achieve. This is a scientifically-proven fact. Our mind does not know the difference between what is real and what is imagined.

This truth was portrayed quite eloquently in the movie, What the Bleep Do We Know? The storyline wove together a woman's addictive battles with quirky animation to depict the impact our thoughts have in every cell of our body. Sprinkled between the real and imaginary scenes were interviews with some of the world's most renowned quantum physicists, spiritualists, and alternative healers who substantiated the movie's suggestions with compelling research and extraordinary possibilities.

One significant scene featured the work of Dr. Masaru Emoto who discovered that:

> "...crystals formed in frozen water reveal changes when specific, concentrated thoughts are directed toward them. Emoto found, "that water from clear springs and water that has been exposed to loving words shows brilliant, complex, and colorful, snowflake patterns. In contrast, polluted water, or water exposed to negative thoughts, forms incomplete, asymmetrical patterns with dull colors..."

This substantiates what was talked about in the previously that when you focus positive, loving thoughts on your dreams your mind starts the process of creating them. If there is no resistance you begin to allow the manifestation. But when those thoughts get ambushed by your doubts and fears you disallow your dreams, and instead, create chaos and frustration.

It has become widely accepted and understood that if terror, betrayal, fear of abandonment or shame, are attached to the manifestation of our desires they will eventually be annihilated by that negativity. As many have seen, when hopes and dreams are externally based on the values of others, instead of on our internal values, we deny the essence of our true self. Manifestation is vibrationally contingent on our being connected to our true self. When we are not connected, we feel a loss—not only of our dreams—but also the loss of our true self!

And again, this loss of our true self evolves when we adapt to another's expectations and become who we think we need to be in hopes of feeling accepted and loved. This loss activates the process of grief. It is involuntary. It is a natural, predictable series of emotional responses encountered any time we experience a loss of any kind. These emotional responses affect the way we think and the manner in which we express our emotions.

What the Bleep Do We Know?—and subsequent scientific research—supports the existence of a biochemical component linked to these emotional responses. What we think, feel, and say plays such a profound role that we literally can (and subconsciously do) use our thoughts, feelings, and statements to impact our cells.

Athletes know this. Cancer survivors know this. They have long known the power of positive, deliberate, intention and affirmation. They employ these techniques with great success.

What most of us do not keep in mind on a day-to-day basis, however, is the fact that when our thoughts, feelings, and statements are negative they produce negative results. Our cells flat-line and become lethargic. They are programmed to energetically attract exactly what we think and envision. If we tell ourselves we are fat— our cells create fat. If we tell ourselves we are a failure—we create situations in which we fail. If we fear getting hurt—we attract hurtful situations. This pattern of negative belief systems, self-negating feelings, and incriminating self-talk may begin in childhood in response to our non-filtered download, but they become magnified the first moment we confront not feeling safe and experience that *essential wound.*

The Essential Wound

Each of us experiences a defining moment in our lives when we realize we are not safe. It is part of the human experience. Again, Hal Bennett, in his book, Follow Your Bliss, was the first to refer to this moment as the *essential wound.* Our psyche experiences a trauma which shatters our basic assumption about our world. It also corrupts the value system we downloaded. Things in our life begin to go awry. What we thought would lead to safety all of a sudden does not. This trauma can be a result of neglect, sexual or physical abuse, or mental cruelty through shame and belittlement. It can be experienced in this lifetime, or can even be carried over from a previous lifetime. The DNA blueprint of our first remembered Soul experience of feeling unsafe has been shown to be carried in the etheric body and can impact the force field of our current incarnation.

In response to this realization, irrespective of its origin, our psyche goes into shock. We either dissociate from the emotion of the event or bury recall of the event, thus banishing the memory deep into the unconscious mind. The stress of these traumas, however, gets recorded in the electrical systems of our bodies and ultimately emerges as symptoms of what is called Post Traumatic Stress Disorder. There are two kinds of PTSD: simple and complex. Complex PTSD usually results from multiple incidents of abuse and violence such as child abuse or domestic violence. Simple PTSD is related to an isolated incident which is beyond the scope of ordinary coping abilities.

Develops into a Post Traumatic Stress Disorder-PTSD

Until recently it was thought that PTSD impacted only combat veterans or victims of isolated, one-time events such as 911 or a natural disaster. The psychological community has come to understand that, in fact, there is another form of PTSD which is now referred to as complex PTSD. Not only are survivors of atrocities such as the Holocaust, torture, war, natural disasters, catastrophic illnesses, and horrific accidents susceptible to PTSD—anyone who is exposed to an on-going threat to his or her safety, (such as physical or sexual abuse, rape, domestic violence, family alcoholism, or any experience which threatens one's basic survival) can develop a form of PTSD.

Remarkably, this holds true even if a person *witnesses* a traumatic event. If, as a child, you observed the abuse of your mother or the abuse of a sibling, you can develop debilitating PTS symptoms from just having been a witness. Traumas of great magnitude shatter our basic assumption about the world and our experience of personal safety. The impact can leave us feeling alienated, distrustful or overly clinging. These responses are buried and emerge only when a trigger brings these feelings back to the surface.

Our affirmations serve as this trigger. Underneath the surface, the electrically-charged emotions related to these traumas are forever encoded in our bodies and are conditioning our cells to attract exactly that which we most fear. The process becomes circular—our fear perpetuates this Post Traumatic Stress response, and our PTS response perpetuates our fear. Fear creates anxiety. Anxiety is the first stage of grief. We are perpetually responding to the never-ending loss of our true self. Why? Because when we feel unsafe, we deny our true self and develop the adapted self as we evolve into the person we think we need to be if we are to experience love and protection.

The Biochemical Perspective

Author, Candace Pert, who is a neuroscientist who is also featured in the film, *What the Bleep Do We Know?)* provides a very compelling, biochemical, explanation for the circular impact of our perpetual grief. When asked why we keep getting into the same kinds of relationships, having the same kinds of arguments, repeating the same patterns, she replies:

> *…Every emotion circulates through our body as chemicals called neuropeptides—"short-chain" amino acids—that talk to every cell of our body deciding what is worth paying attention to. When these peptides repeatedly bombard the receptor sites, the sites become less sensitive and require more peptides to be stimulated. Receptors actually begin to crave the neuropeptides they are designed to receive. In this sense, our bodies become addicted to emotional states. When we have repeated experiences that generate the same emotional response, our bodies develop an appetite for these experiences. Like addicts, we will draw experiences toward us that give us that fix…*

If we are constantly being exposed to neglect and abuse we develop an almost hyper-vigilant anticipation of the abuse—and when we anticipate it, we attract and create it.

Lynn Grabhorn, in her best-selling book entitled, Excuse Me, Your Life Is Waiting, states:

> *…Modern-day physicists have finally come to agree that energy and*

matter are one and the same...everything vibrates because everything—what you can see and not see—is energy, pure, pulsing, ever-flowing energy. Just like the sound which pours out of a musical instrument, some energy vibrates fast from high frequencies, and some vibrate slowly at low frequencies...the energy that flows out from us comes from our highly-charged emotions which create highly charged electromagnetic wave patterns of energy, making us powerful—but volatile—walking magnets. "Like attracts like." When we're experiencing anything that isn't joy or love, such as fear, worry, guilt ... we are sending out low-frequency vibrations ... they're going to attract only cruddy stuff back to us ... It is always a vibrational match...

In my over three decades of experience helping individuals arrest their addictive behavior and heal their childhood and Soul wounds, I have observed this same dynamic from a slightly different angle. I have observed that most of us, when conditioned to anxiously anticipate a certain response, unsuccessfully attempt to manage that anxiety. Our psyches cannot sustain the on-going experience of the tension, and ultimately, symptoms of our PTS develop. In an attempt to manage our emotions we flip between the second, third, and fourth, stages of grief which are bargaining, rage, and despair. This attempt to manage our feeling unsafe becomes what I have coined, our "codependent bargain™".

Our Co-Dependent Bargain™

We cannot heal our core issues and truly manifest our heart's desires until we identify and work with that bargain we made in this lifetime with the parent we identify as the one who could have loved and protected us—but didn't. We assume they didn't because of our deficiency and this becomes the source of our shame. In response to this shame and our perceived "lack," we enter into this unconscious agreement to "earn" their love in hopes they will finally love us enough to keep us safe.

When our Co-Dependent Bargain™ doesn't work we feel tension. This tension is uncomfortable and must be discharged. We discharge it by developing compulsive, perfectionistic, behaviors which later can easily set the stage for our addictions. In our adult life, whatever we do in excess—its intent is in response to this unconscious, and yet ineffective, unmet bargain. Because this bargain is unconscious we engage in this dynamic over and over. Our perpetual belief which permeates every interaction and relationship is that if we can just figure out what needs to be changed or fixed then things will be the way we need them to be and we will feel safe, loved, and protected. This act is a response to the "bargaining" stage of grief. It is an attempt to deal with the first stage of grief which is the anxiety and panic we feel in response to not feeling safe and fearing abandonment.

But it never works. No matter how much we try to be perfect— no matter how much we try to fix things so they will be better—we always fail because unfortunately, the source of the dysfunction is not us—it is the dysfunction in the parental system or our caretaker's addiction, negligence, or inabilities, to provide for us. As children, we did nothing to deserve being unloved. So we can never be "good enough" to impact or change what is wrong so things will get better. We get caught in the vicious cycle of attempting to be perfect— failing—then acting out compulsively or addictively to discharge the energy of that failure. This cycle keeps us active in our compulsions and addictions as well as disconnected from our authentic self and Source. This cycle is enacted by what I have come to call our *cherished saboteur*™.

The Cherished Saboteur™

All of us have that one central character within us who sabotages our best efforts to succeed. When we come up against this relentless part of self—a self who feels bigger than even our most desired goals— we have come into relationship with what I call the *cherished saboteur*™. The foundation of this saboteur is embedded in the co-dependent bargain™. In every endeavor we pursue we encounter this resistance and a loyalty which springs from our original, co-dependent bargain™. This part of self knows nothing else.

This cherished saboteur™ is engrained in our beingness to such a degree that we often come to believe it is our true self. It is the essence of our DNA makeup, the root of our energy disturbances and energetic imbalances. It is this biochemical response which reinforces this pattern over and over and continually bombards the receptor sites with the peptides which disarm us. Its patterns give rise to our righteous indignation as we defend this saboteur's legitimacy. And it's tricky. It can shape-shift—change forms—jump from one area of our lives to another–always leaving us with that one thread in our perfect tapestry which needs to be rewoven–that one brick in our successful fortress which needs to be replaced. That core issue which is embedded in a continual reenactment of our co-dependent bargain™.

Self-preservation—the dance between the Co-dependent Bargain™, Rage, and Despair

When we muster up enough courage to begin the process of confronting our childhood pain, it soon becomes apparent that at a very young age—when faced with an experience which shattered our basic sense of safety—we either became active in early co-dependent behavior, lashed out in anger at others, or shut down, became sullen, depressed, and closed off to feeling anything.

I call this the *fight, flight, or make it right* response! All responses are attempts to cover up the underlying feeling of loss (or grief) related to believing we are not good enough to be loved and protected. Again, we begin to believe the problem is with us. Our parents are not protecting us or making us feel safe because there is something wrong with us. This is the source of our negative self-talk which sets off the cycle of what I call the "shame/blame" game.

The Cycle of Shame and Blame

Our shame is the source of self-incrimination. We assume we need to be perfect in order to be loved and when we fail, we feel shame, or we project the feelings out onto others and blame them for our deficiencies and disappointments. We super-impose the experiences of our past onto the situations of our present. The faces of strangers become the faces of those who betrayed and disappointed us. We forever get caught in the cycle of feeling shame for not being good enough or placing blame on those who disappointed and hurt us. The shame/blame game creates a cycle which is never-ending, and that cycle is the process of grief.

The process of grief has five stages. The first stage is panic and is experienced in the form of our PTSD. To manage this panic, we again fluctuate between the second, third and fourth stages of grief. We bargain, rage, or feel despair. If we get caught in the loop of the second stage, we bargain with the experience by attempting to make deals with the lost object in hopes of retrieving it. If the loss is our sense of safety, we attempt to retrieve that safety by fixing the situation which resulted in the loss in the first place. If a loss such as this occurs in childhood, we develop behaviors whose intent is to win back the favor of the disapproving or abusive parent.

Our bargain goes something like this…*"Mommy, if I am a good little girl and never make you angry—then will you love me enough to make me feel safe?"* Of course, we can never be perfect enough to be reinstated to this sense of safety. So we can perpetually get caught in the bargaining stage of grief enacted through our co-dependent behavior of "trying" … trying to fix a situation over which we actually have no control. We can spend lifetimes trying to be reinstated to this lost sense of safety.

When this does not work, you can shift between the third and fourth stages of grief—anger, and despair. If your anger is turned outward and projected onto others, you are operating in the third stage of grief. If the anger is turned inward in the form of depression or despair, you are operating in the fourth stage of grief. Until your grief is processed through expression and neutralized with a technique such as tapping, you will be forever caught in this vicious cycle.

Our PTSD activates our need to manage this discomfort. We react with either a fight (anger), flight (despair) or make it right (co-dependency) response. We may find moments of peace—but the cycle of our grief is raging just below the surface and emerges whenever we encounter a situation which resonates with our original, essential wound.

The Shame of Our Imperfections

The motivating force behind the grief process—and its perpetual re-enactment—is our feeble attempt to ward off the insurmountable fear of abandonment and loss resulting from the shame of our imperfections. The panic which accompanies this ever-present fear is intolerable. It fuels the inner child's sabotage. It continually circulates through our body sending messages to our cells that not only are we not safe (which triggers panic), but our lack of safety is our fault (which triggers shame). We come to believe we are not worthy and lovable enough to be protected. We enter into that unconscious agreement of our *co-dependent bargain*™ as we hold onto the hope that if we can just be good enough—perfect enough—"they" will come through for us and be able and willing to love us and make us feel safe. This inner belief becomes the foundation of our need to be perfect. Our pursuit of perfection gives us a focus for the tension created by the fear we may fail.

But we do fail. We fail because there is no such thing as perfection. When we fail, we end up back in the middle of the tumultuous emotions of our essential wound—the fear—the panic—the disconnection from our true self. We end up back in the cycle of grief. This cycle is the essence of the twists and bends in our DNA make–up. It is the root of our cherished saboteur's™ energy disturbances and energetic imbalances. It is fueled by this biochemical response which reinforces this pattern and keeps continually bombarding the receptor sites with the peptides which disarm us.

How It Can Be Healed

To become fulfilled and healthy adults who can manifest our heart's desire we have to intervene in this cycle. We have to ***revise our false belief*** that we are not good enough and ***challenge our pursuit of perfection.*** We have to ***grieve the original loss*** of safety—***express and process the anger and despair of the Post Traumatic Stress*** associated with our loss, and ultimately ***reprogram the cellular encoding of our DNA.***

My *Seven-Layer Healing Process* teaches you to use your breathing, guided meditations, journal exercises, and Interactive Tapping™ sequences (to which you were introduced in the last section) to address this.

Revising Your False Belief with Interactive Tapping™

This revision begins by dealing with the mental body and the belief systems which developed in response to your inner child not feeling safe. The mental body or mind carries the need to understand. It is the part of you who reads with such diligence to try to make sense of what happened and understand what needs to happen, for things to change. Knowledge is power. When you come to know that the only true source of safety is the Divine, you step into the empowerment of your Adult Self who can orchestrate our own healing. As John Bradshaw stated in the mid-eighties, "There is no human security!"

The only way to challenge the belief system of your perfectionism—the source of your shame—the belief that you are not good enough—is to operate from the Illuminated, Adult Self. It is he or she who is connected enough to the Higher Source to be able to respond to, and retrieve, the wounded inner child or Soul part who felt the loss in the first place. That wounded self will let go of the old belief system when he or she experiences a different reality in the interaction with this illuminated, Adult you. With the interactive tapping™ sequences you slowly neutralize and, in essence, erase the old belief by assuring the wounded one that the Adult is now present and able to create something new. You begin to create your own reality, and therefore, you are empowered to envision a new experience for this wounded self.

In the *Seven-layer Healing Process*, you are again encouraged to use your breathing to inflate you with the essence of the Divine. You begin your life with your first breath, and you complete your life with your last breath. Each breath, from birth to death, gives you the opportunity to reconnect.

This is accomplished in Layer One of the healing process. You learn how to empower your Adult Self. Once connected, you proceed through the remaining six layers of healing and use the interactive tapping™ sequences to retrieve the adapted self. You neutralize and heal his or her feelings and create whatever reality he or she needs to feel safe. Once empowered in that first layer of healing you are equipped to move through the remaining six layers which begin with separating enough from the wounded one so you can help him or her grieve and feel safe.

Grieving the Original Loss with Interactive Tapping™

Targeting your inner child's grief with interactive tapping™ sequences and the exercises that follow offers a viable method for your Adult Self to neutralize the effects of this anxiety and grief. When this anxiety is neutralized, the inner child witnesses that he or she can survive. In fact, being rescued by the Adult Self is proof of this. You now have a part of you who can escort the wounded self through all of the feelings of grief and the interactive tapping™ sequences provide the vehicle to do so. You step into your Empowered Self with your breathing and then use energy tapping to support your vulnerable self through the stages of grief as you neutralize the franticness of trying to control the situations that are beyond your control.

By first neutralizing your panic, and then addressing your frantic need to bargain, you are able to move into the rage of the loss. The Adult Self helps the inner child get the anger out of his or her body.

And when the inner child has expressed and neutralized the rage he or she can collapse into despair. True despair is standing in the center of the void of the loss. When the Adult Self is able to tolerate that emptiness the inner child has no need to distract with compulsions and addictions. He or she does not have to deny with disruptions. You stand side-by-side with your inner child, naked in the truth of the loss, able to embrace its rawness without fear. The tumultuous emotions of your childhood grief emerge to be neutralized, so the cycle of your PTS can subside. There are entire sections in this book dedicated to processing the grief, both as the Adult and as the inner child. But this release can only be experienced once the truth has been spoken and heard.

This is true whether you are dealing with the current experience of your Adult Self, the memory of an inner child, or the recall of an aspect of your Soul. When you have successfully reconnected with your Authentic Self and neutralized and released the unexpressed emotions, the circuitry of both the physical and etheric bodies is forever changed. You are then able to download a new program into the DNA make-up of each cell.

Reprogramming Your DNA with Source Energy and Interactive Tapping™ *Sequences*

You will see how in the preview of the *Seven-Layer Healing Process,* you are lead through an exercise in which you do this reprogramming. However, for your conscious mind to support your efforts, it is useful to have a conceptual understanding of this exact process.

First of all, DNA is a large molecule, shaped like a double helix and found primarily in the chromosomes of the cell nucleus. The DNA contains the genetic information of the cell. The DNA forms a double helix, two elongated molecular chains (like staircases) that wrap around each other. DNA tells our cells what they have been; what they will continue to be; and what they will become. The DNA is the blueprint for our life processes. Each cell of our bodies contains the complete genetic code for the whole body.

According to Margaret Ruby, founder of *The Possibilities DNA Vibrational Healing School,*

> *"...Our body's communication systems have been broken down due to feelings of limiting beliefs. There is a vibrational interference pattern attached to this limiting belief causing negative, low vibrational emotions, which affect and distort our DNA. When two energy waves (thoughts and feelings) pass the same point and are out of phase, they interact and create a low vibrational, low wave interference that can, in turn, create physical or emotional imbalance...DNA then replicates this interference pattern which has a twist and slight bend to it..."*

These twists and bends have to be neutralized if we are to heal and manifest a productive, successful and satisfactory life.

Dr. Joe Dispenza—also featured in *What the Bleep Do We Know?* comments,"…*the remarkable component to this dynamic is the fact that as our cells split—and they do split and recreate—they carry the energy of the old cell. It does not split with a fresh start. A cell's off-spring carries the imprint of the parent cell at the time of the split. Negativity begets negativity, and positive reinforcement begets positive reinforcement!*"

There are trillions of cells in your body and within each and every cell is the nucleus, the mastermind for the blueprint of your life. The stories recorded in your DNA determine the course of your relationships, your wealth, your health and your career. What happens to you on your life journey is a result of what is written in the life code of your DNA. When this blueprint becomes faulty—the communication between each cell is faulty. This faulty communication is in response to the wounds experienced in childhood. It is established in response to the fears, disappointments, and hurts encountered when you were unable to fend for yourself.

Connecting with your Higher Self, accomplished through breathing and interactive tapping™ sequences, enables the Adult Self to repair this faulty communication. By activating your DNA and reprogramming and infusing it with the vibration of Source Energy, your most illuminated, Adult Self re-establishes a connection with its intuition and then helps the wounded inner child do the same. The twists and bends, which create the interference patterns of the DNA in every cell in your body, are neutralized, and the cells can once again be infused with this vibration of Source Energy.

But not only can the cells be reprogrammed, now, with the new brain science and epigenetics, it is understood that it is possible to even rewire the brain and construct new neural pathways which sustain a healing of this kind.

Rewiring Your Brain with Interactive Tapping™

As you have hopefully gathered, the basic cornerstone of my model is that; "the healing agent for the old wound, which results in your sabotaging behavior, is the interaction between your wounded one and a part within you who can respond with compassion, love, and care." And furthermore, I hope by now I have effectively explained that in order to achieve this healing you must develop a soothing inner voice which can respond to the wound and need of a younger self. But as you have seen, this interaction is often eclipsed by the stress that followed you into adulthood and gets expressed in your day-to-day life. So, instead of being able to respond, you collapse into the wound and react to the current situation in the same way you did as the child.

My understanding of this principle was enhanced when I listened to a New Brain Series, *hosted by Ruth Buczynski, Ph.D. of the* National Institute for the Application of Behavioral Medicine. *In that series I was introduced to the work of* Dr. Richard Hanson *author of the* Buddha's Brain, *and* Hardwiring Happiness. *His work inspired me to integrate some of the new brain concepts into my Seven–Layer Healing Process.* Interactive tapping™ in itself rewires the brain in that it positions a negative experience with a positive one. But i*nfusing this process and modality with this new science makes it even more effective.*

In my Seven-Layer Healing Process the meditative interactions, super-charged with the new interactive tapping™ *sequences, successfully replaces the old reactive experience with a calmer, more compassionate, response. Your brain is then equipped to send your body the new messages that are more life-giving.*

The Adult Self can give a face to those saboteurs who run rampant with their negative statements and destructive behaviors. This Illuminated Self learns how to relate to those wounded ones with care and love and helps them grieve what was originally lost. The essential wound is repaired as the true essence of self is invited back into the vibration of your force field where it can be safe. The body learns how to relax. There is a part of who is willing to learn how to cope and is about to learn how to grieve. This is the promise when you learn how to administer the basic interactive tapping™ sequences that enable you to address your grief.

So What The Bleep Is The Point?—

The point is this—when you look at your essential wound and the cycle of your grief from the perspective of your Soul, you come to realize this whole drama has been an expression of what your Soul signed you up for this time around. It is as if this drama is the class your Soul enrolled you in, in this school term called life. The beauty of this healing is that it empowers us to come full circle. For the essence of our essential wound holds the thread of our Soul's lesson—and our Soul's lesson gives us the opportunity to realize the *true essential wound* is the moment we left the connection with our Source in the first place.

The real sense of loss—which gets projected onto our parents and loved ones—is actually an expression of the loss we feel when we turn away from our Source…and so forth…and so on. There is no yesterday or today or even tomorrow. There is only now…this moment… this expression of Source through you. That is the true rabbit hole. Are you up for the game? Can you see the drama of your life as the entertainment center of your mind and have the courage to return to your true sense of safety found only in Divine? By signing up for this program you have shown yourself you are at least willing to give it a try! For that, you should be proud.

Website Resources for this Chapter

Dr. Masaru Emoto—http://www.masaru-emoto.net/ Dr. Candace Pert—http://www.candacepert.com/ Hal Bennett—http://www.halzinabennett.com/ Lynn Grabhorn—http://www.lynngrabhorn.net/

Margaret Ruby—http://www.possibilitiesdna.com/home.html Dr. Joe Dispenza—http://www.drjoedispenza.com/

What The Bleep Do We Know? http://www.whatthebleep.com/ Post Traumatic Stress Disorder—http://www.headinjury.com/ faqptsd.html

Adamantine Particles—http://www.awakening-healing.com/ AdamantineParticles.html

PROGRAM COMMITMENT

The Importance Of
Choosing An Event

IT IS HIGHLY recommended you begin this program by choosing an athletic event or milestone for which you design a strategic plan for success. It is irrelevant what that event is. Just by choosing an event, establishing a goal, and devising a plan to achieve that goal, you provide your psyche with the structure needed to move into the new you. You give your inner child a goal for which it can work and an event which it can anticipate.

By designing a day-by-day plan you regain the trust of your body through your daily willingness to show up. In return, it gives you a way to integrate the new you.

The Physical, Mental, Emotional, And Spiritual Weave

By EXAMINING THE impact your childhood issues and belief systems have on your daily behaviors you seize the opportunity to compassionately befriend the saboteurs within you who are afraid of success. Each part will be identified and each aspect of you will be given what s/he needs in order to allow you to succeed.

You are being invited to embark on a journey whose structure assists you in moving forward in your growth. As you have already read, each of us has that aspect or habit which sabotages even our best intentions. In this program that aspect is again referred to as your *cherished saboteur*™.

Components And
Time Commitments

THE COMPONENTS OF this program to which you will be committing for a period are described in detail below. In addition, if you also choose to focus on weight management you will be encouraged to engage in proper nutrition and in supplementing your daily intake with workout enhancement support. Proper intake of essential vitamins and minerals is paramount to becoming healthy and fit enough to sustain the changes made emotionally, spiritually and mentally.

#1 Regimented, Conscious Aerobic Exercise/Personal Goal Commitment

This plan is the backbone of your program. It offers your body, heart, mind, and Soul the structure needed to energetically transport you into your new self. When this commitment is woven together with a celebration of a life milestone or ambition it creates a context for the new you to emerge. Exercise goals or physical goals combined with nutritional intentions and lifetime aspirations provide a tangible, measurable barometer for your progress. The results are immediate and encourage perseverance. When you piggyback an additional goal with your physical regimen—such as passing a test, completing a work assignment or even buying a house, your commitment to your Soul

Steps Program enables you to walk, run or stretch yourself into the future you. By combining the two, you invite your body to assist you in attaining a lifetime achievement.

#2 Optional—Daily Phone Check-In With A Buddy

The buddy system suggests you partner up with a friend or family member so the two of you can work the program together. This added support provides the daily element of accountability which ensures success and consistency. This check-in provides the structure needed to keep your commitment fresh. It also gives you a way to learn how to be a friend non-co-dependently. For 5–10 minutes a day you will talk and listen without the need to fix or give advice. It will be the time of day when you recommit by reporting to your buddy what your daily plan is…i.e., what you plan to eat, what you plan to do as exercise, how you plan to reinforce your spiritual intention through affirmations or prayer etc. You can also share your plan to work towards another non-physical goal, such as passing a test or completing a work project or career goal.

#3 Importance Of A Food Plan

What I have observed in working with individuals using this structure is that it is significantly more effective to combine a food management with the material provided in the remainder of this manual. This combination ensures the highest rate of success. Why? Because as you are working on the deeper issues of your psyche, it is common to want to medicate those issues and numb yourself to those issues with the use of food.

Each pound you want to lose has a purpose and if its purpose is not realized, your body will not release it. I do not care how good your plan is or how effective your product line is—I have come to under-stand that getting healthy requires working with more than just the physical form. I have come to understand you are made up of a mental, emotional and spiritual body as well. I have come to understand a balanced, holistic program responds to your entire being—it incorporates nutrition for your mind, heart, and Soul as well as the body.

Most importantly—when it comes to weight management and loss—I have come to understand it does not matter how good your trainer is or how excellent your products are. If your body believes it is serving you by keeping the weight on, it will find a way to do so. Your body is your most loyal servant! It is the intention of this program to help your body serve you wisely!

The only way this structure will assist you in achieving your goals so you can learn to listen to the wisdom your body has to offer you is by quieting your addictive and compulsive need to medicate your body through excessive eating or antagonistic food choices which set your physical system off and activate your cravings and reactions. This repetitive cycle keeps you deaf to your body's natural, innate wisdom.

The effectiveness of the structure is greatly compromised if you cannot listen to your body. No matter how dedicated you are, if you do not have a nutritionally sound replacement and replenishment regimen, your body will not release the weight. You will come to understand your body and its need to hold the weight—but your body will not give it up until it believes you are willing to deal with the issues it has been faithfully holding for you in the first place.

#4 Optional Weekly Phone Coaching Sessions With Cathryn

If you choose to sign up for the coaching sessions done by phone with Cathryn your 60-minute session will provide the one-to-one structure needed to ensure you stay on track and have the opportunity to identify and address any parts of you who might be sabotaging your progress. You and Cathryn set up a designated time and the session begins and ends accordingly. She can be reached directly at 612.710.7720. The focus of these sessions is for you to report your triumphs and challenges and to devise and continually revise a plan of action which ensures your continued success and progression. When you combine the resolution of your emotions with the restructuring of your belief systems and the insight received from your Akashic Records or Higher Guidance, you are guaranteed success. Each weekly session builds on the previous sessions to gradually solidify and secure the structure needed to anchor into your new self.

FIRST THREE DAYS CEREMONIAL OPENING

DAY ONE

THE FIRST DAY of your Soul Steps Program is dedicated to your selecting your space and time and sanctifying it with intention. Taking the time to consciously create the external atmosphere which is going to most effectively support your re-invention process marks the beginning of the construction of the internal structure which will ultimately sustain it.

Selecting And Sanctifying A Place And Time For Your Work—

First, determine the approximate time you are going to set aside daily for this program. Establish when you plan to do your aerobic exercise and when you plan to do your reading, mediations, and homework. Close your eyes and create an imaginary day-timer, which blocks this time out. Block it out in your actual day-timer, or google calendar, as well. This makes your commitment more real and carves out space in your daily life needed to successfully participate in your regimen.

Next, choose the place in your home where you plan to work with

Soul Step structure. Set your intention to claim this space as your healing arena. You will want to select special totems or objects which will make this space personal. Use sage or holy wood to cleanse your area. Many cultures use sage in this manner to purify an area which is going to be used for sacred ceremony. Catholic churches often use frankincense and myrrh. Most metaphysical stores carry ceremonial sage or holy wood. When ready, sit in the center of this space and conduct the following ceremony.

Meditation—Take a deep breath—envision extending a force field of light approximately three-to-five feet all around you as you energetically establish the sense of safety which will be necessary to heal. If you have chosen to use sage or holy wood to cleanse your space...simply light it, set your intention and allow the smoke to absorb anything in that area which does not support your work. Open a window and visually watch the smoke carry the unwanted energy back to the heavens for transmutation. Light a special candle you can then use throughout this program and envision its flame filling that space with a touch of the divine. Open your eyes when you feel complete.

You can either conduct this ceremony one time only or use it to add ritual to your daily practice.

Make the commitment for the next two days to show up in this same space and time to reinforce these intentions energetically. This will ensure your psyche that you are serious about your willingness to follow through with this structure. This first seventy-two hours also gives the different parts of you time to show up at their own pace. Often when we begin something we jump right in and then derail because not all parts of us have arrived at the starting point at the same time. This gradual entry into your program gives those less enthusiastic parts of you a little more time to acclimate to what is about to occur.

Gathering Your Materials—

If you have not already done so you will also want to use this first day to gather the materials you are going to need to work your program. For example, you will want to purchase a special journal and pen to record your responses to the exercises and meditations. You may want to have a tape recorder on hand to record some of the meditations in your own voice, or, if you have obtained the accompanying CD, you will want to have a CD player handy so you can listen to the pre-recorded meditations and overviews. I also recommend you purchase a set of Angel cards and integrate these into your daily spiritual practice. They can also be purchased at bookstores or even through the internet.

Give yourself these first three days to set up your space with special items which will enhance the sacredness of your work. You may want to surround yourself with special stones or crystals; photos from your childhood; pictures of Angels or Guardians who help you feel connected to your Higher Source—or perhaps even books or daily readings which you intend to weave into your connection with Spirit. Just close your eyes and ask your Angels to help you determine what would be useful to have on hand. Keep in mind you can always add to this gathering as you progress in the program. It is just beneficial to set these three days aside in preparation because, by doing so, you give your psyche the message that you are serious enough to dedicate the time needed to adequately prepare.

Meeting Your Healing Team Of Angels And Guardians—

Once you have created your space you will want to sit in meditation and call in the help of your Healing Team. Your Healing Team is made up of Angels, Guides and Loved Ones with whom you feel comfortable. It may be power animals, Indian Chiefs or Priestesses or even loved ones who have crossed over to the other side.

Meditation—Close your eyes and call forth those from the unseen who you choose to provide comfort and support. Then ask if there are any others who would like to be of assistance to you. Ask that they make themselves known. (Often, an archangel or Mother Mary appears. Sometimes characters you would not have suspected show up and offer their services. When this happens, they usually have a special gift to offer to the experience.)

Record your experience in your journal.

Once you have an idea of those who are going to be on your Healing Team think of ways you can make their presence tangible. For example, if Jesus is one of your supporters, bring in a picture or something which holds his essence. If a power animal has come forward, honor its presence by finding a picture or something which will establish that animal's energy in your sacred space.

It is common for the Healing Team to vary throughout this process. For some issues, certain supporters are present while other issues require the support of a different nature. There is no right and wrong way of doing this. Setting this time aside to officially welcome your supporters into your sacred space simply sanctifies the process in which you are about to engage.

Once you have completed the above, give your space and the vibration you have created at least a full circle of 24 hours to acclimate to your specifications. This 24 hour period allows for energy to shift and the new matrix of healing which you have created to solidify.

DAY TWO

The second day of your ceremony is all about setting your intention and pre-paving the journey for the four dimensions of your being— your mind, body, heart, and Soul.

Setting Your Program Intention—

Once your sacred space has had its 24 hours to solidify, you are ready to sit in the center of your space and begin to set your intentions and clarify your goals. This involves establishing the broad strokes for what you want to accomplish during this Soul Steps structure.

Your intention should be simple and to the point. The specifics will come later. All you need to do initially is to acknowledge your willingness to show up for the times you have selected—to begin thinking about the exercise program and food plan which will support your overall goal and to be compassionate with yourself as you learn a new way of being.

Activity—This is most easily done by writing a letter of intent to yourself and your Higher Power which you then date and seal. Put this letter in an envelope and then find a natural place to keep it during your Soul Steps Program. At the end of your journey, you will ceremoniously open it.

Pre-Paving Your Mind, Body, Heart, And Soul For Their Journey—

Next, establish your mind, body, heart and Soul intentions. The following offers you a way to determine the triggers which derail you. You do not have to worry about details at this point—just record whatever you have already uncovered in your inner work. If you are unsure, then simply pre-pave your willingness for discovery by acknowledging to your Healing Team that you trust more will be revealed. This sets in motion an intention and expectation for discovery.

Activity—Ponder which thoughts and feelings exist when you derail. Explore how your efforts to succeed are being sabotaged. What is the self-talk which gets in the way of your moving forward? How do you feel when this occurs? How do you feel before this sabotage takes place? In other words— what is your emotional state before the sabotaging behavior takes over?

Ponder these same issues with respect to your current spiritual practice and the manner in which you now relate to your physical form. This process is similar to taking an inventory. It gives you a sense of the point from which your journey begins.

Once you have completed your current inventory—take a moment to ponder how you would ultimately like to feel, think, connect with spirit and relate to your body. Record your findings in your journal.

Pre-paving your hopes and wishes in this manner notifies your mind, body, heart, and Soul of the expectations with which you are coming into the program.

DAY THREE

Your third day is perhaps the most significant of your entire program because today is when you energetically give your wounded ones permission to emerge and heal. That may sound a bit strange— but the fact is that our emotional selves will stay wounded until they trust there is a pathway for them in which to heal. The pathway is established by the presence of an Adult Self who can respond to the emotional challenge of the original wound with confidence and compassion. It is important to understand that those aspects of you who sabotage your efforts to succeed are not doing so because they want you to fail. They do so because they are afraid of the consequences of your triumphs. Their maladaptive responses to your day-to-day life are attempts to be protective or preventative.

Keep this in mind as you work with the following meditation which will guide you through the "permission ceremony."

Giving Your "Selves" Permission To Heal—

To prepare for this work think for a moment of your most vulnerable soft spot—and a recent situation which triggered it? Then sit in your sacred place and prepare for your inner work.

Meditation—Begin by inviting in your Angels, Teachers, and Guides and by surrounding yourself with the light which then extends out at least three-to-five feet.

Bring your focus to the center of your being and envision the situation which provoked your most tender self. Stay separate from this image— view it as if you are watching a television screen. It is important to stay separate and detached from this situation and observe it from the perspective of the Adult Self. It is the only way you can respond to the wounded one as opposed to collapsing into the old pain and becoming the one who needs to be healed instead of the one who can heal.

When you see the situation—freeze it. Freeze everyone who is involved. See your little one—your wounded one. Step into this scene as the Adult Self and touch your wounded one on the cheek. This character then comes to life. Tell your younger self who you are and explain that you have come back in time to make him or her feel safe and to respond to the unmet need. Invite this little one into your force field where there are safety and protection. Introduce him or her to the Angels and helpers from the unseen—those who appear to lend their support. Allow time for your wounded one to share what frightens or injures him or her. Let this little one speak its truth and experience the response from you and your healing team. Stay with this imagery as your wounded one experiences safety and begins to feel secure.

When the healing has occurred invite your vulnerable self to take refuge in the center of your sacred heart where he or she will forever be protected and kept safe. Once this part of you experiences safety there is an automatic notification which goes out into the universe declaring to all of you who need attention and help that it is now safe to return and be healed.

See this happening—see the representations of the old hurts and wounds and sabotaging behaviors needing to be addressed, coming back into the light. Give them permission to reveal their pain and offer them the promise they will be nurtured and nourished back to health with compassion, love, and care. Assure them that the structure of this entire program is aimed at doing just that. Take a moment now to look up at the horizon and glance at those who wait in the wings to be healed. Know that you are embarking on a journey which will ultimately bring them all home. Open your eyes and record your experiences in your journal.

That completes your three days of ceremonial preparation. You are now ready to begin your Soul Step regimen.

IMPORTANT—PLEASE NOTE: I present this material as a monthly protocol but feel free to pace yourself in whatever way you find useful. This is your program. You will know how quickly to move forward ... when to pause ... and when to ignore that which does not resonate.

THE TWELVE-MODULES—
STEP-BY-STEP

First Module—
Starting The Process

The hardest step to take is that first step and the focus of this first module is to do just that. At the end of this material, you will find a sample daily check-in sheet and weekly review sheet. I suggest you use these or create your own methods to record your progress. It helps you integrate the work you complete and gives you a way to honor the progression of your ever-evolving Future Self.

A FEW GUIDELINES TO GET YOU STARTED

YOU BEGIN YOUR Soul Steps Program by giving form to your twelve module structure. You establish your goals with respect to your exercise regimen; food plan; spiritual practice and any other steps you choose to take with respect to a pre-determined, personal or professional goal. The structure of your program— the day-to-day plan—will build the container which anchors your monthly regimen into your day-to-day life. Once designed, this consistency becomes the seed which grows and evolves into a daily regimen which can serve you in any endeavor at any stage of your life.

"Birthing your program" is simply "showing up" each day for it. Irrespective of what you do or how you "perform," the task this first month is simply to design your day-to-day commitments. Then show up for your daily accountability report by filling in your check-in sheet and, if applicable, conferring with your buddy. (We will talk about the buddy system at our first meeting) The consistency with which you do this will reflect the degree to which you are able to nurture the *infancy* of your new plan.

The focus questions or themes provide insight and direction on how the central issues originating from your infancy period have followed you into your adult life. Becoming aware of these patterns begins the process of neutralizing challenges and building on redis-covered strengths.

As you progress, please remember there is no way you can fail as long as you are willing to check in with yourself and/or your buddy on a day-to-day basis and set your intention for your regimen each day. If you had a difficult day—acknowledge it then recommit and move forward into your current day. Remember, each day gives you the opportunity to begin anew. Your consistency alone begins to build an inner trust which assures your doubters within that you are committed to follow through and show up to respond to what needs to be resolved. In addition to this manual, you will want to purchase a journal you can use to record your responses, thoughts, and feelings.

Identifying the Source of Celebration

In order to proceed, our psyches/personalities need to focus on an upcoming event. The range of celebratory options is immense. It can be any milestone in your life—any transition such as marriage, graduation, retirement or even divorce. It can be a special date such as a birthday, anniversary or stage of life such as cronehood, menopause, child-bearing years or empty nest syndrome.

Combining this special event with a physical goal infuses and honors your celebration even further. The changes made on the outside mirror the changes made on the inside. This combination provides the arena for your day-to-day commitment. The regimen used to train or prepare for your goal carves out the time in your day when you can also put focused attention on becoming the new you. It offers a beginning … a middle and an end…a tangible measure of the progression of your goal. Each step you take, each stretch you make eases your body into the new you. On a daily basis, you set a goal and make a commitment to attaining it. This progressively creates the building blocks necessary to succeed.

WHAT MILESTONE, TRANSITION, UPCOMING EVENT OR LIFE GOAL WOULD YOU LIKE TO CELEBRATE? PLEASE RECORD THE EVENT IN YOUR JOURNAL.

Establishing a Vision for your Future Self

In the next module you will be guided into your mind's eye and travel the timeline to your event so you can meet who you will be when you have acquired your goal. Since time does not really exist, who you want to be already exists in another dimension of time and consciousness. For now, I invite you to simply begin the process by responding to the following journal exercise. This will prepare the seeds you will use in next month's meditation in which you will give form to your future self.

Journal Exercise—To assist this process of giving form to your future self take time now to make a list of adjectives that describe who you want to be when you complete this program. Then proceed with the following to expand your definition further.

To respond to your emotional body—make note of the person you want to be emotionally when you step into this future self. How will this future you respond to your world on a feeling level which is different than how you respond today?

To respond to your mental body—what belief systems will be altered? Make note of the current limiting belief system, and then in a column next to it design the desired belief system.

To respond to your physical body—research the nutritional program and food regimen to which you would like to commit. Make a note of it in your journal and create a plan for how to implement this regimen.

To respond to your spiritual body—determine what spiritual practice you want to integrate into your daily practice. For example, you might select an Angel card each morning or night or choose a spiritual reading from an inspirational source or daily affirmation book, etc. However, you choose to connect—it works best to choose a tangible method. This will assist you in establishing the habit of making daily contact with your Higher Power as you define him/her/it.

Next, translate all you have written into the regimen you want to implement on a daily basis. Use your daily check-in sheets to assist you in this process. Even if you do not exercise every day, it will be advantageous to connect with your Higher Guidance and/or Angels and follow a food plan each day. This structure will help to do so.

REFER TO THE "DAILY CHECK-IN SHEETS" AND THE "7-DAY REVIEW" FOUND IN THE APPENDIX TO LOG YOUR EXPERIENCE.

Second Module—
Hello, Future Self

You, too, have an athlete within waiting to be chiseled from the clay of your present-day self. Whether you run, jog, cycle, play golf, belly dance, weight train, canoe, practice yoga or martial arts, swim or walk, your Future Self is the aspect of you who is ever-striving to attain that precise level of fitness which ignites the highest vibrational frequency, which in turn enables you to align with your most Divine Self.

GIVING FORM TO YOUR FUTURE SELF

IN MODULE TWO you are introduced to the facets of the program that will assist you in stepping into your new self. In the following meditation, you will be guided into your mind's eye and travel the timeline to your event so you can meet who you will be when you have acquired your goal. Since time does not really exist, who you want to be is already in another dimension of time and consciousness.

By actively claiming this vibration of your future self, you set the stage for the vibrational frequency of who you want to be, to attract the vibrational frequency of who you are in your present state of consciousness. Much like a fishing pole line you cast out with the intention of becoming your future self, you will make contact with yourself, then set the line which will draw you to the self you want to become.

If we indeed have been "all things," then somewhere in our Soul's lineage there exists a part of our spiritual self who has learned how to retain the vibrational essence of joy. When we request to meet that Soul Self, we open up to experience that renewed frequency of vibration. It allows us to remember who we once were. Our Soul Self co-mingles with our Present Day Self and together they give birth to the Future Self who will hold this vibration of joy in this body, on this planet, in this dimension of time.

Relax as you allow your Angels to vibrationally chisel away the old and invite forth the vibration of the person you are unfolding to become. Again, this exercise will empower your future self to then attract who you are today; to the person you want to be when you have accomplished your goals.

MEDITATION—"MEETING YOUR FUTURE SELF"

Before we begin, imagine yourself standing someplace in nature— your favorite place—an ocean beach, a river bank, a clearing in the forest or on top of a mountain—wherever you feel closest to your Source. Stand in a column of the current vibration of energy which holds the frequency of all that you are at this moment.

Now imagine your Guidance gathers around you and with the beat of the drum they begin to chisel away, that which keeps you from stepping into the person you want to become. All belief systems—antiquated emotions— images of your old self are being chiseled away now as you allow your Guidance to mold and reform the new you. Stand and respond to their transformative efforts as they dissolve all doubts, assuage all fears, and adjust the vibrational frequency within your physical form so it is repro- grammed to hold your new DNA—that of your warrior God/ Goddess who is strong, present, vibrant and alive. Like a virgin piece of clay, your Guidance molds the new you.

Now, look up. See a column of light ascending from the center of the universe. There is a consciousness associated with this column which feels familiar and engaging—trustworthy. It invites you to come forward. You comply. A band of Angels now descends; each holds a vibration of transcendent light. Like ribbons of color, each vibration of energy swirls around you—adjusting your vibration as the Angels entice the athlete within you to come forward—igniting your passion and infusing your physical form with the vibrational frequency of your highest spiritual essence.

Imagine now as you stand in the center of the multitude of colors that they swirl through you and around you—adjusting your vibration to fit this current dimension of time. Every incarnation which has existed before this time is factored into your new configuration...every strand weaving the old/new you...taking every element of who you have ever been—every element of who you are now—every curve and perfection and flaw of your physical form—is reflected in its state of perfection. Nothing about your mind, heart, body or Soul is accidental. Each aspect of who you have been is now being woven into the new you—the future you who stands in his or her own Light and holds the vibration of your future self. This aspect of you does not feel a sense of urgency, but instead, experiences a sense of calm. This part of you has learned how to hold the energy...this part of you knows how to move with ease and connectedness. Your athlete within is an aspect of your future self. Yes, go ahead. Think of yourself as an athlete. How does that feel? How does it feel to be in alignment with your body and instinc- tively know what to feed it?

On this date, at this moment, become the mother of your athlete within. Give birth to your integrated self who physically holds the balance of emotions with beliefs and spiritual aspirations. Consciously make the choice to stand in this light...to breathe away any vibration that is not in alignment with this light—with this you. Make a conscious choice, a moment to moment conscious choice to stand in this vibration—to operate from this vibration—to hold this vibration as you choose to calm yourself and come back into union—body, mind, heart, and Soul.

Now take a deep breath and know the molding has been done... Open your eyes and slowly return to this moment in time.

Having connected with this future self you are in a position to energetically be drawn to him or her throughout your Soul Steps Program. You have empowered your Higher Guidance to assist you in giving form to this vision and now the vision is tangible and real.

Read the following and record your responses in your journal.

1. *How does this feel? What was your response to this meditation? How do you feel different? Were there any surprises?*

2. *How would you like to reinforce this new vision in your daily program? How can you feel this essence every time you work out? How can you invite the Angels to continue to infuse you with the essence of this new vision? What belief systems need to be dissolved so you can believe in this new you and allow yourself to become him or her? What emotions enhance or challenge your seeing yourself embody the essence of your future self? Ponder these questions and record your thoughts and feelings in your journal.*

3. *You are now ready to begin to "Pick an Event"— listen to the recording for assistance.*

4. *Throughout the month integrate all you have experienced into your daily workouts and inner sessions with self.*

REFER TO THE "DAILY CHECK-IN SHEETS" AND THE "7-DAY REVIEW" FOUND IN THE APPENDIX TO LOG YOUR EXPERIENCE.

Third Module—
Body, Meet My Angels

"Each day of your program you are encouraged to allow your Angelic Presence to enrich your workouts by inviting them to accompany you on the conscious-aerobic journey of the re-invention of self."

STEPPING STONES TO THE HEART OF
SOUL STEPS

ORKING HOLISTICALLY WITH your body and learning to *step from the heart of your Soul* begins when you anchor this intention into every cell, every muscle, and every fiber of your being. It requires that you give your Angels permission to infuse your body with their angelic dust and sprinkle their angelic energy into every aspect of your being. In this next meditation, you will begin that process. We start with the core muscles—the abs. With crunches, pelvic tilts and exercises for the oblique muscles, you will awaken the masculine, feminine and angelic energies within you. Beginning with week-month five, you will continue to take a muscle group each week-month and infuse it with the healing essence of the Angels. You will identify any stored emotions that muscle group has held for you in its posturing to protect you and make you feel safe. Once the muscle group of the month has been notified that you are now willing to do for yourself what it has been doing for you, it will receive permission to let go and to respond in a new and exciting way to your exercise.

Before you begin, choose an Angel card which reflects your need for safety—in your body—with yourself—with others. Record that message from your Angel in your journal.

In each meditation, you will be led through a process inspired by Margaret Ruby's work with reprogramming your DNA in which you will open up the channels between your Master Cell, located in your pineal gland in the center of your head and your Creator Cell which is found at the base of your spine. You will be guided to activate and reprogram the DNA of each cell to enable it to carry a new program of consciousness; ultimately to the cells of every muscle group, you will be focusing on in your strength training and aerobic exercise.

These weekly meditations enable you to challenge your body, not intimidate it…to invite change and transformation; not demand it. Through this imagery, you will be given an opportunity to partner up with your physical form in a conscious manner. This component of conscious exercise invites you to exercise, stretch and flex your body with deliberate and compassionate intent.

Meditation—"Infusing Your Body With The Light From The Angels"

Now let's begin by taking a deep breath and bringing your focus to the center of your belly. Feel that spark of light which rests in the very center of your being—envision that light expanding ever so gently so that every cell within your physical form can now be infused with this light and illuminated with its energy. In your mind's eye, see your entire physical form being illuminated by and infused with this light…and as you do so, envision this light expanding about 6 to 9 inches outside of your physical form—thus creating a column of protective light all around you. This builds a spiritual boundary around you which protects you as you open up your consciousness to higher frequencies…inviting a higher vibrational energy to infiltrate every cell within your body.

Now, bring your focus to the highest place in the Universe you can attain. It is here where you connect with your higher teachers and connect with the grid of unconditionality. It is here where you can extract the healing vibration of the Universe. It is here where you touch the wings of your Angels and where they make contact with you so they can be of service. Make your contact now. Invite your Highest Teachers to be present; your guardians, Ascended Masters, spirit guides, and power animals…ask for their assistance and blessing in this endeavor.

Now bring that new vibration of compassion and love right down to the center of your head into the pineal gland—and into the Master Cell. Infuse the DNA in the Master Cell with this new intent—awakening the chromosomes and the codons—the little computer chips which exist in the nucleus of each and every cell. Know that you are about to download a new program into your cellular makeup as you realign with the natural vibration with which the cells of your physical form long to resonate.

Once your Master Cell has been activated, bring that energy down the back of your head all the way along your spinal column, right to the base of your spine. It is here where you can infuse your Creator Cell with the same intent. Feel the energy of this vibration floating freely between your Master Cell and your Creator Cell—awakening and notifying every muscle, tendon, and ligament of your intention to infuse it with the vibration of the purest form of Light.

Now, having prepared your physical form for this first meditation, I invite you to bring your attention first to your heart. This muscle is involved in the exercise of every other muscle you work. Each time you exercise, flex and stretch any muscle in your body, the capacity of your heart increases as well. Because of this, it is useful to begin by centering your focus in your heart and then extending the vibration of love and compassion found in your heart to the muscle of choice.

Breathe into your heart now—peer into its center. There you will discover a secret chamber called the sacred heart. Within this sacred chamber exists a particle called the adamantine particle. This adamantine particle is the purest form of love which is known to mankind. Feel the vibration of this particle now and envision extending this vibration from the sacred chamber in your heart to the muscles in the core of your being…to your stomach muscles. We will start our series by focusing on this center because it is from this center that the rest of your work extends. Each month we will take a new muscle group and infuse it with the light—but we always begin with the core.

There is a reason for this. Every muscle in your body extends from this center—and each time you exercise these muscles—your upper and lower abs and your oblique muscles, you have an opportunity to acknowledge the inner male, the inner female and to acknowledge the essence of the Angelic realm. It is this combination which makes it safe for you to begin to explore the topic of safety.

Now bring your focus to center on the muscles in your belly. These core muscles—the upper and lower abs and the oblique muscles—govern the strength of your entire being. By focusing on them with deliberate intent you can infuse them with the energy of your masculine self as you do your upper ab crunches; your feminine self as you do your pelvic tilts. You can envision the wings of the Angels wrapping themselves around you in protection as you flex and bring attention to your oblique muscles. Each time you exercise these muscles, envision your body acknowledging the masculine and feminine energy within you and welcoming in the essence of the angelic realm. Record your findings in your journal.

Upper Abs—Welcoming the Masculine Energy

   Now bring your focus to your upper abs. This muscle group holds the essence of your masculine energy—that energy within you which allows you to take action and to implement your creative ideas and desires.

   What is it your upper abs need from you? What is their message? How do they wish to work with you on your higher goal? What action are they willing to take on behalf of your entire body? Make a note in your journal of any information or experience you might have at this time. Even if you are blank—leave this space open to be filled in at a later time. You are not accustomed to listening to your body and having a conversation with it. It may take you time to learn how to decode its language. Be patient— give yourself and your body time to get to know each other as you partner up on this shared goal. Record your findings in your journal.

Lower Abs—Welcoming the Feminine Energy

   Next, bring your focus to your lower abs. As you sit in your seat, gently tilt your pelvic muscles as you acknowledge the essence of your feminine energy. Your feminine energy holds your creativity—your ideas—your gifts to bring to the world...when the feminine and masculine energies work together, you create and deliver magic—one without the other leaves you stumped. Some have great ideas which never get delivered— others are active in their delivery but lack content—as you bring focus to the upper and lower abs you can infuse them with your intention to work together in this endeavor—not only with your exercise—but with any task you choose in your life...for your body holds the opportunity to, teach you how to move forward with deliberate intent. Now with your focus located on your lower abs, ask what the feminine aspect of you needs to come fully into expression? How does your feminine energy want to partner up with you for your higher goal? As you flex these muscles ask your feminine energy what it needs to assist you in your integration? Again, be patient. Each time you exercise and flex your lower abs you will have the opportunity to ask her what it is she has to offer you and what it is she needs. Take a moment now to make any notes in your journal.

Oblique Muscles—Aligning with the Angelic Energy

When you feel complete, bring your focus to your oblique muscles. Envision these muscles as the expression of the wings of your Angels. Breathe in as you refer back to the card you chose from your deck of cards. How does the meaning of that card now highlight the essence of your Angels being infused in your oblique muscles and your desire to hold that intention as they envelop your core?

When you feel complete bring your focus once again to the center of your Master Cell. Set your intention for your Master Cell to be infused with this new program—holding this new communication between you and your inner male—your inner female and your direct connection with the Angel of the week. Every time you exercise between now and our next session you have the opportunity to further your relationship with your core—with these aspects of you. It is at this core that your blocks or issues with respect to safety can emerge. Acknowledge the presence of these issues so you can begin to heal them. Allow the essence of your inner male and female and the presence of the Angel of the month to enrich your workouts and bring a more holistic and conscious focus to your relationship to your body and yourself.

"When we open ourselves to hear our angels' messages, every aspect of our lives becomes more peaceful."

Doreen Virtue, author of Angel Therapy and Angel Medicine

Once completed, record your thoughts and feelings in your journal. How can you integrate this experience into your workouts and into your daily living?

As you work with this, day to day, you may want to listen to the core muscle meditation in its entirety without journaling - for your convenience, here it is:

REFER TO THE "DAILY CHECK-IN SHEETS" AND THE "7-DAY REVIEW" FOUND IN THE APPENDIX TO LOG YOUR EXPERIENCE.

Fourth Module—
In Walks Your
Cherished Saboteur™

"History, despite its wrenching pain, Cannot be unlived, But if faced with courage Need not be lived again..."

"On The Pulse of Morning,"
a poem read by Maya Angelou, 20 January 1993
At the Inauguration of William Jefferson Clinton

MEETING THE CHERISHED SABOTEUR™

IN THE LAST Module, you began the process of infusing your physical form with the energy and light of your Angels. This week we will explore the essence of what I refer to as your cherished saboteur™.

As was discussed in a previous section, we all have one central character within us who sabotages our best efforts to succeed. When we come up against this relentless part of self—a self who feels bigger than even our most desired goals—we have come into relationship with what I call the *Cherished saboteur™*. The foundation of this saboteur is embedded in the co-dependent bargain™. In every endeavor we pursue, we encounter this resistance and a loyalty which springs from our original co-dependent bargain™. This part of self knows nothing else.

This cherished saboteur™ is ingrained in our beingness to such a degree we often come to believe it is our true self; it's patterns give rise to our righteous indignation as we defend this saboteur's legitimacy. It's tricky. It can shape-shift—change forms—jump from one area of our lives to another...always leaving us with that one thread in our perfect tapestry which needs reweaving—that one brick in our successful fortress which needs to be replaced—that core issue which is embedded in a continual reenactment of your co-dependent bargain™.

The Co-Dependent Bargain™ in More Detail

Our Co-Dependent Bargain™ was made in this lifetime with the parent we identify as the one who could have loved and protected us—but didn't. We assume they didn't because of our deficiency— which became the source of our shame. In response to this shame and our perceived "lack", we enter into this unconscious agreement to "earn" their love in hopes they will finally love us enough to keep us safe.

When our Co-Dependent Bargain™ doesn't work, we feel tension. This tension is uncomfortable and must be discharged. We discharge it by developing compulsive, perfectionistic behaviors which can easily set the stage for our addictions. In our adult life, whatever we do in excess, it is in response to this unconscious, ineffective, unmet bargain.

Because this bargain is unconscious, we engage in this dynamic over and over. Our perpetual belief, which permeates every interaction and relationship, is that if we can just figure out what needs to be changed or fixed, then things will be the way we need them to be and we will feel safe, loved and protected. This act is a response to the "bargaining" stage of grief. It is an attempt to deal with the first stage of grief which is the anxiety and panic we feel in response to not feeling safe and fearing abandonment.

It never works. No matter how much we try to be perfect—no matter how much we try to fix things so they will be better—we always fail because unfortunately, the source of the dysfunction is not us—it is the dysfunction in the parental system or our caretaker's addiction, negligence or inability to provide for us. As children, we did nothing to deserve being unloved. Therefore, we can never be "good enough" to impact or change what is wrong so things will get better. We get caught in the vicious cycle of attempting to be perfect—failing—then acting out compulsively or addictively to discharge the energy of that failure. This cycle keeps us active in our compulsions and addictions as well as disconnected from our authentic self and Source. This cycle is the source of our saboteurs—of those behaviors which derail us and keep us from coming fully into the commitments and intentions of the life we deserve to live. It is the essence of our DNA make–up, the root of our energy disturbances and energetic imbalances. It is this biochemical response which reinforces this pattern over and over and continually bombards the receptor sites with the peptides which disarm us.

In the following material, you will be given a method by which you can begin to identify the essence of your cherished saboteur™. This part of you will emerge in each of the worksheets and will give us a direction for our next session. If working this material alone— the material in the Healing Formula section will give you methods by which you can begin to work with this aspect of you—that part of you who continues to derail you.

Let's begin by looking at a brief overview of the seven stages of development, adult patterns, and lessons of the Soul. This introduction will enhance your selection of the statements which resonate with you.

A much more detailed explanation of each of these stages is offered in the Module dedicated to that specific time period.

Seven Stages, Seven Patterns, Seven Lessons

If your life is not working, it most likely indicates you are disconnected from your authentic self and are, therefore, unable to achieve true mastery in your day-to-day life. There are three primary sources of challenge which explain this disconnection. Either: a) your childhood wounds haunt you, b) the adult blueprints remain ineffective or c) your spiritual evolvement has not been adequately anchored into your day-to-day life and into your physical form.

If there are still wounds from your childhood which need to be addressed, they will haunt you until you address them. If, however, you have done a significant amount of work on your inner child issues and still find your life is not working, then perhaps you have healed the childhood pain but have failed to redesign the belief systems dictating the patterns for failure and success in adulthood.

Your unique blueprint is based on the experiences you endured in childhood and the belief systems and accompanying behaviors which originated from these experiences. To redesign them, you will need to identify the wound and determine the belief systems, as well as the connective, dysfunctional behaviors which prohibit you from achieving the mastery you desire. It is also common, however, that the process of anchoring spiritual evolvement into daily pursuits and into your physical form has not occurred and therefore true mastery in adulthood cannot be attained.

The dysfunctional patterns we develop in childhood not only manifest as maladaptive blueprints in adulthood; they also hold the keys to our possible spiritual lessons. In other words, *the progressive developmental stages of childhood evolve into the progressive steps of adult mastery, which open the door to the progressive lessons confronted in one's pursuit of spiritual empowerment.* A predictable, identifiable and similar process is evident in the progression of each of these areas of development.

The process is circular. By pulling a thread from one area of development, one can begin the process of healing the other two areas because the lessons of the Soul are revealed through the wounds incurred in childhood which manifest as ineffective blueprints in adulthood, which impact mastery in our day-to-day pursuits which, when confronted, give us clues about the lessons of the Soul. It is circular. It is multidimensional—and any block prohibiting this circular flow requires a multidimensional healing. The following section gives you a brief overview of these stages, patterns and possible lessons. Each developmental stage and its counterpart are covered more fully in the Module in which that stage is the focus.

Where It All Begins

We all have one thing in common…we all were once children… and having been children, we each progressed through predictable stages of development as we matured into adulthood. Not one of us escaped this progression, and not one of us completely masters the tasks which challenge us along the way.

These mastered or unmastered tasks follow us into adulthood and either enhance or hinder our success and our ability to maximize our true potential.

The tasks challenged in each childhood stage become the blueprint for how we accomplish success in adulthood and how we relate to the lessons of our Soul.

Examining these tasks and mastering the unresolved issues from childhood gives us the key we need to reach adult maturation with success. Once these steps have been climbed, their lessons can be applied to each and every pursuit we encounter, for each of the developmental stages inherently contains the unique, yet universal ingredients needed to pursue even our most intimate spiritual tasks.

The following material will help you see the circular flow of these potential issues and give you an idea of how they are carried from the unmastered tasks of childhood into adult patterns and perhaps reflect the issues of your Soul.

Infant Stage (Birth to 18 months of age)

The developmental task in childhood is to learn how to trust, to bond, to experience safety. Interaction is based on mirrored reaction and feedback from the outside world—this exchange enables the individual to take form...to develop an identity and an ego. The process takes approximately 18 months before a solid form is established.

The pattern carried into adulthood is to give birth to an idea or principle; to give it form; to develop trust in, and to bond with, a parental projection such as a corporation, church or spiritual source, or any other external structure...or conceive of a new idea or new self-image. This is also evident at the beginning of a new, intimate relationship, or in recommitting to a new form of intimacy in an established relationship.

And the lesson of the Soul is to attain and maintain trust in a spiritual source. The task is to mentally attain and hold a belief system of unity with a Divine Power and to physically anchor the spiritual energy into our day-to-day activities.

Toddler Stage (18 to 36 months of age)

The developmental task in childhood is to learn about boundaries and limitations between self and others, self and environment...to begin to deal with the tension of saying No and hearing No, and to learn how to cope emotionally when experiencing boundaries.

The pattern carried into adulthood is to experiment with and to explore limitations between self and external structures—i.e., where do I end and the outside world begin; where do I end and loved ones begin? The same is true regarding job responsibilities, etc. How can I say No in my day-to-day world and how do I deal with others saying No? How do I deal with limitations being set on me due to circumstances or situations?

And the lesson of the Soul is to experiment with and to explore limitations between earthly and spiritual self. What limits does my physical form have to put on my spiritual beingness? When have I been wounded with respect to setting limits? When have I suffered or been harmed for speaking my truth?

Young Inner Child (3-6 years of age)

The developmental task in childhood is to learn how to negotiate between good and bad, right and wrong, positive and negative aspects of self. Most have developed the cognitive ability to determine what is acceptable and what is not acceptable. You begin to make choices accordingly…you begin to compromise who you are in an attempt to avoid risking the loss of rejection or abandonment. This is the origin of shame and blame.

The pattern carried in adulthood is to assess your internal value system in comparison to an external one. We have bonded significantly enough with our position, an idea or a person, yet we begin to see where we may not be acceptable and so the process of making choices which ensure our connection begins to be made. This lesson also involves sorting out what is going to work for us and what is going to have to be challenged. We begin to speak our truth and attempt to work things out in a negotiating manner. This is the adjustment phase when we juggle our values with another person's values or the values of an organization or corporation, and we attempt to mediate agreement or peaceful coexistence.

This lesson involves "process!" The first and second lessons were bonding and conceiving, then butting up against the limitations and boundaries.

This lesson involves the process of working with those limitations and finding an acceptable resolution.

The lesson of the Soul is to learn how to express compassion for self and others…to be non-judgmental of self and others…to confront and dissolve multidimensional shame and guilt…to find the threads of shame in our Soul's history when we may have turned away from our Source.

Grade School Self (6 to 12 years of age)

The developmental task in childhood is to fit in with peers. We go away to school for the first time and represent our family in the outside world for the first time. It becomes important to be the same as others and to fit in…to not be excluded. We are also introduced to task completion and confront the need to excel in some area of interest.

The recognition step prepares us as individuals to enter the refinement phase where true mastery can occur. Endeavors we pursue have their own identity after these first four steps, but it is the last three steps in adolescence which put our individual signature on it.

The pattern carried in adulthood is to find outside activities and interests, and to develop a support system which supports our inner value system. We need to find a group with whom we fit in…to find a hobby or work which gives us the experience of excelling and succeeding and being "good" at something.

The lesson of the Soul is to identify the moments in our Soul's history when we may have joined groups which led us away from our Source…or placed false loyalty on to a false source. We may need to examine our success at establishing a co-creatorship between our Higher Self and our Human Self and recognize and show appreciation for all that we have had to endure in human form.

Young Inner Teen (12 to 15 years of age)

The developmental task in childhood is to get comfortable with discomfort…to reconcile our experience of being self-conscious and to build self-confidence within a peer structure in which we can own who we truly are.

The pattern carried into adulthood is to learn how to deal with self-consciousness with respect to the outside world. As we move into mastery and autonomy, we go through a stage where our new self-image is uncomfortable and does not quite fit. This dynamic emulates the process we go through as an adolescent when we move into a new frame of reference with respect to our body, with hormonal changes and a new social structure with respect to becoming interested in others sexually. Universally, we are moving into a new arena, and yet, just as we felt as a teenager, we may not feel comfortable with the new image of ourselves or our new role…our concept of success is tried on…but is not quite tailored to us yet.

And the lesson of the Soul is to determine when, in the history of the Soul, we may have been uncomfortable with holding the frequency of Light or acted inappropriately in expressing our creative and sexual passion.

Adolescent (15 to 17 years of age)

The developmental task in childhood is to carve out a definition of self. This is often done somewhat rebelliously because it involves a breaking away from the old system and the old definition experienced in our family. "…To be different means to be separate…" Our task is to achieve individuality and to feel comfortable with a sense of self as we prepare to go into the adult world.

The pattern carried into adulthood is to break away from any external structure which has been used as the source OF identity… to break away from any role or negative, self-limiting image which holds failure. This process can involve rebelling against any external structure which has served as the basis of the definition of self and then replacing it with a new, more current and refined definition of self.

This is the step where the true signature is put on our endeavors or relationships…where an idea or job becomes "ours!" It is a time when we settle into our roles with others. We have more comfort at being who we are and can allow the rest of the world to accept or reject us. Our reference point for self-worth is no longer externally projected. It is now internalized and based on the process of self-referencing.

And the lesson of the Soul is to learn to relate, without rebellion, to a Highest Source. This may lead to an examination of when we carried a false sense of bravado or an ego-laced attachment to power and fame and misused our spiritual attainment.

Young Inner Adult (17 to 21 years of age)

The developmental task in childhood is to successfully move into the adult world with all of the skills necessary to be a mature and emotionally well-balanced individual.

The pattern carried in adulthood is the achievement of maturity which is then taken into the world. The goal is to move into mastery in relationship to external structures…to name and claim our talent and share it with the world at large…irrespective of what form it takes. We are seasoned and comfortable with our achievement. We have learned how to attain and maintain true intimacy with loved ones.

And the lesson of the Soul is to examine our history of expressing our God nature in the real world and to learn how to successfully express our Spiritual values through our day-to-day activities.

Taking An Inventory of the Childhood Issues as They emerge in Day-to-day Life

Take a moment to respond to the following worksheets of the respective inventories. These statements reflect how these issues may be emerging in your day-to-day adult life. They are categorized into the specific seven developmental stages. Again, this inventory will help you explore the ways your issues from childhood are impacting your adult patterns and Soul tasks. By identifying the stage of development to which you most relate, you will begin to create a profile of your wounded one's themes.

I suggest you respond to all seven worksheets and then look them over and begin to decipher where patterns and repetitions appear.

Inventory for Self-Image

Read the following statements and check those with which you resonate.

Infant Stage (Birth to 18 months)

_____1. I struggle with knowing who I am.

_____2. I have difficulty clarifying my own ideas.

_____3. I sometimes do not even feel I have a right to be alive.

_____4. I often feel I do not belong and can't find my place in the world.

Toddler Stage

_____1. If I say No, I fear abandonment.

_____2. I find it difficult to say No to those with whom I am involved.

_____3. I fear if I say yes, I will be expected to say yes all of the time.

_____4. I fight the limitations (rules) I experience in my external world.

Three to Six-Year-Old

_____1. I am judgmental and critical of myself.

_____2. I am judgmental and critical of others.

_____3. I'm not clear about my strengths and challenges.

_____4. I feel I give my power to another when I agree but really don't.

Six to Twelve-Year-Old

_____1. I don't feel seen for who I am by those in my life who I value.

_____2. I don't have many outside interests that I pursue with regularity.

_____3. I wish I could find a good support system of like-minded people.

_____4. In order to fit in, I will adjust my values to those of my peers.

Young Inner Teen (12—15)

_____1. I feel self-conscious about my talents.

_____2. I dislike exposure and prefer to stay hidden.

_____3. I feel the right to claim my true self but awkward in doing so.

_____4. I don't like being too vulnerable.

Adolescent (15-17)

_____1. I don't really know what I like or dislike.

_____2. I like to shock others with my ideas of what is important.

_____3. I am very determined about what I want to accomplish in my life.

_____4. I find other people's opinions about me irrelevant.

Young Inner Adult (17—21)

_____1. I like to hang around others who think and act as I act.

_____2. I wish I could feel authentic – but most of the time I don't.

_____3. I find it difficult to be honest about what I really feel or think.

_____4. I don't feel comfortable exposing who I am and how I feel.

Inventory for "Belief Systems"
Read the following statements and check those with which you resonate.

Infant Stage (Birth to 18 Months)
_____1. I wouldn't say I really think for myself.

_____2. It's hard to clarify my thoughts about matters of the world.

_____3. If someone asks me my opinion, I pretend I do not have one.

_____4. If someone asks me to come up with a plan, I panic!

Toddler Stage (18 to 36 months)
_____1. My ideas are usually different than the mainstream.

_____2. I base my ideas on the ideas of others.

_____3. I seldom have an idea of my own and am influenced by others.

_____4. I assume most people think as I think.

Three to Six-Year-Old
_____1. I feel embarrassed when I feel wrong.

_____2. I have strong opinions even when given new information.

_____3. I don't like people that think differently than I do.

_____4. I keep my thoughts to myself for fear of being judged.

Six to Twelve-Year-Old
_____1. It is important to me that others agree with what I think.

_____2. I have creative ideas and want to be acknowledged for them.

_____3. It is essential that the organizations to which I belong believe as I do.

_____4. I study what others think so I can think that way as well.

_____1. I express my thoughts but only if I know they are going to be accepted.

_____2. I cautiously test other's opinions to see if they think as I do.

_____3. If I state a truth that is different than others, I feel ill at ease.

_____4. It makes me feel nervous when I say what I think and feel judged.

Adolescent (15—17)

_____1. I speak what I think no matter what anyone else says.

_____2. I like to say things that shock others.

_____3. My thoughts may be inconsistent, but they are mine.

_____4. If someone disagrees with me, I will defend my view to the end!

Young Inner Adult (17—21)

_____1. My thoughts are not very formed and are ever-evolving.

_____2. I get nervous when I can't determine what I want to be when I grow up.

_____3. My behavior seldom matches how I think.

_____4. I get uncomfortable expressing my thoughts.

Inventory for "Family, Friends, and Romance"
Read the following statements and check those with which you resonate.

Infant Stage (Birth to 18 months)

_____1. It's hard to identify my interest in someone new.

_____2. My relationships with family members feel stagnant and confined.

_____3. Many of my relationships lack depth and trust.

_____4. I have difficulty initiating contact in new relationships.

Toddler Stage (18 to 36 months)

_____1. I dislike having to say No to a friend or loved one.

_____2. I would rather not ask than to risk being told No.

_____3. I fear if I say yes once, I will be obligated to always say yes.

_____4. If I don't know what I want I remain quiet and simply go along.

Three to Six-Year-Old

_____1. It is difficult for me to articulate what I feel about something.

_____2. I regret it if I state an opinion which is challenged.

_____3. If another's opinion differs from mine, I assume theirs is wrong.

_____4. If I feel I another my power when I agree but really do not.

Six to Twelve-Year-Old

_____1. I want more acknowledgment from those I love.

_____2. I feel invisible and unseen by my family members.

_____3. If I disagree with my partner, I stay silent.

_____4.Even if I have strong feelings, I will still agree with others.

_____1. I am very cautious when I exhibit a new behavior with others.

_____2. I get nervous when I attempt to break away from family ideas.

_____3. I figure nothing is going to change anyway, so why even try?

_____4. I would rather avoid others that are different than me.

Adolescent (15-17)

_____1. Even though my family does not agree with my beliefs, I speak them nonetheless.

_____2. Even if I agree, I enjoy disagreeing just for the fun of it.

_____3. I often find my values are unique and stand out.

_____4. I would rather be dishonest than risk losing a close friend.

Young Inner Adult (17—21)

_____1. My relationships are not really based on mutual trust and appreciation.

_____2. I do not do very well with differences in the relationships I have with others.

_____3. If someone challenges my belief system, I have a hard time defending my position.

_____4. I am uncomfortable with others who "agree to disagree."

Inventory for "Sexuality and Creativity"
Read the following statements and check those with which you resonate.

Infant Stage (Birth to 18 months)
_____1. I find it hard to express my creative ideas.

_____2. I feel like a creative person but don't do much with that feeling.

_____3. My sexual expression is more physical in nature than emotional.

_____4. I have difficulty initiating sexual contact.

Toddler Stage (18 to 36 months)
_____1. I have a hard time saying No to sexual advances.

_____2. I have a lot of creative ideas but not much discipline to manifest them.

_____3. I am afraid if I give in once, I will feel obligated to respond every time.

_____4. I have no idea what I like or want sexually, so I remain quiet.

Three to Six-Year-Old
_____1. I have a hard time setting realistic goals for my creative efforts.

_____2. I feel passionate about my ideas but fear being judged if I express them.

_____3. I don't like to be around someone who is experimental with their sexuality.

_____4. I feel ashamed and shy about my sexual feelings.

_____1. My sexual preferences pretty much fit the societal norm.

_____2. My creative thoughts, which I share with few, are somewhat avant-garde.

_____3. I create a great deal but feel I get little recognition for my efforts.

_____4. I have strong sexual preferences but keep quiet to avoid criticism.

Young Inner Teen (12—15)

_____1. I feel awkward about my sexuality.

_____2. My passion for life and for love frightens me.

_____3. I would rather eat, smoke, drink or addict than let my passion emerge.

_____4. I avoid people who obviously have different sexual preferences than I do.

Adolescent (15-17)

_____1. I like to experiment with sexual preferences even if they are different.

_____2. I have creative talents but do not express them.

_____3. I find my sexual values are unique and stand out.

_____4. I am a person with great passion and will compromise it for nothing.

Young Inner Adult (17—21)

_____1. I wish I could see my sexuality as an extension of the Universal Source.

_____2. Sexuality is sacred, but I don't find many partners who feel the same way.

_____3. If my creative projects are challenged, I feel they have little worth.

_____4. I know I am passionate about life but am afraid to express it.

Inventory for "Job or Career"

Read the following statements and check those with which you resonate.

Infant Stage (Birth to 18 months)

_____1. I have difficulty trusting the value of my ideas.

_____2. If offered a position in a new job, I can't decide what to do.

_____3. The thought of being in business for myself terrifies me.

_____4. I experience great anxiety when beginning a new position.

Toddler Stage (18 to 36 months)

_____1. I find it hard to say No to my employer.

_____2. I would rather not ask for special treatment than to risk being told No.

_____3. If my boss is angry or in a bad mood, I assume I made a mistake.

_____4. If a co-worker asks me to do something, I do it even if I don't want to.

Three to Six-Year-Old

_____1. I worry a great deal about what my co-workers and boss think of me.

_____2. I don't think many of my co-workers are as competent as I.

_____3. If I agree to do something, I stick with it until it's done.

_____4. I feel irritated when others do not have the same value for integrity as I.

_____1. I want more acknowledgment from those with whom I work.

_____2. I feel overlooked by my superiors.

_____3. I think about going into business for myself, but fear I wouldn't succeed.

_____4. I dread giving presentations and avoid promotions because of this.

Young Inner Teen (12—15)

_____1. I feel very cautious when I try a new behavior at work.

_____2. I get nervous if I do something at work which calls attention to me.

_____3. If I don't like something, I keep quiet; why try to buck the system?

_____4. I have some ideas which excite me but I don't share them with anyone.

Adolescent (15-17)

_____1. I am determined to speak my mind, even if it gets me into trouble.

_____2. Even if I agree, I like to disagree with my co-workers, just for the fun of it.

_____3. I enjoy testing the company's rules.

_____4. I have strange ideas and I enjoy shocking others with them.

Young Inner Adult (17—21)

_____1. I wish I enjoyed what I do for a living.

_____2. I don't know what I want to do when I grow up.

_____3. If an evaluation challenges my self-image I feel deflated.

_____4. If only I could have had more training before I could go into business for myself.

Inventory for "Prosperity and Abundance"

Read the following statements and check those with which you resonate.

Infant Stage (Birth to 18 months)

_____1. I have difficulty conceiving of myself as a wealthy person.

_____2. Abundance seems really out of my immediate reach.

_____3. I am so used to struggling I don't know how it would feel to have money.

_____4. I have great wealth I just don't know what to spend it on.

Toddler Stage (18 to 36 months)

_____1. I devise a budget plan but then do not stick to it.

_____2. I wish I could spend money wisely, but don't.

_____3. I don't make a lot of money because I am afraid it would change me.

_____4. If I do get money, I feel a need to spend it right away.

Three to Six-year-old-Stage

_____1. I want just enough money to meet my needs.

_____2. I feel everyone else has more than I.

_____3. I don't like to be around people who have a lot of money.

_____4. When abundant, I feel uncomfortable if I see someone who is not.

Six to Twelve-Year-Old

_____1. It is important to me to "keep up with the Jones'."

_____2. My job pays well and I like others to know this.

_____3. I feel less prosperous than most around me.

_____4. I feel abundant but keep it quiet rather than risk rejection or criticism.

Young Inner Teen

_____1. I feel inadequate when it comes to managing my money.

_____2. I don't have much passion for life or love.

_____3. I believe if I do what I love, the money will follow.

_____4. I avoid people who obviously have significantly more or less money than I.

Adolescent (15—17)

_____1. I spend money on items that most others would not.

_____2. I don't like spending time on anything that doesn't fit with who I am.

_____3. I refuse to spend money on items which are harmful to the planet.

_____4. I purchase only those things which reflect my individual spirit.

Young Inner Adult (17—21)

_____1. I wish my abundance was a direct extension of the Universal energy.

_____2. I feel abundant in my life but know there is room for improvement.

_____3. I do what I love; I just wish the money would follow.

_____4. When I look at the world, I wish I saw more abundance and prosperity.

Inventory for "Body Image and Physical Health"
Read the following statements and check those with which you resonate.

Infant Stage (Birth to 18 months)

_____1. I would like to exercise but have difficulty getting started.

_____2. I find it impossible to decide what kind of exercise plan I want to follow.

_____3. I have a hard time staying present in my body and often dissociate.

_____4. I addict to food or drugs to stay disconnected from my body.

Toddler Stage (18 to 36 months)

_____1. I start an exercise plan but have trouble sticking with it.

_____2. I can adhere to a food plan very strictly, and then I splurge.

_____3. I have a hard time setting realistic physical health goals.

_____4. I am not good at assessing the best food plan for my system.

Three to Six-Year-Old

_____1. Even if my exercise plan becomes too restrictive, I stick to it.

_____2. I am judgmental of my body type and wish it were different.

_____3. I wish I were more in shape, but don't have the time to exercise.

_____4. I am uncomfortable with people who "let themselves go."

Six to Twelve-Year-Old

_____1. I want my peers to acknowledge how good I stay in shape.

_____2. I am very conscientious about my eating habits and like acknowledgment.

_____3. I feel unaware of my body.

_____4. It is important my body is acceptably met by society's standards.

Young Inner Teen (12—15)

_____1. I am self-conscious about my body.

_____2. If someone criticizes the way I look, I believe what they say.

_____3. I wish I could accept my body, but somehow am unable to do so.

_____4. I do not like to eat in front of others.

Adolescent (15—17)

_____1. I know exercising is good for me, but it is such a fad, I refuse to do it.

_____2. Even though certain foods do not agree with me, I eat them anyway.

_____3. I eat, drink or addict when I am angry.

_____4. I don't like to relax, it makes me too nervous.

Young Inner Adult (17—21)

_____1. I wish I accepted my body just the way it is, but I don't.

_____2. I try to eat in a healthy and responsible way but am not really good at it.

_____3. I like would like to exercise at least 3 - 5 times a week but.....

_____4. I want to feel more comfortable in my body than I do now.

Review your responses to each area. Are there certain stages of development which emerge? Did specific themes become apparent? Record what you have learned about yourself in this experience. Make a note of the stage or stages of development you resonated with most predominantly. Please Record Your Responses To Your Answers. What Did You Learn In The Process That You Can Now Apply To Your Daily Workouts And Your Day-To-Day Life?

In the following modules, you will be working with the respective stages of development and identifying how the unmastered tasks and achievements from that time in your life either hinder or enhance your participation in this program. You will look at each stage of development from the eyes of your Soul and the perspective of your cherished saboteur™. To set that intention, review your responses and begin to ascertain your theme-then prepare yourself for this brief, introductory meditation.

Meditation: Close your eyes—when you have a sense of your theme, bring your focus to the center of your being and call forth that part of you who represents this theme—the part who is a composite of the vulnerable part of you who has manifested and enacted this wound. How does this part of you present itself in the present moment? Keep in mind that this cherished saboteur™™ *often changes forms and emerges in the most unlikely manner. As the week's progress, you will come to know this part of you much more fully—you will see how it attempts to protect you even when it sabotages your efforts to achieve. It is cherished because it sacrifices everything to remain loyal—even if that loyalty is unwarranted. As you move through each week you will begin to develop your own formula for befriending this part of you. You will design the backbone for a lifetime formula which will allow success.*

You will be introduced to each developmental stage; given ways to identify the impact the experience from that time of your life has had on your adult life. You will be provided with insight into the potential lessons of your soul; given an overview of the muscle group which may be holding the issues from each stage and offered information on how the energy centers or chakra centers of the etheric body carry the themes of each developmental stage. All of these methods will enable you to work with this saboteur and bring its efforts into alignment so it works for you and for your highest and best. For now…set your intention for transformation—communicate that intention to every cell and fiber of your being…breathe it in…hold it. When it feels right, bring your focus back to the center of your being with the assurance that your contract is about to be rewritten and your healing is about to begin. What you will experience is a very comprehensive approach to holistically heal through your commitment to and implementation of "conscious aerobic exercise.

REFER TO THE "DAILY CHECK-IN SHEETS" AND THE "7-DAY REVIEW" FOUND IN THE APPENDIX TO LOG YOUR EXPERIENCE.

Designing The Backbone Of Your Lifetime Formula For Success

Your efforts in this last module familiarized you with the structure of the generic program. You gave form to your Future Self; established your first goal and flushed out the cherished saboteur™. You are now equipped to tailor your regimen to your specific strengths and challenges and create a structure which will serve you for a lifetime of successful pursuits. The structure you are about to develop will be the one you will use repeatedly to attain future goals.

As you progress in your Soul Steps program you will have the opportunity to study your responses to what you have designed by observing your program through a finer lens. The lens provided through the delineation of each of the seven developmental stages assists you in looking at the issues of your cherished saboteur™ from a variety of angles. The Adult Self engages in this study on behalf of the wounded self. Its intent is to identify the context of the situations in which your wounded self feels victimized and to respond accordingly so this part of you can be freed to once again trust. The cherished saboteur™ only sabotages your efforts to succeed when he or she experiences the current situation as a threat to survival and is attempting to self-preserve and remain safe.

You will be guided through the essence of each developmental stage and invited to examine how your experience from that time in your life either enhances or challenges your ability to succeed in attaining your desired goals. The impact of your experience from each developmental stage will vary—some will carry more weight than others. However, by the completion of this Program, you will have obtained a kaleidoscopic profile of every angle of your cherished saboteur™ and be equipped to identify it—irrespective of the manner in which it emerges in your attempts to succeed.

Once you "know" who inside is afraid and what he or she needs—you are never again ill-equipped to respond. The partnership developed between your body, mind, heart, and Soul; your Angels and/or your Higher Guidance ensures your ability to succeed. Your commitment to your exercise enables you to anchor your success into every cell and every fiber of your being. This is the reward of engaging holistically in "conscious aerobic exercise." You never again fear your inability to cope because when you identify that you are out of alignment, you have the tools to realign.

In this next Module, as you begin to review your program with more depth, you meet the aspect within who either compromises or augments your efforts and ability to give form to new endeavors. You actually began working with the remnants from the infant stage of development the minute you signed up for this program and began to design your day-to-day regimen. As you read the following material, reflect on what has worked and what has not worked in your first four modules. Keep this in mind as you review the following material on the stages, patterns, and lessons related to this first developmental stage. Use the following focus questions for your discovery.

Fifth Module—
The Infant

From Abandonment To Union

"Your body does not lie. Your body relates to you, the Adult Self, like an infant relates to his or her Mother. When you think of your body in this fashion, how good of a parent do you feel you are?

THE INFANT WITHIN (Birth to 9 months)

THE FIRST DEVELOPMENTAL stage in childhood is infancy. The task in infancy is to develop a sense of trust and safety in relation to our environment. This is accomplished through the relationship we have with our mother or primary caretaker. From Her, we learn, body to body, what it means to be safe. If she transmits acceptance, calmness, and security, we internalize that experience to the depth of our physical being and trust it is safe to exist, develop and take form. When we experience this sense of safety and trust, we develop the capacity to experience mastery in every area of life. However, if our primary caretaker is tentative about her mothering skills, ambivalent about motherhood, distracted from her maternal tasks because of an external life crisis which demands her attention, we internalize unrest, feel unsafe and relate to our environment in a tentative and ambivalent manner.

FOCUS QUESTIONS TO PONDER WHICH RELATE TO THE INFANT STAGE OF DEVELOPMENT:

Begin by asking yourself these questions to get a bird's eye view of how you relate to this stage of development.

Safety—Do I feel safe in my body…with myself…in my relationship to a God/Higher Power…in the world and, if working with another, with my buddy? What does safety mean to me…to my inner child?

Trust—Do I trust myself to follow through with my commitments? Does my inner child trust me? Do I trust others; my Higher Power? Do I consider myself trustworthy?

Ability to Bond—Do I feel connected to and bonded with my body…with Mother Earth…with others? What are my strengths and challenges with respect to giving form to this program…to planting the seeds of my plan? Do I feel bonded with God/HP?

Faith and Abandonment—How do I define faith? In what do I have faith? Have I ever felt abandoned by my faith or have I abandoned my faith in myself, others or God/Higher Power? Does my inner child have faith in me? Do I have faith in my body?

With these thought-provoking questions in mind, now turn your focus to exploring the context of these issues which originated in the first stage of development from birth to approximately eighteen months of age.

Developmental Tasks In Infancy (Birth to Eighteen Months)

As infants, we cannot assess when our mother's reactions are in response to us and when they are in response to external circumstances. We self-reference every event and organically assume responsibility for all reactions to us. These reactions become the blueprint which ultimately dictates the degree of safety we feel in trusting others and in allowing ourselves to become attached to them. If in infancy, we are not safe to trust, we cannot bond. If we cannot bond, we cannot successfully attach. This inability results in a longing. We long for that attachment. Our sense of safety is built on healthy ego development which involves being able to adequately attach. Once we attach, we then have something from which to detach.

It is this attachment/detachment process the personality uses to establish an identifiable and separate form. The mirrored reactions and interactions we experience with our primary caretaker in these early months enable us to begin to develop our unique identity. This exchange enables us to claim our right to exist and thus take form.

How Patterns May Have Been Carried Into Adulthood

If as a child, we had difficulty taking form, we will not have the internal point of reference needed in adulthood to give form to anything in our day-to-day lives. The adult challenge which relates to this developmental stage is to give form to ideas, goals, to a self-image, body image, financial plan, and exercise plan or to anything in our lives we want to create. Every endeavor we pursue requires a beginning, a seed, a birth. Every inspiration which leads to action begins with the birth of an idea which is then nurtured and given substance and form. If the original blueprint for conception and formation is faulty, the process of giving birth to that which we want to manifest will be faulty. Just as an infant has to endure and survive the birthing process before it can obtain the feedback which allows it to take form, the universal challenge of the first step to adult mastery is to have our ideas and goals survive their own birth so they can develop and thus take a tangible form.

Once the idea has taken form or the goal has been established, the second component of this first step to mastery is to successfully bond with the external object of choice. This requires developing trust and faith in the idea or goal sufficiently enough to "bond" with it. This bonding may also occur with a parental figure, such as a corporation, a church or spiritual source; a significant other or any external structure. We may simply "bond" with the creation of a new idea or bond through a heartfelt commitment to a new pursuit such as the desire to attain financial security or engage in a physical exercise regimen. It is this experience which gives us the foundation to conceive of a new idea or to give birth to a new goal and then to nurture this idea or goal until it develops a substantial and tangible identity of its own.

Potential Spiritual Lesson

A potential spiritual lesson which can extend from this developmental stage and this step of mastery is the theme of needing to attain and maintain trust in a spiritual source, a power greater than that which our personality knows. The challenge may be to mentally attain and hold a belief system which incorporates unity with a divine power and to then be able to anchor that spiritual energy into our day-to-day activities and endeavors.

Difficulties in any of the above areas may indicate you would benefit from exploring the origin of such difficulties. This soul theme may have even been mirrored in your childhood experiences of the religious organization in which you were raised. You may have experienced inconsistencies in the church doctrines which eroded your trust in the organization and therefore in the spiritual source which it represented. Now, in your present day life, you may find it difficult to trust and put your faith in any power greater than self. It is hard to believe and have faith.

How do you relate to what you have just read? Review the times in your adult life when you have been confronted with starting something new. How did you commit? Do you have a difficult time bonding with a new idea or pursuit? How does your past experience now relate to your experience in this program? Record any findings in your journal. Then proceed to look at the issues from this stage of development from the perspective of the following specific areas of concern. You already previewed these areas of concern when you responded to the statements last week as you were flushing out the essence and obtaining the profile of your cherished saboteur™. The following glimpse will make this assessment more specific. It may be useful to refer back to your response to the first sections of each of those sheets.

A Review of How Tasks From Infancy Emerge as Goals in Adulthood with Respect to Specific Areas of Concern:

The following offers a brief overview of how unresolved issues from your infant stage of development may be impacting you in these specific areas of concern. The statements have been repeated here to assist you in your evaluation.

1. Body Image—Physical Body—Goal is to make inner commitments to goals for physical form, physical fitness…to become and stay present in body without numbing out or dissociating.

_____1. I would like to exercise but have difficulty getting started.

_____2 .I find it impossible to decide what kind of exercise plan I want to follow.

_____3. I have a hard time staying present in my body and often dissociate.

_____4. I addict with food or drugs to stay disconnected from my body.

2. Self Image—Emotional Body—Goal is to be able to feel good about who we are…about our value system and living within an acceptable expression of what we feel about ourselves and about life in general.

_____1. I struggle with knowing who I am.

_____2 .I have difficulty in clarifying my own ideas.

_____3. I sometimes do not even feel I have a right to be alive.

_____4. I often feel I do not belong—like I cannot find my place in the world.

3. Belief Systems—Mental Body—Goal is to give form to the solidified view of self…to develop a definite sense of self…acquiring the ability to describe self objectively…I AM _____. "Wait, I am my own person." It's to come to that realization.

_____1. I don't really think for myself.

_____2. I find it challenging to clarify my thoughts about matters of the world.

_____3. If someone asks me my opinion, I pretend I do not have one.

_____4. If someone asks me to come up with a plan, I panic!

4. Spirituality—Spiritual Body (Spiritual Path or Recovery Program)—Goal is to give birth to the idea that there is a power greater than self. This can be done by giving form to the practice of our chosen spiritual path, by officially joining an organization or spiritual group or by making a commitment to a spiritual leader.

_____1. I have difficulty trusting in a Higher Source.

_____2. I am unclear about my views of a Higher Source.

_____3. I feel a need to belong to an organized, spiritual community.

_____4. I intellectualize the concept of a Higher Source but do not feel it.

5. Family and Intimate Relationships—Goal is to acknowledge an interest in forming a relationship with an intimate partner or to rekindle an interest in deepening an existing relationship.

_____1. I have difficulty determining if I am interested in someone new.

_____2. My relationships with family members feel stagnant and confined.

_____3. Many of my relationships lack depth and trust.

_____4. I have difficulty initiating contact in new relationships.

6. Sexuality and Passion—Goal is to own not only our physical passion but emotional passion as well…to give form to our sexual preferences and to acknowledge our self as a sexual being with sexual needs…owning our sexuality as opposed to being detached from our sexuality…also to give form to our passion for something creative in life by birthing an investment in an idea or goal.

_____1. I find it hard to express my creative ideas.

_____2. I feel like a creative person but don't do much with that feeling.

_____3. My sexual expression is more physical in nature than emotional.

_____4. I have difficulty initiating sexual contact.

7. Prosperity and Abundance—Goal is to give birth to a vision of what kind of wealth we want to have…what does wealth look like, who are we as a wealthy person? The goal is to create a vision of wealth so the seed can be planted…defining what is feasible and within reach of our vision of self so that we can indeed become a wealthy and prosperous person.

_____1. I have difficulty conceiving of myself as a wealthy person.

_____2. Abundance seems out of my immediate reach.

_____3. I am so familiar with struggling I can't imagine having money.

_____4. I have great wealth—I just don't know what to spend it on.

8. Job, Career or Climb on the Corporate Ladder—Goal is to establish a vision of what we want to do…to give birth to the commitment to create it or to seek and accept a position for which we have been hired. If we are involved in the corporate world already, this step may involve applying for a new position and then developing trust in the organization as we determine if it will live up to promised perks such as vacation and sick time being honored; health benefits being provided and profit sharing being offered.

_____1. I have difficulty trusting the value of my ideas.

_____2. If offered a position in a new job I can't decide what to do.

_____3. The thought of being in business for myself terrifies me.

_____4. I experience great anxiety when beginning a new position.

As you peruse the above material, contemplate how the issues of this developmental stage interface with your daily life and perhaps reflect the issues and lessons of your Soul. Then turn your focus to your body and to the muscle group which may hold this essence of your trust and need to feel safe.

WORKING WITH THE CHEST MUSCLE WHICH CORRELATES TO THIS STAGE OF DEVELOPMENT

When we encounter life situations with which we are unable to cope, the unexpressed emotional energy of those situations gets stored in the muscular tissues and fibers of the body. Each muscle group holds a theme of these issues. All of our frozen feelings are lodged in the muscular structure of our physical form and will be unleashed as we proceed with our athletic endeavors. Again, the body does not lie. As you, week after week, bring focus to the different areas of emotional challenge carried over from childhood, your body will release the unexpressed energy related to that challenge.

In this next section, I invite you to work with the specific muscle group which may carry your issues related to this stage of development. The area of the body which most often carries the theme of trust, safety, and fear of abandonment is the chest area because the chest muscles are the umbrella for the heart. When we begin to work with this muscle group; strengthen it and flex it, we dislodge any issues of the heart this area may have housed.

Our heart muscle is the chief muscle which is strengthened through aerobic exercise. Our heart is also the chief area which responds to the pain of abandonment, mistrust, and fear. The sacred chamber of our inner heart is where we place our children within so they can feel safe. It is the foundation of inner trust and must, therefore, be addressed in the infancy of your program.

Chest Muscle Meditation: *I invite you now to bring your focus to your chest and to the area of your heart. Breathe into it and ask your heart to reveal any issues it may have held for you. Listen and record your responses in your journal. Learn to understand the language of your body and it will always reveal your most beneficial next step.*

THE SEVEN ENERGY CENTERS OF THE BODY

Mastering the art of balance between the emotional, mental, spiritual, and physical bodies involves mastering the influx of energy which flows between these four bodies. Energy is the vitality of our existence and in order to master the containment and expression of it, we need to understand it. Each of us has seven primary energy centers which connect our spiritual body to our physical one. They are referred to as chakra centers. They operate on subtle levels and are invisible to the naked eye, yet affect every aspect of our life.

In effect, these seven centers act as transformers—or sending and receiving stations—negotiating the flow of energy which comes from us and to us moment to moment. They are situated in the etheric fields of our being along the spinal column at the base of the spine, the pelvic area, midway between the base and the navel, near the heart, throat, and third-eye area and at the top of the head. As we come into contact with each of these chakra centers we are given an opportunity to master another dimension of energy. They correlate to the seven stages of development because they hold the vibrational agenda for learning how to contain and dissolve the tension associated with each developmental task. Each challenge presents a rite of passage which escorts us to the next developmental stage or progression of mastery.

These chakras are the central processing centers for every aspect of our being. Blockage or other energetic dysfunction in the chakras usually give rise to disorders in the body and disrupts how we think, feel and connect with our Angels and Higher Guidance. A defect in the energy flow through any given chakra will impair the entire energy field's ability to process energy—affecting all levels of the being. The energy field is a holistic entity; every part of it affects every other part.

Again, it is important to understand that these chakra centers do not actually exist as "objects" in the physical body. They are energy patterns which vibrate at an energetic frequency on the etheric level and produce a certain hue or intrinsic color associated with that specific chakra. In other words, each energy center has its own *true color* of the visible light spectrum associated with it. An introduction to the nature of each energy center is provided in the respective stages of development to which they correlate.

THE CHAKRA CENTER WHICH CORRELATES TO THIS STAGE OF DEVELOPMENT IS THE ROOT CHAKRA

The first chakra is located in the spiritual body near the base of the spine. It governs the issues of survival on the physical plane and connects us to the earth. We cannot evolve spiritually without having a secure base in the physical world. When this energy center is vibrating at its highest frequency the color is that of a violet flame. It is this color which assists in the transmutation of earthly challenges regarding survival and issues with respect to trusting and feeling safe. As we encounter physical traumas and life events which are wounding, the chakra energy center begins to spin at a slower rate and takes on a denser, reddish tone.

When working with the issues of the personality it is often helpful to first accelerate the frequency of the spin by flooding it with the pure color of ruby red. Ultimately, however, the goal is to bring that frequency to its true vibrational color of violet. Energizing this energy center with this color balances your needs in the physical and strengthens your connection to both Mother Earth and the spiritual realm.

This energy center is associated with the infant self and the infant's needs because the infant carries our basic need for survival. It is from birth to approximately the age of eighteen months when we learn to trust that our basic needs will be acknowledged and met. In adulthood, this pattern is reflected in the mechanics of our daily living. If your base connection with the physical plane was faulty—as will be evident in your exploration of the infant stage of your development—your energy pattern emanating from this center will be distorted and create disturbances which will need to be addressed and balanced.

Root Chakra Meditation: *Take a moment to bring your focus to the bottom of your spine. Imagine a ball of energy rotating and being infused with a brilliant color of ruby red. Allow this energy center to spin out the issue related to your fears of abandonment, safety, and trust and be realigned to harmony and union with your Higher Guidance. See your Angels now touching this area of your spine and using their angel dust to calm any fears and assuage any doubts of being loved, protected and safe. See the energy center shifting in color from the deep ruby red as the issues are purified and replaced to that of the illuminated violet flame which will keep this area balanced and in a state of purity. When you feel complete, take another deep breath, open your eyes and record what you experienced in your journal.*

To bring closure to this week's work, reflect once again on how your cherished saboteur™ emerges with respect to your feeling safe and in your attempts to begin new endeavors. What has your Adult Self learned which will now assist it in responding to the needs of this wounded self so the tendency to sabotage can be dissolved? Record your answers in your journal.

Closing Meditation: *Now close your eyes and see this wounded infant self in front of you...ask what is needed in order for this wounded one to feel safe. Respond to that need and then invite this little one to reside in the center of the sacred chamber of your heart where he/she will be safe. Fill your heart center with the golden light of love and the healing light of the violet flame. Then bring your attention to the center of your head and ask that the master cell is re-activated with this new DNA vibration of safety and trust. Feel the energy pulsating through your body as it travels down your spinal cord to your creator cell where this same intention is decreed. Take a deep breath and ask that every cell in your body now holds this new DNA patterning and that the muscles which have resonated with the disturbance now be relaxed, aligned and harmonized. Take a deep breath and record your experience in your journal. As you progress through your week keep these experiences fresh in your mind and in your intentions.*

REFER TO THE "DAILY CHECK-IN SHEETS" AND THE "7-DAY REVIEW" FOUND IN THE APPENDIX TO LOG YOUR EXPERIENCE.

Sixth Module—
The Toddler

From Betrayal To Trust

For the toddler, mastering the art of discernment is based upon feeling secure enough to experiment with what does and does not feel good and then developing the ability to distinguish between the two—to instinctively notice the contrast of feelings between the two. In adulthood, we draw from this mastery to make the conscious choices which dictate the quality of our life

THE TODDLER WITHIN (18-36 months)

IN THE LAST Module, you gave form to your plan and you are now ready to move to the second phase of mastery. This phase involves stepping back from the structure you gave birth to and discerning what is working and what part of your plan will need to be modified or adjusted. Your focus shifts from conception and formation to separation and discernment.

This discernment will allow you to identify the limitations of your program. It will assist you in examining your food plan; your exercise regimen or in determining if the goals you have set for yourself are realistic. It will help you examine the limitations you may feel in your relationship to your Higher Power and help you be honest with yourself as to how you are implementing your spiritual practice. It can assist you in setting limits with your behaviors…in creating boundaries between the addict or co-dependent within you and the part of you who seeks recovery and growth. It can give you information revealing which belief systems need to be revised; which feelings need to be owned and processed and how your blueprint for success or failure with respect to your program needs to be modified.

Your ability to effectively step back (separate from) and assess (discern) your program will mirror the successes and challenges you encountered in the Toddler Stage of Childhood which occurred between the ages of eighteen months and three years. Keep this in mind as you review the following material on the stages, patterns, and lessons. Use the following focus questions to deepen and enhance your discovery.

FOCUS QUESTIONS TO PONDER WHICH RELATE TO THE TODDLER STAGE OF DEVELOPMENT:

Ability to Say and Hear No—Use this week to explore your comfort or discomfort with saying and hearing No. How do you respond when someone says No to you? Do you feel shame for having asked? How do you feel when you say No to others? Can you say No with compassion or does it have to be with a force which masks your discomfort? Can you say No and feel calm or is it followed by a sense of guilt, perhaps even shame? In which relationships do you experience difficulty hearing and saying No and in which relationships do you feel accepting and confident of hearing and saying No?

Discerning Separateness and Having the Ability to Set Personal and Emotional Boundaries—Boundaries enable us to experience where we end and where another begins. Boundaries are what keep us from merging with others and taking on their feelings—being able to ascertain what is ours and what is another's. Use this week to explore the potential issues you may have with merging with others emotionally. Do you lose your identity when you become involved with others? Do you merge with your significant other and begin to take on his or her feelings? Do you feel secure enough to be separate and able to say, "This is yours, not mine..." Spiritual boundaries are what allow us to feel trust that what we are "intuiting" is of a higher nature and not mere "psychic interference." How much do you trust your connection to Spirit? Also, explore how well you are able to set boundaries with respect to your body's needs.

Claiming Our Right To Choose—Our ability to claim this right is based on our trust of self and our ability to discern what feels divinely accurate and what feels toxic. Often we ignore the fact that we have the right to choose how we feel; how we respond and react. Instead, we allow ourselves to be unconscious and pushed along by fate, "the universe," our Higher Power or the choices of others. Subtly, we can give up the responsibility of holding ourselves accountable for our choices. Notice this week if there are any areas in your life which you rationalize the circumstances. Are there some areas of your life in which you own your choices more comfortably? In what areas of your life do you choose to remain a victim?

Ambivalence—Ambivalence is feeling two ways about the same thing at the same time—part of you wants to excel and part of you wants to sluff off—part of you wants to progress and part of you wants to stay stuck—part of you wants to be accountable and part of you wants to be a victim and blame others. Ambivalence results when we expect ourselves to feel only one way about the circumstances in our lives instead of a myriad of ways which need to be addressed and resolved. Ambivalence is a way we keep ourselves from moving forward and from coming into the third option which is compassionate acceptance of who we are and of what we do at all times. If we are truly accepting of ourselves there are no dichotomous feelings. We do not feel divided because we are accepting of our diversity, fragmentation, and inconsistencies. Ambivalence results when we are unable to embrace our human and Higher Self with the same degree of reverence for both. Integration is being able to hold the duality of both experiences with gratitude and value. Examine the areas of your life where you feel split or torn between two distinct feelings and these two feelings result in your experiencing your life in black and white terms—all or nothing terms—as opposed to feeling integrated with respect to your duality.

Developmental Tasks In The Toddler Stage (Eighteen Months—Three Years)

This stage of development is when you first began to experiment with being separate from your caretaker and experienced a taste of the independence resulting from that separation. Remember, you cannot separate if you never attached. This step of mastery builds on the first step. Your separation and independence enable you to step back and discern what works and what does not work. As a toddler, you begin to trust yourself enough to make adjustments in your behavior and to experiment with who you are. For the toddler, mastering the art of discernment is based upon feeling secure enough to experiment with what does and does not feel good and then developing the ability to distinguish between the two—to instinctively notice the contrast of feelings between the two.

The toddler years were the first time in your development when you were mobile enough to walk away from your caretaker and verbal enough to refuse and protest. This was when you began the transition from dependency to autonomy. It is a process which continues throughout your life. Learning how to establish and maintain personal boundaries was essential if you were to succeed at establishing a sense of self. Boundaries were emotional and physical separations from your caretaker. Boundaries were the manner in which you established your independence. They enabled you to experience control over yourself and your environment.

Learning to say "no" gave you this sense of control. Hearing No was also important. Having a caretaker who gave you clear boundaries helped you feel safe. It gave you clear limits and an idea of what was expected of you. It also gave you a way to experience your separateness. It gave you the opportunity to begin to experience the tension of your separateness.

You were, for the first time, exposed to the life-long conflict of choosing between self and others. "Do I respond to the needs of others or meet the needs of self?" You vacillated between compliance and defiance as you refined your definition of self. Working with this struggle set the stage for you to learn how to distinguish between what you felt and what others felt...distinguish between what felt good to you and what did not feel good to you. It taught you how to discern contrast.

How Patterns May Have Been Carried Into Adulthood

To successfully mature into emotionally healthy adults we needed to have experienced in childhood that it was acceptable to say "no" without being punished and encouraged to hear "no" when it was for our safety and protection. Few of us received this encouragement because it required our caretaker to allow us the luxury of experimenting with testing their limits and setting our boundaries. The healthiest way a caretaker can do this is by providing a set of choices which empowers the toddler to choose between two acceptable options. This empowers the toddler and yet allows the parent to still be in charge of the parameters of choice. Most often our caretakers were ambivalent about letting go and therefore gave us mixed messages about our acting independently.

They may have responded with a rigid structure or with no structure at all. If they responded rigidly we would have never been able to develop the internal structure needed to establish our own separateness. Instead, they would have overpowered us, forcing us into submission through ridicule and/or abuse. If they provided no structure, then we would have experienced difficulty in discerning where they ended and we began because we would have no clear point of reference for the division between us. If, as toddlers, we were given too much control over our lives we would have begun to melt into boundariless oblivion. We would have experienced tension in response to feeling unprotected and unsafe. Either approach from our caretakers would have left its mark.

In adulthood, this impairs our ability to experiment with and to explore limitations between ourselves and external structures. It makes it difficult to assess where we end and the outside world begins... to determine where we end and our loved ones begin. It makes it challenging to have a clear idea of the expectations of our responsibilities at work. We may be ill-equipped to say No in our day-to-day world, to set limits for ourselves with our bosses, loved ones, and friends. Likewise, we may find ourselves confused about how to deal with others saying No...with how to deal with limitations being set on us due to circumstances or situations.

In order to be prepared for the third stage of development which teaches us how to make adjustments and modify or revise any life goals we have established, we will need to learn how to assess what is working and what is not. We do this by experiencing the "contrast" between how we feel when the energy in our lives flows and how we feel when it seems blocked.

Carrying this ability to experience contrast into adulthood enables us to begin to consciously assess what we want and do not want. It puts us in a position to consciously set intentions regarding what we want. Through prayers and affirmations, we begin to focus on creating and attracting that which we have discerned we want.

This practice is called "deliberate creation." It involves identifying what we want, envisioning those wants and, through prayers and affirmations, mastering the ability to command universal law of attraction to manifest and attract what we want. The vibration you attain through mastery of this ability is the vibration of joy—because the frequency of energy required to intend in this manner is a joy! Joy is an expression of trusting ourselves enough to be able to set boundaries and limitations.

Potential Spiritual Lesson

A potential lesson which extends from this developmental stage and this step of mastery is the need to experiment with and explore limitations experienced between your earthly and spiritual bodies or your personality and your Soul. You might find yourself pondering the limits your physical form has created for your spiritual beingness. You may begin to have memories of being wounded when you set limits or of times when you suffered or were harmed for speaking your truth. It will also become apparent as to how well you deal with the ambivalence of being in the density of your physical form versus the freedom felt in the spiritual world.

The unresolved issues of your Soul and the themes your Soul charted to focus on during this lifetime may have originated from a time when you first separated from the Universal Source and had to deal with the limitations of body and the temptations of the earthly plane. Most often the experience of boundaries and limitations which emerge in adulthood carry the same vibration of how we responded to these issues when experienced in other times and other places. These Soul experiences may even carry life and death themes. There may be times in the history of your Soul when you were abandoned or killed for saying "No" or for claiming an independent position in response to a structure or a person in authority. If this pattern resonates with you, for further exploration and examination I recommend you refer to and apply the Ten-step Healing Formula provided for you in the next section. Before you proceed, record any thoughts or findings in your journal. Then look at the issues of this stage of development from the perspective of the following specific areas of concern. You already previewed these areas of concern when you responded to the statements in the fourth week of your program when you were flushing out the essence and obtaining the profile of your cherished saboteur™. The following glimpse will make this assessment more specific. It may be useful to refer back to your responses to the toddler sections of each of those sheets.

A Review of How Tasks From the Toddler Years Emerge as Goals in Adulthood with Respect to Specific Areas of Concern:

1. Body Image—Physical Body—Having given form to your commitment to a physical program or goal in the previous stage, these goals pertain to actually putting these goals into action so you can evaluate their effectiveness. You will be asking questions such as—How realistic is my plan? What are its limitations? Can I succeed? You will examine where you can say No to what you agreed to limit and where this is a challenge. You will ask yourself "Can I follow through with my plan? What are my limitations?"

_____1. I start an exercise plan but have trouble sticking with it.

_____2. I can adhere to a food plan very strictly, and then I splurge.

_____3. I have a hard time setting realistic physical health goals.

_____4. I am not good at assessing the best food plan for my system.

2. Self-Image—Emotional Body—This goal is to begin to test the acceptance of your individuality. You explore which situations reward you for being who you are and which situations disapprove of your independence? What happens when you do say no? How do you respond if you are confronted with the limitations of the structure by an authority figure? How are these issues emerging in your program? Are you being able to set limits with your toddler self who wants to derail the adult from staying on task with the program's regimen?

_____1. If I say No, I fear abandonment.

_____2. I find it difficult to say No to those with whom I am involved.

_____3. I fear if I say yes, I will be expected to say yes all of the time.

_____4. I fight the limitations (rules) I experience in my external world.

3. Belief Systems—Mental Body—The goal now is to examine how your belief system is fitting in with what you are creating in your program—in your life. What thoughts support your newly defined self and what thoughts challenge the concept of a new you? When

do your thought patterns support your efforts? In which situations does your self-talk compromise your efforts? These issues are all evidence of the belief systems which may need to be redesigned using the exercises included in the generic healing formula presented in a later chapter.

_____1. My ideas are usually different than the mainstream.

_____2. I draw most of my opinions from those of others.

_____3. When I do have an idea of my own I can easily be influenced by others.

_____4. I assume most people think as I think.

4. Spirituality—Spiritual Body—(Spiritual Path or Recovery Program)

When you get to this place in your program, the goal is to explore how you are relying on the dogma of a path or philosophy you have chosen to follow to set limits on your life for you. You may also witness, at this stage of your program as well as any other endeavor, a healthy rebellion beginning to form…"Where do the limits of this path or organization blend with my own and where do they conflict?" At this early stage, however, most often, the excitement of joining a group or organization overrides the need for autonomy. So we tend to choose, at least initially, in favor of the limits of the external structure rather than relying on our own internal one.

_____1. I feel most secure when I abide by the rules of my spiritual organization.

_____2. I feel rebellious against the rules of my organization.

_____3. I act differently when I am in church and when I am not.

_____4. Unclear about what I believe, I follow an organized dogma.

5. Family and Intimate Relationships—The goal with respect to relationships is for you to begin to examine the boundaries needed in relation to loved ones…how do family members and loved ones respond when I say No to them? Is it well received? How do I

deal with hearing No? Again, determine if you can say No or Yes without resentment or engulfment.

_____1. I dislike having to say No to a friend or loved one.

_____2. I would rather not ask for a favor than risk being told No.

_____3. I fear if I say yes once, I will be obligated to say yes the next time.

_____4. If I do not know what I feel or want I remain quiet and simply go along.

6. Sexuality and Passion—Your goal with respect to this area is to begin to explore the limitations and boundaries of your own sexual choices and examine the degree to which you are able to say No or Yes and retain your authenticity. You will begin to identify the degree of passion involved in a project or a goal…"How do I have to make this scheme more manageable…more realistic to accomplish these tasks? How can I make it work? How can I put the passion of my design into action with scrutiny?"

_____1. I have a hard time saying No to sexual advances.

_____2. I have a lot of creative ideas but not much discipline to manifest them.

_____3. I am afraid if I give in once, I will feel obligated to respond every time.

_____4. I have no idea what I like or want, so I remain quiet.

7. Prosperity and Abundance—Your goal here is to set appropriate limits on your spending, to see where you need to set limits on your budget and where you have been too restrictive. You will begin to ask yourself if you see the world from a perspective of scarcity or prosperity. If you're in debt and borrow against tomorrow, you might examine if that action shows scarcity or lack of faith that what you need will be given.

_____1. I don't believe that "the money will always be there."

_____2. I devise a budget plan but then do not stick to it.

_____3. I wish I could spend money wisely—but don't.

_____4. I do not make a lot of money because I am afraid it would change me.

_____5. If I do get money I feel a need to spend it right away.

8. Job, Career or Climb on the Corporate Ladder—Your goal here is to begin to explore and resolve any tension between your personal needs and the companies' expectations…to experiment with setting limits and saying No (i.e. Am I expected to stay late and what happens when I say No?) as well as testing limits of corporation and hearing No. (i.e. Can I be late without recrimination… can I abuse time spent at lunch…can I call in sick without consequence?) You will also be developing a realistic perspective as to what the company can provide you in terms of advancement, room to grow…recognizing the realistic limits of the corporate structure.

_____1. I find it hard to say No to my employer.

_____2. I would rather not ask for special treatment than risk being told No.

_____3. If my boss is angry or in a bad mood I assume I made a mistake.

_____4. If a co-worker asks me to do something I do it even if I don't want to.

As you peruse the above material, contemplate how the issues of this developmental stage interface with your daily life and perhaps reflect the issues and lessons of your Soul. Then turn your focus to your body and to the buttocks muscles which often posture the essence of your issues involving setting limits, establishing boundaries and developing a sense of your independent self.

WORKING WITH THE BUTTOCKS MUSCLE WHICH CORRELATES TO THIS STAGE OF DEVELOPMENT

The area of the body which most often carries the energy related to setting boundaries and being able to say yes and no with integrity is the buttocks area. These muscles are the strongest, most powerful muscles in the body when given permission to develop and hold their power. They also hold the energy of the inflated ego—i.e. the phrases of being a *pain in the butt* or *a tight ass*—which suggests a rigidity in one's nature.

These muscles are also the central muscles related to the core muscles and work hand-in-hand with them to hold the body tall and erect and to carry one's pride. If you feel out of touch with your power you may find you have a difficult time isolating your buttocks muscles enough to even focus on strengthening them. When you begin to work with this muscle group and strengthen and flex it, you will dislodge any issues this area may have housed.

This week, as you bring your focus to the different areas of emotional challenge carried over from your toddler years, consciously give your body permission to release the unexpressed energy related to these issues.

Buttocks Muscle Meditation: *I invite you right now, however, to bring your focus to your buttocks area. Breathe into it as you ask the muscles in your behind to reveal any issues they may have held for you. Listen and record your responses in your journal. Learn to understand the language of your body and it will always reveal your most beneficial next step.*

The Chakra Center Which Correlates to This Stage of Development Is the Second Chakra

The second chakra is located in the center of your belly right beneath the spleen near your pelvic area. It is related to the emotional body and the issues of balance and harmony, boundaries and limits.

Its highest frequency color is also that of the violet flame but when it takes on the density of day-to-day activities and vibrationally slows down, its hue appears more of a pumpkin orange. When you are attempting to find balance in your emotions and learning how to establish your place in the world by learning to say no and by hearing no, it is useful to focus on this center with healing light. Breathe into this center and ask for assistance in being able to express your emotional needs in a calm and effective manner. Envision yourself saying no or yes with ease and speaking your truth with confidence.

Second Chakra Meditation: *Take a moment to bring your focus to your pelvic area. Imagine a ball of energy rotating and being infused with a brilliant color of vibrant, tangerine orange. Allow this energy center to spin out any issues related to your fear of being rejected or abandoned if you set your limits and declare your right to be autonomous. Ask that this vibrational spin dislodge all blockages to your speaking your truth with honesty and assurance. See your Angels now touching the location of your second chakra as they use their angel dust to calm any fears and assuage any doubts of saying or hearing no and of stepping into your own sense of independence. See the energy center slowly shifting in vibration as it begins to reflect the color of the transmuting violet flame. Know that this imagery is assisting your personality in shifting its more dense vibration to the higher vibration of your spiritual self. When you feel complete, take another deep breath, open your eyes and record what you experienced.*

To bring closure to this week's work reflect, once again, on how your cherished saboteur™ emerges with respect to your ability to discern what does and does not feel good and your ability to extend this discernment into your assessment of any new endeavor. What has your Adult Self learned which will now assist it in responding to the needs of this wounded self so the tendency to sabotage can be dissolved? Once you have given this the mental attention it needs, close your eyes and proceed.

Closing Meditation: *See this wounded self in front of you. Ask what is needed in order for this wounded one to feel safe. Respond to that need and then invite this little toddler to reside in the center of the sacred chamber of your heart where he/she will be safe. Fill your heart center with the golden light of love and the healing light of the violet flame. Then bring your attention to the center of your head and ask that the master cell is re-activated with this new DNA vibration of feeling secure enough to establish a sound sense of boundaries and with a willingness to set limits with yourself and others.*

Feel the energy pulsating through your body as it travels down your spinal cord to your creator cell where this same intention is decreed. Take a deep breath and ask that every cell in your body now holds this new DNA patterning and that the muscles which have resonated with the disturbance now be relaxed, aligned and harmonized. Take a deep breath and record your experience in your journal. As you progress through your week, keep these experiences fresh in your mind and in your intentions.

REFER TO THE "DAILY CHECK-IN SHEETS" AND THE "7-DAY REVIEW" FOUND IN THE APPENDIX TO LOG YOUR EXPERIENCE.

Seventh Module—
Young Inner Child

From Shame And Guilt To Unconditional Love

The developmental stage between the ages of 3–6 presents all of the basic tasks we need to master in order to achieve balance on the physical plane. This stage prepares us to stay conscious of our body as we encounter the core issues of judgment and projection, shame, blame, and guilt. If we are unsuccessful, we dissociate from our bodies and are therefore unable to be present in our relationship to the external world.

YOUR YOUNG INNER CHILD (Ages 3-6)

YOU ARE NOW at the juncture of your program you began to step back and look at what you have designed with discernment. You are now ready to move to the phase which involves building on the positive and negative aspects discerned last week by making the appropriate adjustments. Week by week you will be constructing a plan to deal with the saboteur you flushed out in week four. Each week you gather more information regarding the behaviors sabotaging your efforts. In the toddler stage, these behaviors were the result of the encroachment or abandonment experienced in response to your new found independence. The behaviors exhibited in this next stage of development are the fears experienced as a toddler that then evolve into the character traits exhibited as a three-to-six-year-old. By this time in childhood, we begin to assume any problem which occurs is our fault and we begin to experience shame and guilt.

We also begin to feel self-consciousness in our body and a discomfort with our natural sense of curiosity. These issues relate back to this stage of development because it is this time in your life when you first encounter the tasks of dealing with these aspects of your character. How you feel about yourself and your body; how you deal with and respect the positive and negative qualities in yourself and others are related to how you experienced these issues when you were between the ages of three and six. The following focus questions will set the tone for your exploration. Read them and then keep them in mind as you read the following material. They will enrich your exploration of this stage of development in your own life.

FOCUS QUESTIONS TO PONDER WHICH RELATE TO THE THREE-SIX YEAR-OLD STAGE OF DEVELOPMENT

Judgments and Projections—What are your primary judgments? What are the chief gripes which irritate you? How do those irritations mirror issues within you which need to be addressed? Notice, during the week, the times you become judgmental, then take that judgment to the next level—owning what it says about you…and your need to work on this issue.

Guilt and Shame—Reflect on recent times when you felt guilt and times when you felt shame. What is the source of each feeling? How do you experience the difference between each feeling? Notice when you feel shame. Are you feeling out of control? How do you attempt to regain your composure? How does your shame get projected out onto others as blame? Experiment with responding to the shameful and guilty parts within you with compassion. Explore as you read the following, how this healing interaction may dissolve your shame and guilt.

Natural State Of Curiosity—Do you worry about what others will think and your ability to inquire about things which interest you and cause you to wonder? How comfortable do you feel in allowing that child-like wonderment to be expressed? Do you stifle it for fear of looking "stupid", if so, when and with whom?

Judgments Regarding Intimate Relationships—When you turn your attention to your relationships with others—how does what you feel towards them reflect how you feel about yourself? Where do you give your power away to others and where do you see in others what you want to see in yourself? Which relationships mirror self-love and which ones mirror discomfort and judgment?

Developmental Tasks in the Three-To-Six-Year-Old Stage

In this stage of development, you begin to work with the positive and negative aspects of who you are. The foundation for this exploration was laid during the years of three to six because that was the time in your life when you first confronted the fact that when you were good (acting like the adults in your life expected and wanted you to act) you were rewarded, but when you were bad (acting in ways that were unacceptable to these adults), you were punished. The rewards may have been in the form of praise or you may have been given special food, toys or outings. Punishment may have been emotional; you may have been humiliated or teased, or your parents may have ignored you. Perhaps you were punished physically— spanked, slapped, or sent to your room. Fearing punishments and desiring rewards, you quickly learned what was acceptable and what was not.

Your developmental task during this stage was to learn how to negotiate between the good and bad, right and wrong and positive and negative aspects of self. You had developed enough cognitive ability to determine what was acceptable and what was not acceptable and could, therefore, calculate which behaviors brought rewards and which behaviors resulted in punishment. You began to make choices accordingly. You also began to compromise who you were as a way to avoid risking rejection or judgment. It is for these reasons this stage of development is the origin of shame and guilt.

You are also, by age three, figuring out how to relate to other people. You know what to do to get what you need. Unfortunately, if you were raised in a dysfunctional home your needs were probably ignored or even ridiculed. You may have been the object of anger because you even *had* needs. The words you heard others use to describe you became the words you adopted to describe yourself. If you were told you were bad you would begin to believe you are bad. If you were told you were stupid, you would begin to believe you are stupid. If you were teased or told to shut up anytime you were curious and asked a question, you would learn it was not safe or wise to inquire about anything. If you were shamed, humiliated or teased about your body; if you were violated or your physical boundaries were not honored, you would grow up to believe you had little right to physical or emotional privacy and that your body was bad or perhaps even evil. These beliefs would have become the foundation for who you became as an adult.

How Patterns May Have Been Carried Into Adulthood

This stage of development sets the arena in adulthood for our ability to negotiate with the positive and negatives of any life situation and our capacity to know how to make the necessary adjustments. As an adult, if we are to successfully discern strengths and challenges we have to have developed a healthy relationship with our humanness. This means developing the ability to relate to ourselves with compassion. We have to be able to assess our positive and negative qualities and blend the good with the challenging to not only create but to also accept and revere our authentic self. This solidified self-empowers us to negotiate our differences with others and to reach an acceptable compromise without feeling overpowering or disempowered.

To be successful in our adult activities we also need to have developed the ability to assess our internal value system as it compares to an external one. For example, in your career or job, you may have bonded significantly enough with a position or the ideas of a company to where you can determine what aspects of the company resonate with who you are and where you need to make adjustments to fit in. You would then draw on what you learned in this third stage of development to determine how to make these adjustments without losing your integrity or sense of self. If the mastery of your ability to assess was thwarted, your adjustments in adulthood will be faulty. They will be shame-based and laced with fear of what others may think or do instead of based on a viable, internal sense of self.

The same can be said in our relationships with others. This blending, which requires compromise, is built on a clear understanding and acceptance of the person we are—identifying where we can bend and where we need to stay true to ourselves so we do not violate our own value system. This negotiation and adjustment phase involves sorting out what is going to work for us and what is going to have to be challenged. In relationships, this emerges as our need and ability to begin to speak our truth and attempt to work things out in a negotiating manner. It is in this adjustment phase of our relationships when we juggle our values with the other person's values or the organization or the corporate value system and try to mediate agreement or at least peaceful coexistence.

This is the "process" stage. The first and second stages involved bonding and conceiving—then butting up against limits and boundaries. This step involves the process of working with those limitations and finding acceptable solutions.

This developmental stage represents all of the basic tasks we need to master so we can be balanced on the physical plane. It allows us the opportunity to experiment with staying anchored in our body as we encounter such issues as judgment and projection, shame, blame and guilt, and comfort or discomfort with our bodies. This is the key developmental stage when we anchor into our bodies and consciously experience all of the density of the physical plane. Therefore, special topics need to be covered and addressed with respect to this stage of development because the impact these issues have on your adult life is paramount to your developing the ability to succeed in your pursuit of mastery.

Our Initial Dilemma—The Socialization Process

When we take a physical form we are subjected to a socialization process which serves to shift us from trusting our God-Self to trusting those in charge of us on the physical...i.e., parents. We are taught to externally reference that it is not safe to trust ourselves or our God-self.

We learn very quickly who we are and what we do is not always acceptable. We can begin to lose trust in ourselves to discern right from wrong. If we are not given the guidance to experience life and learn its lessons based on our inner truths, we learn to discount our inner knowingness and to rely on, instead, the adult figures who can use guilt and shame or withdrawal and fear, to socialize us so we fit into a world of others who do the same. It results in a community full of people who are attempting to get their needs met in a horizontal manner—by looking to each other—instead of looking up to their God-Self and the Divine for their vertical connection which can then illuminate their connections to others.

Parents often believe they have to "imprint" their child with a sense of right and wrong. It is my experience that the God-Self already carries that programming for each of us and that as parents we can ally with that God-Self and help the child learn to believe in and trust his or her basic goodness. Between the ages of three to six a child begins to separate from his or her God-Self and develop the ego self. If as children we are given the message that we are basically good and we can trust ourselves, the ego can be illuminated with the essence of our God-Self instead of severed from it. If this was the case, in the process of healing our childhood we have the opportunity to make up for this and to give this to our children within.

Our Body and Our Need to Respect It as Sacred

One of the issues many of us need to heal is our relationship with our bodies. We have spent many years, and perhaps lifetimes, de-valuing our bodies and its needs believing the physical form is too dense and of such a low vibration that we need to tend to our spiritual path instead of our bodily needs. I have found that since I am in body and must do my spiritual work from this plane, it is absolutely essential for me to hold sacred this physical form which enables me to do this work.

In exploring this for myself, I realized that the "I" who I identify as my human and physical self had a right to be in an equal relationship with my connection to the God-Source or my higher or God-Self. This thought inspired me to begin to explore how I became disconnected from respecting my body in the first place.

I came to realize that as children we are taught to be shy about our bodies, that our curiosity about our bodies is not acceptable and that, at best, the body is an object to be taken care of but not to be taken too seriously. However, since every mineral and cell found in our bodies is also found in the make-up of Mother Earth, wouldn't it be wonderful if, as children, we were taught to respect our bodies as a gift from Mother Earth. To learn that she has given of herself to give us a physical form that can house the gift of spirit we have received from God.

If, in childhood, we could learn to respect the land and the trees as our relatives, the rocks and the rivers as the libraries of the earth; if we could be taught to listen to the land, to say hello to Grandfather Sun and to bid Grandmother Moon good-night; if as a child we were taught that it is from Mother Earth and her animal and mineral creatures from which our food comes; if we were taught that we, too, come of the earth, we would be so much more connected to ourselves, to the earth and to the God-source around us. Being taught to relate to one's body in this way would allow us, as children, to stay connected to our physical form, to accept our curious nature and to respect and to expect to be respected for our physical boundaries and needs. Relating to your inner children in this manner can at least begin to facilitate your own connection to your physical form and could undo some of this disconnection which took place in your own life. It can restore your trust in your body to tell you what it needs so you can make the appropriate choices.

One of the ways I have tried to re-instate my connection to Mother Earth and my physical form is that at meal time I not only thank God for the meal, but I also thank the food, the farmers, the grocery store clerks—every person or element which has been involved in getting this food from its source to my table. It re-educates my inner child regarding the sequence of nourishment and sets the stage for her to not be so disconnected from her origin. It also serves as a metaphor for my inner child and facilitates a reconnection to appreciating the gifts of Mother Earth as well as those from the God-Source.

Judgments and Projections

Children observe they do not judge. They are taught to judge by the adults around them when good and bad is applied to their responses to their world. Children, at a very early age, speak the truth and often their parents become mortified. Parents get embarrassed because they look at their child as an extension of themselves and fear being judged. Children do not know how to use tact. They speak the truth without judgment. I believe it is a parent's reaction which then becomes internalized and places a value of right and wrong on any person, place or thing.

For instance, when a child sees a person in a wheelchair, the child naturally stares and comments on how this is different. Parents often silence the child who then gets the impression that there is something wrong with being in a wheelchair. This very exchange sets up a prejudice. A separation between another human being and the child is implanted and the foundation for the superior/inferior value system is imprinted. There are many examples, but the fact remains that whatever we experienced in childhood gets internalized as our values and is carried into our adult lives where they are projected onto others in a manner in which we feel entitled to judge another as good or bad, right or wrong.

I believe there is a difference between having an observation about someone and having an observation laced with an emotional charge, which is really a judgment. This judgment then gets projected onto others. Rather than focusing on changing someone else, we can, when emotionally charged, look at what that projection carries for us and use that information to further illuminate our own path. Most often the judgment stays suspended and sustains the essence of there being something wrong with the other person. That pattern of wanting everyone else to be like us and striving to be the same as others get locked in and begin to slowly erode our sense of self which is essential if we are to trust our innate wisdom. This disconnect is the origin of a great deal of dysfunction.

Dealing with Shame

Shame is when we feel we are not good enough. The first time in our lives when we have the cognitive ability to associate the feeling of not being good enough with the way we behave and the manner in which the adults in our lives react to that behavior is between the ages of three to six. When the adults in our lives do not like what we do, they attempt to control our behavior by humiliating us, neglecting us, abandoning us or sometimes even abusing us.

Shame can also result from being sexually abused. Our perpetrators can blame us for their sexual inappropriateness and we can, therefore, begin to feel as though the abuse was our fault. We come to believe that we did something to deserve it.

Shame can even occur if our parents or caretaker made us "too" important in their lives. If we were over-indulged, we can sense that our parent/s is living vicariously through us. This results in a tension that we may let them down. If we sense the parental expectation is for us to always be the best at everything we do we can become burdened and fearful we will let them down. We develop the fear that we will be left, humiliated or even violated if we fail to live up to that parental expectation.

Either source results in our coming to believe that the fault lies with us. We develop this belief because it would be too painful, in fact almost impossible at such a young age, to admit the adults in our lives are incompetent. We cannot afford to feel that powerless and unprotected. So, instead, we take it on as our deficiency. We say to ourselves, *"If only we were better, then we would be loved and protected."* Or we tell ourselves, *"I'd better be perfect so I don't let "them" down."*

This inner belief becomes the foundation of our need to be perfect. Our pursuit of perfection gives us a focus for the tension created by the fear we may fail. It gives us the illusion we have some control over a situation which is beyond our control. This creates a dynamic which I call "functional shame" because it allows us to survive in childhood but ultimately prevents us from becoming self-fulfilled adults.

In order to become fulfilled and healthy adults, we have to give up the *false belief* that we are not good enough and challenge our *pursuit of perfection.* This requires we give up the antiquated hope that our parents will become who we need them to be. As a child and as an adult, giving up this hope is more than we can bear. So we remain loyal. We unconsciously hold onto the hope that if we can just be good enough—perfect enough—"they" will come through for us and be able and willing to love us and make us feel safe.

In adulthood, the "they" expands beyond our parents and gets projected onto our intimate relationships, our relationships with co-workers and onto any person who is a candidate to protect, love or value us. We overdo in hopes of winning their love. Time and time again we become involved in relationships in which we feel we must overdo to warrant being loved. Each of these dysfunctional relationships ultimately gives us the opportunity to heal our shame.

To look at this dynamic from the eyes of the Soul we would be taken into times in our Soul's history when we felt too unworthy or imperfect to hold the Light of our Source. Spiritual shame resulted when, in response to our "free choice," we were unable to hold the light, and instead, made choices which resulted in our turning away from Source.

We begin by going back to a recent or current experience when we felt shame. We trace this thread back to the first remembered time we felt that same sensation in our childhood. We re-parent our inner children and help them accept that it was not their fault. We help the inner children begin to believe they are enough just the way they are.

Our Co-dependent Bargain™

We cannot heal our shame until we identify and work with the bargain we made in response to our shame. Again, I call this bargain the co-dependent bargain. It is made in this lifetime with the parent we identify as the one who could love and protect us—but didn't. When we assume they didn't because of our deficiency, we frantically engage in an unconscious bargain to act in a manner which will "earn" their love in hopes this will finally ensure we will be kept safe.

When our co-Dependent bargain™ doesn't work, we feel tension. This tension is uncomfortable and must be discharged. We discharge it by engaging in compulsive and addictive behaviors. Whatever we do in excess—its intent is most likely in response to this unconscious, and yet ineffective, unmet bargain.

Because this bargain is unconscious, we engage in this dynamic over and over. Our perpetual belief is that if we can just get it right and figure out what needs to be changed or fixed then things will be the way we need them to be and we will feel safe, loved and protected.

It never works. No matter how much we try to be perfect—no matter how much we try to fix things so they will be better—we always fail because unfortunately, the source of the dysfunction is the system—not us. We can never be "good enough" to impact or change what is wrong so things can get better—but we get caught in the vicious cycle of the attempt. We fail—then act out compulsively or addictively to discharge the energy of that failure. This cycle keeps us active in our compulsions and addictions as well as disconnected from our authentic self and Source. This cycle is the source of our cherished saboteur's™—of those behaviors which derail us and keep us from coming fully into the commitments and intentions of our pursuit of mastery.

Our goal is to realize that it isn't our fault that our safety must be found vertically and not horizontally! It must be anchored in our relationship to the Angels and to our Higher Guidance and not to those in the physical world of our day-to-day lives.

However, in order to even think to look vertically instead of horizontally, we need to first become aware of our own addictive and compulsive behaviors. This includes confronting our own co-dependency. It means exploring our own unique Co-Dependent Bargain™ and the degree to which we focus on others instead of ourselves. It means we need to determine the degree of tension which surrounds our co-dependent behavior and honestly address the degree to which we use our compulsions and addictions to mitigate that tension.

Potential Spiritual Lesson

A potential lesson which extends from this developmental stage and this step of mastery is learning to express compassion for self and others; learning to be non-judgmental of self and others, confronting and dissolving multidimensional shame and guilt and finding the threads of shame in our Soul's history when we may have turned away from our Source.

It is this source of Soul issues which can escort us into the trials and tribulations of being a physical being in a spiritual world. I have never worked with an individual who did not have at least one central life theme which originated at this stage of development and which was in need of resolution. Remember this as you begin your exploration. Record your thoughts and findings in your journal. Then proceed to look at the issues from this stage of development from the perspective of the following specific areas of concern. You already previewed these areas of concern when you responded to the statements in the fourth week of your program when you were flushing out the essence and obtaining the profile of your cherished saboteur™.

The following glimpse will make this assessment more specific. It may be useful to refer back to your responses in the respective section of each of those sheets.

A Review of How Tasks From This Stage of Development Emerge as Goals in Adulthood with Respect to Specific Areas of Concern:

1. Body Image—*Physical Body*—The goal is to come to terms with our body type and begin to focus on how we can maximize our healthy and strong physical characteristics and how we can compensate or progressively work with our limitations. It is a time when the physical goals can be refined with acceptance and harmony.

_____1. Even if my exercise plan becomes too restrictive I stick to it.

_____2. I am judgmental of my body type and wish it were different.

_____3. I wish I were more in shape but don't have the time to exercise.

_____4. I am uncomfortable with people who "let themselves go."

2. Self-Image—*Emotional Body*—With respect to our self-image this marks the stage in our adult lives when we begin to realistically assess our strengths and our challenges and develop a strategy for how to capitalize on the strengths and compensate for the challenges. The goal is to do this without judgment or, for that matter, without attachment to feeling shame *or* pride.

_____1. I am judgmental and critical of myself.

_____2. I am judgmental and critical of others.

_____3. I don't have a very good understanding of my strengths and challenges.

_____4. I do not respond well even to constructive criticism.

3. Belief systems—*Mental Body*—The goal with respect to your belief systems is to observe the polarities in your thought processes. Notice in which situations you get into a power struggle with someone else or even with yourself. Once recognized, own the projection and work with mediating a compromise between the opposing beliefs. Trust that both sides hold an aspect of your truth which needs to be partnered with its extreme opposite. This mental processing serves to bring more balance to your life.

_____1. I feel embarrassed when I hear something I feel I should have known.

_____2. I have strong opinions—and even with new information—I do not adjust.

_____3. I do not like to hang out with people who think differently than I.

_____4. I keep my thoughts to myself for fear of being judged.

4. Spirituality—*Spiritual Body*—(Spiritual Path or Recovery Program) What we see in Step Two of the Twelve Steps of A.A. is where your ideas did or did not match with your chosen path, you begin to make the necessary adjustments and begin the process of accepting the differences without judgment, without blame or shame.

_____1. I feel uncomfortable following some of the principles of my organization.

_____2. I fear others will judge me for my spiritual beliefs.

_____3. I feel judgmental and condemning of others if they don't follow the rules.

_____4. I trust the direction of my spiritual leader more than my own intuition.

5. Family and Intimate Relationships—The goal in relationships is for you to begin to examine the differences in value systems between you and your loved ones and/or intimate partner and explore ways in which both parties operate in the day to day activities. You will want to begin the on-going process of making adjustments and attempting to find an approach which incorporates both styles of operation. This is also the step when you make peace with what your loved ones can and cannot offer. You realize you can either get stuck in judgments—theirs or yours—or you can use the judgments and projections as mirrors for personal growth.

_____1. It is difficult for me to articulate what I feel about something.

_____2. If I state an opinion which is challenged, I wish I had remained silent.

_____3. If another's opinion differs from mine, I assume theirs is wrong.

_____4. When I give in and agree with others, I feel I give them my power.

6. Sexuality and Passion—Again, the goal is to refine your sexual preferences without shame or blame, accepting the views of others while being able to stand solidly in your own preferences or likes and dislikes. With respect to a passion for a project or the expression of one's creativity, the goal is to begin to mix passion with realistic action. Goals are set which incorporate the pluses and minuses of an idea, adjustments are made to accommodate this information. The limitations confronted in the last stage of mastery which related to the toddler issues are now worked with in such a way that a new plan can emerge which is more solid and more reflective of your inner values.

_____1. I have a hard time setting realistic goals for my creative efforts.

_____2. I feel passionate about my ideas but fear being judged if I express them.

_____3. I don't like to be around others who experiment with their sexuality.

_____4. I feel ashamed and shy about my sexuality.

7. Prosperity and Abundance—The goal now is to begin to balance what you have and what you don't have…to mix your spiritual affirmations for wealth with a concrete plan of action. It is also effective to begin to examine your definition of prosperity and abundance. Value shifts may occur which enable you to feel abundant with what you have as opposed to what you dream of having. You can become more realistic as you deal with judgments towards self or others and give up the comparison game of being better or worse off than others.

_____1. I want just enough money to meet my needs.

_____2. I feel everyone else has more of everything than I.

_____3. I don't like to be around people who have a lot of money.

———4. When I am well off I feel uneasy being around someone who is not.

8. Job, Career or Climb on the Corporate Ladder—You now begin to learn your company's rules and it's value system as you assess how your internal value system interfaces with that of the company's value system...asking if it is compatible, tolerable. You will address if the goals of the company match your internal goals... ask questions such as..."What do I have to do to be accepted? Is the company's position or philosophy acceptable to mine? With respect to the profession in a self-employed position, you can begin to deal with the pros and cons of being self-employed and make adjustments to accommodate.

———1. I worry a great deal about what my co-workers and boss think of me.

———2. I don't think many of my co-workers are as competent as I.

———3. If I agree to do something I stick with it until it's done.

———4. I feel irritated when others do not seem to value integrity.

As you peruse the above material, contemplate how the issues of this developmental stage interface with your daily life and perhaps reflect the issues and lessons of your Soul. Now turn your focus to your body and to the area of your upper arms because it is this muscle group which mirrors the partnering between your polar opposites and carries your shame, guilt, and hesitancy to express your curiosity with ease.

WORKING WITH THE BICEPS AND TRICEPS WHICH CORRELATE TO THIS STAGE OF DEVELOPMENT

The biceps and triceps mirror the energy related to the three-to-six-year-old stage of development. These muscles are polar opposites, and yet, constitute a pair which needs to be balanced with equal attention. The arms are also the vessels of the personality and Soul. They reach out and connect to the outside world and pull back as a way to conserve the energy of our individuality. Three-to-six year-olds use their arms to reach for support; to point to unknown items about which they want more information; to brace them against the world as they learn how to balance their individual needs with the expectations placed on them by others. Remember, this is the time of your life when you first began to experience shame because it was the first time you could cognitively assess how the adults in your world were responding to you. Decisions about how you behaved were made accordingly. Your upper arms record and mirror your experience of these decisions.

The biceps carry the thrust forward and outward, representing the child's relationship to his or her external world. The triceps, on the other hand, carries the essence of self—and the art of bringing the energy back into one's own force field. *Experiment right now with flexing your biceps and then pulling the energy back into yourself by tightening the triceps. Feel the tension between reaching out and pulling back.*

It is during this stage of development we perfect our ability to interact with our environment and the upper arm area carries all of the experiences related to the successes and challenges of this endeavor. When you begin to work with these two, polar-opposite, muscle groups and strengthen and flex them, you will dislodge any issues this area may have housed. This week, as you bring your focus to the different areas of emotional challenge carried over from your three-to-six-year-old, consciously give your upper arms permission to release the unexpressed energy related to these issues.

Bicep Muscle Meditation: *I invite you right now, however, to once again bring your focus to your biceps and your triceps area. Breathe into them and bring the focus to the partnership between these two polarities. Both are in need of flexing if the arm is to be strong. As you bring attention to this area of your body and experience harmony in your upper arms, envision that you also begin to experience harmony in the interplay between meeting your own needs and meeting the needs of others. Resonate with the dance presented to you from this stage of development when the central task confronted was the need for balance, reciprocity, and compassion. Recognize if you just focus on your biceps and ignore your triceps, the over-all functioning and strength of your arms will be compromised. Invite your upper arms to reveal any issues of shame or guilt—all or nothing thinking—concerns about expressing your natural state of curiosity, and/or judgments and projections they may have stored for you. Listen and record your responses in your journal. Learn to understand the language of your body and it will always reveal your most beneficial next step.*

THE CHAKRA CENTER WHICH CORRELATES TO THIS STAGE OF DEVELOPMENT IS THE SOLAR PLEXUS CHAKRA

This third chakra is your personal power center, the center of the will. It is located in the solar plexus near your navel and relates to your ability to show confidence and strength. The highest frequency of light associated with this chakra is purple with golden and ruby flecks but when it takes on the density of day-to-day activities and vibrationally slows down; its hue appears to be more of a lemon yellow.

This chakra center relates to the adrenal gland and governs your force and energy in exhibiting your personal power. By first energizing it with the color of lemon yellow, you will begin to smooth out the rough edges of your will, thus enabling the color to return to its natural state of purple with the golden and ruby flecks. This will then assist you in expressing your personal power in a non-aggressive but firm manner. The third chakra correlates with the issues of the three-to-six-year-old and your ability to negotiate between the positive and negative qualities within you and others.

Solar Plexus Chakra Meditation: Take a moment to bring your focus to your solar plexus or navel area. Imagine a ball of energy rotating and being infused with a brilliant color of vibrant, lemon yellow. Allow this energy center to spin out any issues related to your fear of being judged or being ridiculed. Ask it to purify your own tendencies to judge, project—to blame and then feel shame. Determine if there is angst because of a fear of being exposed or a fear of "looking foolish or stupid"? If so, ask that this energy is freed for transmutation as well.

Allow the force of the violet flame to transmute all fears, worries and displaced emotions relating to this stage of development. See your Angels now touching the location of your third chakra as they use their angel dust to calm all fears and regrets related to the blame/shame dynamic or to your feeling judged or judging others. See the energy center slowly shifting in vibration as it begins to reflect the color of the transmuting violet flame which ultimately restores it to its highest hue which is purple with gold and ruby flecks. Know that this imagery is assisting your personality in shifting its more dense vibration to the higher vibration of your spiritual self. When you feel complete take another deep breath, open your eyes and record what you experienced.

To bring closure to this week's work reflect once again on how your cherished saboteur™ emerges with respect to your ability to dissolve your shame with compassion and your guilt with forgiveness and acceptance. What has your Adult Self learned which will now assist it in responding to the needs of this wounded self so the tendency to sabotage can be dissolved? Once you have given this the mental attention it needs, close your eyes and proceed.

Closing Meditation: *See the three-to-six-year-old in front of you. Ask what is needed in order for this wounded one to feel safe. Respond to that need and then invite this inner child to reside in the center of the sacred chamber of your heart where he/she will be safe. Fill your heart center with the golden light of love and the healing light of the violet flame. Then bring your attention to the center of your head and ask that the master cell is re-activated with this new DNA vibration of compassion and acceptance for self and others. Feel the energy pulsating through your body as it travels down your spinal cord to your creator cell where this same intention is decreed. Take a deep breath and ask that every cell in your body now holds this new DNA patterning and that the muscles which have resonated with the disturbance of shame, guilt, and judgment now be relaxed, aligned and harmonized. Take a deep breath and record your experience in your journal. As you progress through your week, keep these experiences fresh in your mind and in your intentions.*

REFER TO THE "DAILY CHECK-IN SHEETS" AND THE "7-DAY REVIEW" FOUND IN THE APPENDIX TO LOG YOUR EXPERIENCE.

Eighth Module—
Grade School Self

From Rejection To Acceptance

Perhaps the most profound pattern which originates from this developmental stage is the pattern
of sabotage related to being loyal to the dysfunctional parenting unit. Seldom have I worked with an
adult on their inner child issues without us having
to confront this grade-school self. This dynamic
emerges and sabotages any effort which would
result in surpassing his or her parent's expertise or
succeeding in areas where the parents were unable
to excel. The purpose for this is embedded in the fact
that, as children, we need to think of our parents as
all-knowing. It is the only way we can survive.

THE GRADE SCHOOL SELF (Ages 6-12)

YOU JUST BEGAN your work with your Co-Dependent Bargain™ and examine the sources of your shame and guilt as you explored the nurturing and critical aspects of self. Through the focus questions, you were invited to assess your issues with respect to judgment and projection. You were given the opportunity to trace how your judgments get projected onto others in your current life, as well as how your shame gets projected onto your body and your performance in this program.

In this upcoming material, you will build on this new found knowledge. As you enter into the realm of issues from your grade-school self you will be invited to explore how these concerns and strengths interface with your peers, co-workers, friends, acquaintances, and family. You will be visiting potential issues involving feeling left out—your discomfort or pride related to your inclusion or exclusion in the "in crowd." Competition with self and others will also emerge for examination. You may review how you have compared your progress to others in the past and identify when you felt either superior or inferior. Although either experience can breed stress, bringing awareness to these feelings will give you the opportunity to confront how you deal with feeling "better than" or "lesser than" someone else. This whole teeter-totter of comparison with others can result in tension irrespective of the side to which you slide. Much to your surprise, you may find that feeling superior to others brings about just as much fear as feeling inferior.

Some may confront memories of being chosen first on the baseball team—or being first in a spelling contest. Yet others will revisit feeling left out—feeling inept and less than their peers. Your upcoming participation and performance in your chosen event will give you an opportunity to flush out your blueprint with respect to your follow through, comparison with others, and your ability to step into your "athletic" self.

You will also begin to build on your experience with your co-dependent bargain™. You will begin to identify and work with the part of you who may be remaining loyal to your antiquated family system.

This pattern is perhaps the most profound remnant left from this stage of development. There were many social tasks to be completed at this stage of your life. In order to succeed you would have had to have ample emotional energy to concentrate on their mastery. If there was stress in your family—if your emotional energy was tied up with survival rather than progression—your mastery of these tasks would have been thwarted. To understand this dynamic more fully let's examine these developmental tasks with a little more depth. The focus questions are woven into the body of this discussion because they will be easier to relate to if they are presented in context.

DEVELOPMENTAL TASKS DURING THE SIX-TO-TWELVE-YEAR-OLD STAGE OF DEVELOPMENT

How well you fit into your social groups, the degree of comfort you feel with your co-workers and close friends, the degree of success you experience when you have to perform or compete, and the success you experience in a career or when you start and complete projects are all related to how well you mastered these tasks when you were between the ages of six and twelve. These years are called the middle years because they span the time between the rapid physical growth of your first six years and the marked changes which arise with puberty. Your attention was more on mastering tasks of a social rather than a psychological nature. Your focus moved from being internally referenced to being externally referenced.

FOCUS QUESTIONS TO PONDER WHICH RELATE TO THE SIX-TO-TWELVE-YEAR-OLD STAGE OF DEVELOPMENT

Exclusion versus Inclusion—Around the age of six is perhaps the first time you moved from the safety (or lack thereof) experienced in your family and entered the outside world. You began to focus on issues involving your relationship with peers. "Do I fit in? Am I the same as others or different? Am I accepted by my peers?" Whatever experience you had at this time in your life followed you into adulthood and is now reflected in how well you feel you belong or how much you fear being excluded.

Mastery or Fear of Public Speaking—Another area of exploration which emerges is the degree of comfort you experience when you speak in public. Since this was the time in your life when you were first expected to get up in front of your class and give reports and presentations, your comfort or discomfort will be related back to these childhood experiences. If you are able to do this with ease then you developed the confidence necessary to feel comfortable with such visibility. This confidence is also evident whenever you are expected to give presentations in your work and other environments. Since, other than death, public speaking is the number one fear, few moved through this task with ease.

Task Completion (Beginning and Completing Projects)— Completing tasks and learning the discipline needed to begin and finish projects is also related to what you experienced during this time in your life. Starting and completing tasks is a skill which needs to be learned—it is not innate and you are not "lazy" if you did not master it. Many factors influence your success at mastering this ability. It depends upon how much assistance you received from your caretakers in following through with your homework. It can be influenced by how secure you felt in your peer groups. It can also be affected by how much emotional energy you had to devote to this lesson. If you were distracted from this focus by family dysfunction—if your energy was directed towards worrying about what was going on at home— whether your mother was drinking or your father had found a job— then you would not have had the emotional energy to focus on such task developments and your mastery would have been stifled.

You may have grown up having great challenges in completing projects and now interpret this trait as evidence of your being lazy or unmotivated. In truth—many adults are unable to begin and complete projects because they simply were never taught how to put one foot ahead of the other as a way to take the steps necessary to succeed. Those who are able to complete tasks with ease were often forced to focus on this area of their life as a way to survive. They were the parentified child who was selected as the member of the family who had to hold the order. Even though this accomplishment can be experienced as a source of strength in adulthood, it can carry the underpinnings of grief and sadness because of its origin.

Loyalty to Your Dysfunctional Family System—Perhaps, however, the most profound pattern which originates from this developmental stage is the pattern of sabotage related to being loyal to your dysfunctional parenting unit. Seldom have I worked with an adult on their inner child issues without us having to confront this grade-school self who developed a loyalty to one or both parents. This dynamic emerges and sabotages any effort which would result in that person's surpassing their parent's expertise or succeeding in areas where their parents were unable to excel. The purpose for this is embedded in the fact that, as children, we need to think of our parents as "all-knowing." It is the only way we can survive. We hold onto the unconscious belief exhibited in the plea of our Co-Dependent Bargain™ that if only we can "do what is needed" then our parents will be able to become the parents we need them to be in order to survive. As we grow into adulthood we take this unconscious belief into our day-to-day lives.

We remain loyal to the contract and sabotage any efforts which would result in our succeeding in areas our parents have been unable to experience success. Why? Because it is too frightening for this part of self to excel and surpass his or her parents—this brings on too much grief and fear of being alone. We would then be expected to be the experts of our own lives and that fear alone can catapult us into despair, a sense of isolation and/or a fear of failure. So, instead, we become preoccupied with our weight, finances, dysfunctional relationships or any dysfunction which allows us to feel less accomplished than our parents.

How These Patterns May Have Been Carried Into Adulthood

So how does all of this material filter into your adult life? The pattern exhibited in adulthood which relates to this stage of development is found in your need to be recognized by your peers and acknowledged for your accomplishments. Your agenda is to find outside activities and interests. You begin to search for a support system which matches your inner value system. You begin to gravitate towards a group which mirrors your specific styles and one in which you feel you "fit." You may also find you begin to develop hobbies or a line of work which gives you the feeling of accomplishment. You may find your psyche can and is drawn to success in at least some areas of your life. As long as that one sacred area which surpasses your parents is left untouched you can proceed without risk of being disloyal to the parent with whom you still long to connect.

This stage of development and adult pattern reflect the transition made from being a novice to being seasoned. You will see this represented in your present level of achievement in your career or in the manner in which you relate to loved ones and family members. You may see evidence of these threads emerging in the way you attract prosperity; create your life's passion; relate to your sexuality, your body in general and your sense of self and adult belief systems about success. This transition prepares you for entry into your refinement phase of adolescence when true mastery can occur.

Potential Spiritual Lesson

This time in your life and the issues which emerge in this stage of the pursuit of your mastery offer the opportunity to look at the moments in your Soul's history when you perhaps joined a group which led you away from your Source or perhaps a time when you displaced your loyalty onto a false source. Record any findings in your journal. Then proceed to look at the issues from this stage of development from the perspective of the following specific areas of concern. You already previewed these areas of concern when you responded to the statements in the fourth week of your program when you were flushing out the essence and obtaining the profile of your cherished saboteur™. The following glimpse will make this assessment more specific. It may be useful to refer back to your responses to the sections related to this stage of development on each of those sheets.

A Review of How Tasks of This Stage of Development Emerge as Goals in Adulthood with Respect to Specific Areas of Concerns:

1. Body Image—*Physical Body*—Often what emerges at this juncture is a desire to be acknowledged for achievements with respect to your physical form or food program. You notice you want to feel comfortable in your body—not oblivious to it. If you have dissociated from your body due to abuse, you might begin to want to come home and recognize your physical form as a vital part of your healing. There exists a desire to feel connected, grounded and aware of your body and its presence.

_____1. I want my peers to acknowledge how well I stay in shape.

_____2. I am very conscientious about my eating habits and like acknowledgment.

_____3. I feel out of touch with my body.

_____4. It is important my body fits in with society's standards.

2. Self--Image—*Emotional Body*—Self-Image is dependent upon receiving outside and external validation and recognition. You may notice you want to be seen as the person you are…to be more visible. You can also begin to pursue mastery in some outside interest and have a need to be recognized for this mastery…but the mastery still has to be within the acceptable limits of the external world such as peers or family.

_____1. I feel self-conscious about my talents.

_____2. I dislike exposure and prefer to stay hidden.

_____3. I feel the right to claim my true self, but feel awkward in doing so.

_____4. I don't like being too vulnerable.

3. Belief systems—*Mental Body*—During this stage, you will notice that you want your beliefs to match those with whom you relate. To be the same is to be accepted and the goal at this stage is to fit in—so you will be drawn to those who think as you think. Your

family's belief system will become less important as you seek to find a like-minded peer group to support you in your new efforts.

_____1. I express my thoughts but only if I know they are going to be accepted.

_____2. I cautiously test another's opinions to see if he/she thinks as I.

_____3. If I state a truth which is different than others I feel uncomfortable.

_____4. I feel nervous I will be judged if I say what I think or feel.

4. Spirituality—*Spiritual Body*—(Spiritual Path or Recovery Program)

At this stage of your spiritual path, you begin to identify heavily with another dogma or the teachings of someone outside of self. Most are not quite ready to claim their own views and put their own signature on their spiritual belief. Many still seek an outside authority such as a Guru or spiritual teacher to determine the steps of their path.

_____1. I feel invisible and unseen by those in my spiritual community.

_____2. I have not found a path or community to which I want to belong.

_____3. I have difficulty speaking my truth about my spiritual beliefs.

_____4. My spiritual beliefs are different than those of my family.

5. Family and Intimate Relationships—You will find you still want to fit in with your family but the stirrings of breaking away are under the surface…and fitting in with peers will begin to have more dominance. You might notice there are silent bargains maintained which sustain your being able to fit in with the "in" crowd rather than break the molds. A compromise of your authentic self will take precedence over risking the loss of peer approval. Unfortunately, the price paid is your own authenticity.

Your need for approval can also be based on being counted on for "being there for others, for doing for others" at the expense of self—which is a perpetuation of the theme of the codependent bargain which now gets projected onto relationships with peers.

_____1. I would like to be more acknowledged by those I love.

_____2. I feel invisible and unseen by family members.

_____3. If I disagree with my partner I stay silent rather than risk disapproval.

_____4. Even if I have strong feelings I will still agree with others.

6. Sexuality and Passion—As an adult, you might notice your desire to make sexual choices which are acceptable to the norm and fit in rather than stand out. If everyone in your peer group is promiscuous, you may feel pressure to conform. You may find you are less able to set your own standards based on your own inner values because of your need for outside validation. Passion may be something you have a hard time defining at this point. You may become aware of the inner urges of your authenticity, but you feel too dependent on outside approval to "go for it." Sometimes people can feel as though they are a victim of their own passion because of the losses which might result if they act from their own source of passion which may be "unacceptable."

_____1. My sexual preferences pretty much fit into the societal norm.

_____2. My creative thoughts, which I share with few, are somewhat avant-garde.

_____3. I am very creative but feel I get little recognition for my efforts.

_____4. I have strong sexual preferences but keep quiet to avoid criticism.

7. Prosperity and Abundance—The challenge at this stage is to determine if your financial goals are based on your value system or an external one. You may find you base your financial goals on your need for recognition so you set goals which are in alignment with society's values and not your own. You may discover you spend money on things which will win approval from others as you try to "keep up with the Jones" so you can fit in with friends, neighbors, and family. It is important to keep in mind this is a phase and not become too judgmental of yourself as you explore these tendencies.

_____1. It is important to me to "keep up with the Jones."

_____2. My job pays well and I like others to know this.

_____3. I feel less prosperous than most around me.

_____4. I feel abundant but keep it quiet rather than risk rejection or criticism.

8. Job, Career or Climb on the Corporate Ladder—Your work-related desire related to this stage will be to find a support system within the company…to find your niche of like-minded co-workers with whom you fit in. You might find you don't want to stand out… don't want to lose your job. You may discover you are attempting to get promoted for being "good" and "appropriate"—not "creative" and "individual." Many stuck at this stage find they shy away from taking risks which could jeopardize their secure positions.

_____1. I feel very cautious when I try a new behavior at work.

_____2. I get nervous if I do something at work which draws attention to me.

_____3. If I don't like something I keep quiet. Why buck the system?

_____4. I have some ideas which excite me but I don't share them with anyone.

As you peruse the above material, contemplate how the issues of this developmental stage interface with your daily life and perhaps reflect the issues and lessons of your Soul. Then turn your focus to your calves because it is this muscle group which holds the essence of this stage of development and the issues of fitting in and being successful at completing projects and attaining goals.

Working with the Calf Muscle Which Correlates to This Stage of Development

The area of the body which most often carries the energy related to the six-to-twelve-year-old is the calf area of each leg because they are the muscles which spring us into action and propel us forward. They carry us from one place to another bridging the experiences of our inner world with the impressions of the world which exists beyond us. They represent one of the most predominant expressions of our athleticism…visible when taut…their development necessary for success. If we feel powerless and immobile, often our calf muscles will be the first to show signs of having atrophied.

We also use our calf muscles to rise above situations…to peak at something we cannot quite grasp and to get a glimpse of something which we determine is just right outside of our reach. By flexing our calf muscles we are able to stretch beyond our immediate limits and expand our horizon. This replicates exactly what we are experimenting at this stage of development. We are stretching beyond who we were in our families and testing the new world of our peers. When you begin to work with this muscle group and strengthen and flex it, you will dislodge any issues this area may have housed.

This week, as you bring your focus to the different areas of emotional challenge carried over from your grade-school self, consciously give your body permission to release the unexpressed energy related to these issues.

Calf Muscle Meditation: *I invite you now, however, to bring your focus to the area of your calf muscles. Breathe into them and ask them to reveal any issues they may have held for you. Listen and record your responses. Learn to understand the language of your body and it will always reveal your most beneficial next step.*

CORRELATION OF THE FOURTH OR HEART CHAKRA TO THE SIX-TO-TWELVE-YEAR-OLD STAGE OF DEVELOPMENT

The fourth Chakra is located at your heart center and is the center of your intuition. The color associated with this energy center most commonly is emerald green but actually, when it is vibrating in its purest, most loving frequency, it puts off more of a pink hue because it holds your experience of love and forgiveness. This chakra governs your connection to others—your interactions with others and in the world.

It governs your thymus gland and correlates with the issues of your six-to-twelve-year-old within because it was at this time in your life that you first began to relate to the outside world in an interactive way. It is then that you felt you had to measure up to an outside standard and develop the skills to hold your own in this arena.

It is this part of self who often needs the most attention when it comes to being able to feel love and trust in your heart. By balancing this center first with the color emerald green and then with the healing color of soft, loving shades of pink, you will be able to cleanse yourself of false loyalties and augment your ability to love and be loved.

Heart Chakra Meditation: *Take a moment to bring your focus to this area. Imagine a ball of energy rotating and being infused with a brilliant color of emerald green which then fades into the healing color of shades of pink. Allow this energy center to spin out the issues related to your fears of not fitting in—of feeling isolated and alone—judged and criticized by your peers. See your Angels now touching the location of your fourth chakra as they use their angel dust to calm any fears and assuage any doubts about being able to succeed. When you feel complete, take another deep breath, open your eyes and record what you experienced. See the energy center slowly shifting in vibration as it begins to reflect the color of the trans-muting violet flame which ultimately restores it to its highest hue of the soft, healing shades of pink. Know that this imagery is assisting your personality in shifting its more dense vibration to the higher vibration of your spiritual self. When you feel complete take another deep breath, open your eyes and record what you experienced.*

To bring closure to this work, reflect once again on how your cherished saboteur™ emerges with respect to your fears regarding your ability to succeed and be accomplished. What has your Adult Self learned which will now assist it in responding to the needs of this wounded self so the tendency to sabotage can be dissolved? Once you have given this the mental attention it needs close your eyes and proceed.

Closing Meditation: *See the six-to-twelve-year-old in front of you. Ask what is needed in order for this wounded one to feel safe. Respond to that need and then invite this inner child to reside in the center of the sacred chamber of your heart where he/she will be safe. Fill your heart center with the golden light of love and the healing light of the violet flame. Then bring your attention to the center of your head and ask that the master cell is re-activated with this new DNA vibration of acceptance and a renewed sense of belonging to a group of your choice. Feel the energy pulsating through your body as it travels down your spinal cord to your creator cell where this same intention is decreed. Take a deep breath and ask that every cell in your body now holds this new DNA patterning and that the calf muscles, which have resonated with the disturbance of being left out, of not succeeding or being able to accomplish your goals, can now relax, align and harmonize. Take a deep breath and record your experience in your journal. As you progress through your week, keep these experiences fresh in your mind and in your intentions.*

REFER TO THE "DAILY CHECK-IN SHEETS" AND THE "7-DAY REVIEW" FOUND IN THE APPENDIX TO LOG YOUR EXPERIENCE.

Ninth Module—
Inner Teen

From Self-Consciousness To Self-Confidence

Suddenly, it becomes apparent we cannot move forward until we release some of the remnants of our past. The body will just not let us. We have brought our consciousness into the physical realm to such a degree that those issues will no longer stay hidden. We have the choice to either deal with them and get better or keep them buried and remain the same. We cannot do both.

THE YOUNG INNER TEEN (Ages 12-15)

IN THE PAST few weeks of your Soul Steps Program, you were invited to build on what you experienced with your co-dependent bargain™. You began to identify and work with the part of you who may be remaining loyal to your antiquated family system. In fact, you may have realized that this pattern was the most profound remnant left from the six-to-twelve-year-old stage of development. There were many social tasks to be completed in that stage of your life, and each of these tasks has most likely been reflected in the manner in which you have shown up for your program to this point.

In this upcoming module, you will have the opportunity to build on what you experienced, and bring forth all of the aspects you have reclaimed and healed from the first twelve years of your life. Stepping into puberty and entering the twelve-to-fifteen-year-old stage of development marks the beginning of your transition into adulthood. Any transition involves grief. We grieve who we were as we step into the person we are becoming.

Often, in fact, at this stage of development—in any endeavor pursued—we derail and get off course because to sustain excitement we have to experience our feelings…all of our feelings. For whatever reason, any residual grief lurking below the surface makes itself known at this stage. Perhaps the veil is thinned by the vibration of self-consciousness so prevalent at this juncture. Whatever the reason, if there is any residual grief, it emerges during this phase of development—irrespective of what we are pursuing—be it a career, an intimate relationship or even a long, desired goal.

For most of us it suddenly becomes apparent we cannot move forward until we release some of the remnants of our past. The body will just not let us. We have brought our consciousness into the physical realm to such a degree that those issues will no longer stay hidden. We have the choice to either deal with them and get better or keep them buried and remain the same.

The need for resolving this grief is reflected in the young, inner teen's self-consciousness and his or her unbearable fear of exposure.

This fear is often covered up by a sense of impending doom. Heaviness hovers until its origins are addressed and belief systems can be revised. It is for this reason that an overview of the grief process has been included in this week's material. Read the following to familiarize yourself with the essence of grief. If you are working with Cathryn or another professional directly, it would be useful to deal with your responses further in your one-to-one sessions. Processes to work with your grief are also covered in more detail in a later section. For now, however, this overview will enable you to identify your feelings of grief if they do emerge.

Grief: the Recipe For Sustained Joy

In order to obtain and maintain the holistic health needed to succeed and experience the joy we need to be: a) connected to a Higher Source, b) responsive to the needs of our body and the emotional needs of our children within, and c) able to establish and maintain a nurturing support system. Often, however, we become too consumed with the stresses of everyday life to have the energy needed to obtain— let alone sustain—any of the above.

If we are constantly worried about survival we do not have the time to pray and meditate which would keep us connected to God. If we are constantly worried about day-to-day issues and do not have the energy to be concerned about what we put into our bodies— we do not take the time to exercise. If we are always wrapped up in warding off the next crisis we have little time to participate in relationships in the healthy manner required to build a nurturing support system. Few know how to manage day-to-day stress because few have mastered the fourth, yet chief, an ingredient of emotional well-being—the ability to know how to embrace this process called grief.

Most of us will allow ourselves the luxury of grieving a major loss such as the loss of a loved one, a divorce or the loss of a job or our home. But truth be known, grief is a process with which we are involved every minute of our day. We are constantly reacting to one or more of the five stages of grief—even when we do not identify our reactions as such. The first four stages of grief are: 1) panic and denial;

2) bargaining or an attempt to control; 3) anger, and 4) despair. The fifth stage of grief is resolution. It is experienced as a state of serenity and joy. In the moments we do not feel serenity and joy, we feel stress. It may emerge as a pure sense of anxiety and panic or a need to control. It may get expressed as anger, despair, or frustration, but every feeling experienced by mankind that is not serene and peaceful is a feeling which can be related to one of the other four stages of grief.

Seldom do we recognize this fact, however. Instead, we react unconsciously to our day-to-day stress unable to identify the feelings associated with these reactions. We cannot resolve that which we are unable to name. This creates even more anxiety and panic. Many of us are perpetually caught in this state of panic and nervousness. When this state becomes unmanageable, we numb out with maladaptive and addictive behaviors. Consequently, stresses related to daily living never reach a resolution. They just continue to accumulate until we reach a breaking point and erupt with emotion or numb ourselves into complete oblivion with our addictions.

Since 9/11 our society has become even more imploded with unresolved daily stress. We are a society in mourning with few tools to grieve. The events of terrorism, wars in foreign lands, and the effects of natural disasters coupled with the current stresses of home, work, and school leave us afraid and confused—triggering childhood wounds and activating fears and doubts about our ability to cope. It is common, as children and as adults, to act out this unexpressed confusion, fear, grief, and tension through compulsive, addictive and self-defeating behaviors. We may eat, drink, drug or smoke too much or even love, shop, work, gamble or worry too much as we slowly begin to live our lives out of fear rather than faith—compulsion rather than choice—isolation rather than unity. Our efforts at home, school, and work get compromised as we long to anchor our safety in a place which cannot be bombed or destroyed by Mother Nature.

So what is the solution? In this day and age is it possible to live life peacefully, non-addictively—with promise and joy? What is it that we fear most? Is it alienation … childhood wounds … adult fears of survival …or even our own success?

All of these carry their own weight, but the underlying cause for our engaging in maladaptive and addictive behaviors is the simple fear we will not be able to cope. In this program, the fear is related to not trusting we will be able to cope with the success our program can bring. Success means more awareness. The more conscious we become, the more those things we have wanted to deny rear their ugly little heads. Remember, our bodies do not lie. Our bodies reveal our deepest fears.

Whether it is in the area of career, family, prosperity, love or creativity—we fear that what we have will be taken away and what we want will never manifest. The underlying fear that we will be unable to cope with the loss of dreams, hopes, friends, money, jobs and/or material possessions unconsciously weighs on us as we are bombarded constantly by the inevitability of such crises.

How do we ward off the anxiety of our fears, doubts or resentments? What is the process which can bridge us from seeing the world from the eyes of our human self—our everyday Adult Self who experiences trial and suffering—to viewing the world through the eyes of our Higher Self who can observe the world and its events as opportunities for expansion? How can we rediscover and learn how to sustain our joy? We can embrace our grief.

Embracing the process of grief is the antidote
for our fear we will be unable to cope.

Most, however, relate to grief as a process which is endured and revered only when there is a measurable loss which has a beginning and an end. Few perceive it as a natural response to the very challenges faced on a daily basis. But if grief is not processed and embraced, these challenges accumulate, erode hope, lead to rage and despair, and manifest as physical ailments or even suicidal ideation.

If we can learn how to grieve, even the most minute losses, we can successfully deal with our moment-to-moment feelings and return to a state of serenity. What's serenity? Serenity is not a state of mind that becomes fixed. It is a state of mind we continuously attain, lose and regain through the process of grief. By being able to deal with and resolve the anxiety which accompanies our daily losses and embrace the momentary anger and disillusionment, we are able to return to a state of resolution and trust.

When we feel trust we can stay connected to our source. We can nestle safely in the comfort of the arms of our Higher Power and feel bigger than our fears. But most of us are constantly caught in a battle with our fears and our fears keep us distracted from trusting. We swing between being afraid and being in the process of trusting and feeling grace. Often fragments of us are in both places at the same time.

What can we do when we slip from the safety and comfort of trusting our Higher Power into the depths of our fear we will not survive? We can embrace the process of grief. Again, we are already perpetually involved in the process of grief; we just do not identify it as such. For instance, one experiences the five stages of grief when confronting the simple loss that accompanies missing a phone call.

Picture for a moment those times you have come into your house with your arms full of groceries. The phone is ringing. You hurriedly drop the bags and rush to the phone. In these days you may check Caller ID and identify that the caller is definitely someone with whom you want to speak. However, just as you do this your voicemail kicks on and you have missed the opportunity to receive that long-awaited call. What is your response?

Whether identified as such or not it is most often the first stage of grief, *denial*. You may find yourself clicking the receiver as if you can "will" the person back. Then you slip into the second stage of grief as you *bargain* with the dead phone as you hear yourself plea, "Please don't hang up," even though the other party has already done so. This is often followed by an expression of *anger or disappointment*. "Damn, why did you hang up? Why could I have not gotten here sooner?" For some, the response may be even more colorful, but this reaction is quickly absorbed into a *despair or sadness* that the opportunity has been lost. What happens then? The sadness gives way to the knowledge that the person will indeed call back. Or you recall that you have that *69 on your new phone package, and you instantly try to reach the person. However you come to terms with this incident, the *resolution* does ensue.

You have denied the phone call was missed; tried to plea, bargain or fix this fact to make it different; felt anger in response to the loss which then gave way to despair followed simply by the resolution that you can either reach them or they will call you back. In a period of about 10 seconds, you have experienced the process of grief.

If you want to be equipped with the tools to live your life non-addictively, with feeling, then embrace the process of grief. Befriend this process. Use it as a way to work through all of life's challenges and disappointments. Don't deny them—but resolve them by identifying the stages of grief that you experience in response to your daily losses. Graciously move through those stages so you can return to a state of grace and resolution.

If you do not process these feelings they can manifest emotionally in your codependent behavior which keeps you stuck in the bargaining stage of grief. You can get locked into the third stage of grief which is anger by becoming edgy or critical, or in the stage of despair which is masked by lethargy and depression and then emerges somatically in illnesses or physical ailments. If you are willing to actively engage in the process of grief you will have a method by which you can deal with whatever life hands you.

Learn how to breathe through your anxiety, let go and give up your attempts to control the outcome of situations over which you have no control. Give yourself permission to beat on a pillow, scream in the mirror or throw a tantrum in the safety of your own home as you rid yourself of the energy of your anger. Learn how to befriend the void and emptiness of your despair so that place within you can be cleansed and prepared for you to bring in something new. Find that point of reference within for your serenity and then make it your goal to constantly process whatever keeps you from sustaining a sense of calm and connection.

Part of the human experience is to bump up against glitches in your day-to-day life. No matter how good you are—you are going to have to deal with life's challenges. You are going to get stuck in traffic jams. You are going to get hooked into old family roles or simply have "bad days." If you can become comfortable with the process of grief you can live fearlessly, with the assurance that you will indeed be able to cope. If you can cope, you can love. If you can cope you can succeed!

So, What Is Grief? Grief is the natural response to loss and it usually follows the five distinct stages previously discussed. Although these stages do not always progress sequentially, all of these emotions are present in the process of grief. Any loss which has been buried will most likely emerge during this Soul Step Program because your body is bringing to the surface those issues which prohibit you from attaining the progress you so desire.

Much of our adolescent years were spent actively involved in the stages of grief. In fact, the progression through adolescence can be viewed as a progression through the five stages of grief. In the initial stage, which occurred between the ages of twelve and fifteen, as we confronted self-consciousness and struggled to feel confident, we were dealing with the first two stages of grief; anxiety and bargaining. We bargained with who we were becoming and felt anxious about leaving behind who we were and what we knew. Yet, the transition did occur. And we did shift to the new us.

Developmental Tasks of the Twelve-to-Fifteen-Year-Old

Moving into the twelve-to-fifteen-year-old stage of development marks the beginning of your transition into adulthood. Most of us made this shift physically much more quickly than we did mentally or socially. We spent most of our adolescent years trying to settle into who we were becoming. All of the tasks mastered up to that point in our development paved the way for this transition. The bonding and trust we learned as infants provided the security we needed to risk relating to the opposite sex. The ability to set limits and to say No provided us with the foundation needed to establish and discern boundaries. The mediation between the good and bad aspects within prepared us for the comparisons which so ruthlessly emerged in the early teen years. The social and educational skills mastered in grade-school set the tone for the academic and social adventures which greeted us as budding young adults.

Each of these agendas has been mirrored in the successes and challenges you have encountered in showing up for your exploration. You have prepared the foundation for your plan; worked with the dichotomous feelings and confronted the co-dependent bargain™. You have looked at the sources of shame and guilt, your false loyalties, your need to please, and your fear of being excluded. All of the above paved the way for you to now step into the emerging you with a sense of ownership which is often associated with a fear of exposure. Why? Because whatever you were able or unable to master before you turned twelve became major building or stumbling blocks. Even under the best of circumstances, the move into adolescence is awkward. Discomfort with the sexual attraction you felt towards others and your struggles with social awkwardness and isolation became key issues. The need for peer approval became even greater because your entire self-image rested in the judgments of those around you. The following discusses these themes more fully.

Dependency on Peers for Approval—In our adult lives, it is important to feel we can ask someone what they think. We all need feedback. Dependency on another's opinion, however, is another thing. This form of dependency results when we completely lose sight of what we feel or think because we are so heavily influenced by the opinions of others.

Indicators of a dependency such as this are evident when you have to poll your friends before you feel confident about making a decision. This is further indicated if you continue to do this— over and over again. Asking for feedback and asking someone else to tell you what to do are two distinctly, different agendas. Asking for feedback invites those close to you to shed light on the areas of your life to which you may be blind. However, the ability to take that feedback and co-mingle it with your own intuition results from trusting yourself and your connection to your Source.

As a teenager, this was a way we felt connected to our peers and became a part of the "in-crowd." As an adult, this dependency can become a problem. In your pursuit of mastery, it can hinder your enjoyment of what you have achieved thus far in your goals. Your successes will only be valid when compared to the successes of others. Between twelve and fifteen years, teens are primarily involved in same-sex activities. When sexual interest did begin to spark, however, few knew what to do with it. This new interest was also accompanied by rapid physical changes. The teen years were a time riddled with baby fat, acne, and voices that cracked. The emotional and physical bodies were at odds. It was a time when we were perhaps the most self-conscious physically and yet the most compelled to take emotional risks. This tension between the emotional and physical agendas is what made us feel so hopelessly awkward.

Social Awkwardness—A carry over from this stage of our lives is revealed in our level of comfort or discomfort in social situations. If we were unable to learn how to cope with our sense of self-consciousness then we would have never developed that internal sense of self-confidence. This would be most apparent when we find ourselves in social situations in which we fear judgment. Those experiences when you feel exposed—when it is as if you are walking across a lunchroom and all eyes are on you—are threads from this stage of development. If these situations in your adult life are still gut-wrenching then this is a stage which will need some work. If you never learned how to cope with this discomfort and how to contain that anxiety without acting it out, then as you progress in your maturity, you will have to face those issues and learn what was never learned.

Using Compulsions and Addictions as a Way to Cope—So what did most of us do to quiet these anxieties? We withdrew and began a long history of resolving this angst through compulsive and addictive behaviors. If your coping mechanism involved using chemicals then you learned how to cope with discomfort by drinking, smoking dope, doing mind-altering drugs or simply by smoking cigarettes or overeating. If you were physiologically predisposed, you may have even activated an addictive disease or your co-dependency may have taken root. Perhaps your will to survive emerged and you assuaged your discomfort by channeling that discomfort into competitive sports or academic ventures. This certainly would have taught you how to manage and cope with your discomfort but, at some point in your life, you would still need to learn how to work with and resolve your discomfort.

Irrespective of how you directed this surge of hormonal energy—it was directed in some manner and that manner, destructive or constructive, would have followed you into your adult life. It would have set the stage for your challenge between self-confidence and self-consciousness with respect to entering new situations, new groups and new ventures.

Sexual Promiscuity—The last theme which needs to be addressed with this age is sexual promiscuity. Sexual promiscuity is a learned behavior. It was either learned from watching your parents misuse their sexual energy or developed in response to having been sexually abused and incorporating this experience into your blueprint for being loved. The result is that you learn to use your body to get your needs met…to "attract" love because that is what you learned as a child.

What results is a shame-based approach to one's sexuality. If you were molested as a child, on some level you sensed this was wrong and you internalized this "wrongness" as being related to something you did. You could have also been told you were being molested because you were the "chosen one…" you were special…so the way in which you would attempt to meet your needs for feeling loved and accepted could be through sexual activity. How? By your using your newly budding sexuality to manipulate your world in hopes of getting your needs met. The context of this sexual acting out is embedded in the fact that as a child your body was exploited and you developed the belief system that the manner in which you could get your needs met was by physicalizing your need for love.

For some, the sexual molestation began at this age. Because a young teenage body is developing, it can suddenly be exploited by others. Perhaps a step-father began to turn to you to meet his sexual needs. By not protecting you, your mother unconsciously allowed and even sanctioned it. Incest cannot happen unless there is a breakdown in the communication between the daughter and the mother. If a strong bond exists then the daughter would feel free to tell her mother what was happening and the abuse would stop.

For many, their attempts to get help were met with accusations, ridicule, and disbelief which only compounded the guilt, fear, and tendency to take responsibility for the abuse and make it your fault. If you had never developed clear boundaries and had witnessed one or both of your parents being promiscuous, you may have been more inclined to become promiscuous yourself. If you were experimenting with drugs and alcohol, this activity would have contributed to the loosening of your inhibitions.

How These Patterns May Be Carried Into Adulthood

As we move into mastery and autonomy we go through a stage where we experience discomfort with our new self-image. We may feel as though we don't quite fit into this new self. It mimics the issues we experienced between the ages of twelve and fifteen when we were moving into a new frame of reference with respect to our body, our families, and our peers. Our hormones were running rampant and this created great anxiety and discomfort. Our self-confidence was compromised by our self-consciousness. This experience is often recreated in any new endeavor which we pursue.

We go through that period when we have moved into a new area of expertise, yet, we do not feel quite comfortable with our new role. Our concept of success is tried on, but it needs adjustments. These alterations are made in the next stage of development which is adolescence. It is then when we become comfortable enough with the new role to pepper it with our own unique ingredients.

This stage of development and adult patterns reflect the transition made from being a novice to being seasoned. You will see this represented in your present level of achievement. This transition prepares you for entry into your refinement phase of adolescence when true mastery can begin to occur.

Potential Spiritual Lesson

So what might the potential spiritual lesson look like? The answer to this would be found in exploring when, in the history of the Soul, you experienced discomfort in holding the frequency of Light or lacked the self-confidence to appropriately express your creative and sexual passion. There may have been a time in your Soul's past when you began to attain spiritual mastery but felt insecure with your new powers and, therefore, acted without integrity.

You may discover a spiritual situation when you moved into a position of authority before you felt confident enough to hold that energy and you were left with an uneasiness of having possibly bitten off more than you could chew. The lessons related to this stage of development which would be reflected in this stage of your journey have to do with a discomfort with the newness. You may have completed some goal and now, all of a sudden, fear new expectations will be put upon you from some unknown source. As you work with these issues keep your mind open to their origin.

A REVIEW OF HOW TASKS FROM THIS STAGE OF DEVELOPMENT EMERGE AS GOALS IN ADULTHOOD WITH RESPECT TO SPECIFIC AREAS OF CONCERN:

1. Body Image—*Physical Body*—We claim our right to our physical forms, our right to be here, our right to have the physical form of our choosing. It is an empowering step, yet our confidence is still somewhat wobbly and can be thwarted by external judgment.

_____1. I am self-conscious about my body.

_____2. If someone criticizes the way I look I believe what they say.

_____3. I wish I could accept my body, but somehow am unable to do so.

_____4. I do not like to eat in front of others.

2. Self-Image—*Emotional Body*—Building on the foundation of acceptance we begin to take ownership of our unique talents and therefore can show our real self more to the external world.

However, we do so with great self-consciousness. We still feel quite awkward in being so vulnerable, but some inner force dictates that we take that risk.

_____1. I feel self-conscious about my talents.

_____2. I dislike exposure and prefer to stay hidden.

_____3. I feel the right to claim my true self, but feel awkward in doing so.

_____4. I don't like being too vulnerable.

3. Belief Systems—*Mental Body*—Now we are able to take even more risks with what we believe and are moving away from a should-based existence, but we do so with some reluctance and anxiety regarding possible rejection. We learn how to say just enough to test another's reaction, and if it is positive, we proceed. If it is negative, we retreat.

_____1. I express my thoughts but only if I know they are going to be accepted.

_____2. I cautiously test another's opinions to see if he/she thinks as I.

_____3. If I state a truth which is different than others I feel uncomfortable.

_____4. I feel nervous I will be judged if I say what I think or feel.

4. Spirituality—*Spiritual Body*—(Spiritual Path or Recovery Program)

Once we have created a support circle with those of like-minds who can accept and recognize us for our beliefs we have a model for beginning the process of internalizing this acceptance and recognition. We begin to take ownership of our vision of a Higher Power and test our inner reality by externalizing it. We can be somewhat guarded about our newly defined beliefs. We are not sure we can trust ourselves to be able to make sound judgments. We may still feel awkward about trusting our inner knowingness, but nonetheless, the definition of our beliefs is gathering momentum.

_____1. I am clear about beliefs but don't express them for fear of being judged.

_____2. I experience anxiety if my spiritual beliefs are too visible.

_____3. I have specific ideas about spirituality which I keep private.

_____4. I feel anxious if I have to present my beliefs in any public manner.

5. Family and Intimate Relationships—In our close relationships we begin to risk new ways of being with those we love, but we can be shy and quick to pull back into the old patterns due to our self-consciousness. In our primary relationship, we move into wanting to experiment with more authenticity but are still very cautious. We do not want to "rock the boat" or lose the relationship.

_____1. I proceed with great caution when I exhibit a new behavior with others.

_____2. I get nervous when I attempt to break away from family ideas.

_____3. I figure nothing is going to change anyway so why try to be different.

_____4. I would rather avoid contact with some family members than deal with the discomfort I feel at being different than them.

6. Sexuality and Passion—The goal of this phase is to explore our sexuality, but we feel quite awkward in identifying ourselves as sexual beings. This is usually due to societal and parental programming. Our sexual energy is tied into our passion and creativity because the energies come from the same energy source, so often we experience this same awkwardness with respect to owning this passion and our creativity. We may become "closet creators"—creating in the privacy of our own homes but still shy about putting it out into the world. Self-conscious about being judged and fearful we are unable to channel this energy appropriately and responsibly, we can block it and deny it due to this lack of trust.

_____1. I feel awkward with my sexuality.

_____2. My passion for life and for love frightens me.

_____3. I would rather eat, smoke, drink or addict than let my passion emerge.

———4. I avoid people who obviously have different sexual preferences than I.

7. Prosperity and Abundance—We may begin to play with the concepts "creative lifework" or "right livelihood," but we do not quite know how to put those principles into practice. We can begin to shift from manifesting abundance based on horizontal principles to manifesting it according to our higher wisdom and inner knowingness.

———1. I feel inadequate when it comes to managing my money.

———2. I don't have much passion for life or love.

———3. I believe if I do what I love the money will follow.

———4. I avoid people who obviously have significantly more or less money than I.

8. Job, Career or Climb on the Corporate Ladder—This step marks the first step towards mastery in that it is the first time we entertain the idea of developing a new self-image or a new role in the company that carries more power and status. We may begin to want to climb the corporate ladder and excel, but we are somewhat tentative and self-conscious with new prospects.

———1. I feel very cautious when I try a new behavior at work.

———2. I get nervous if I do something at work which draws attention to me.

———3. If I don't like something I keep quiet. Why buck the system?

———4. I have some ideas which excite me but I don't share them with anyone.

As you peruse the above material, contemplate how the issues of this developmental stage interface with your daily life and perhaps reflect the issues and lessons of your Soul. Then turn your focus to your body and to your hamstrings—the muscles which carry the essence of this stage of development because they operate behind the scenes and yet are essential to the overall movement and agility of our entire physical being.

WORKING WITH THE HAMSTRING MUSCLES WHICH CORRELATE TO THIS STAGE OF DEVELOPMENT

The area of the body which most often carries the energy related to the young inner teen is the hamstring area which runs along the back side of each leg. These muscles are essential to overall movement and flexibility, and yet, are often overlooked because they hide behind the more powerful quadriceps which extends from the hip to the knee.

The hamstrings are lean muscles which work hand-in-hand with the back muscles, quadriceps, and lace around the calf muscles. They are connecting muscles just as the young inner teen stage of development connects the psyche into the young budding adolescent physical form. The hamstring muscles are also central to the core muscles and work hand-in-hand with them to hold the body tall and erect and to carry one's pride. When we begin to work with this muscle group and strengthen and flex it, we will dislodge any issues this area may have housed.

This week, as you bring your focus to the different areas of emotional challenge carried over from your young teen years, consciously give your body permission to release the unexpressed energy related to feeling self-conscious and uncomfortable in your body. Reflect on this time in your life which invited you to stretch into a new version of yourself, just as the hamstrings need to be stretched and exercised if they are to hold the rest of your body in proper alignment.

Hamstring Muscle Meditation: *I invite you right now, however, to bring your focus to your hamstring muscles. Breathe into these muscles and ask them to reveal any issues of discomfort or self-consciousness they may have held for you. Listen and record your responses. Learn to understand the language of your body and it will always reveal your most beneficial next step.*

THE CHAKRA CENTER WHICH CORRELATES TO THIS STAGE OF DEVELOPMENT IS THE THROAT CHAKRA

The throat chakra is related to speaking our truth with integrity. Our words hold a vibration and carry our spiritual attunement out into the world. As we explore our self-consciousness with a sense of confidence and get comfortable with a higher vibration of energy, our speech reflects this higher consciousness in the words we choose and the manner in which we speak. The three chakras after the heart are considered the higher chakras and therefore naturally hold a higher vibration of color which is more aligned with both the physical and spiritual bodies.

Chakra Meditation: *Take a moment to bring your focus to your throat area. Imagine a ball of energy infusing this area with the brilliant color of summer day sky blue. As the throat area becomes more balanced and able to hold a higher frequency of light, the color glistens with shades of blue which fluctuate with the vibration of your spoken word...the more harmonious your speech, the softer the tones of blue. Allow this energy center to spin out any issues related to feeling self-conscious thus increasing your ability to feel more comfortable with the new vibration of adolescence. See your Angels now touching the location of your fifth chakra as they use their angel dust to calm any discomforts and assuage all fears and anxieties related to becoming more and more comfortable in your new physical form. When you feel complete, take another deep breath, open your eyes and record what you experienced.*

To bring closure to this week's work reflect once again on how your cherished saboteur™ emerges with respect to your fears regarding your ability to feel confident and to cope with the discomfort of the unknown and the unpredictable. What has your Adult Self learned which will now assist it in responding to the needs of this wounded self so the tendency to sabotage can be dissolved? Once you have given this the mental attention it needs close your eyes and proceed.

Closing Meditation: *See the twelve-to-fifteen-year-old in front of you. Ask what is needed in order for this wounded one to feel safe. Respond to that need and then invite this inner child to reside in the center of the sacred chamber of your heart where he/she will be safe. Fill your heart center with the golden light of love and the healing light of the violet flame. Then bring your attention to the center of your head and ask that the master cell is re-activated with this new DNA vibration of self-confidence and a sense of comfort with the uncomfortable—a sense of trust in that which is unpredictable. Feel the energy pulsating through your body as it travels down your spinal cord to your creator cell where this same intention is decreed. Take a deep breath and ask that every cell in your body now holds this new DNA patterning and that the hamstring muscles master this tension and learn how to cope with that which cannot be controlled. Take a deep breath and record your experience in your journal. As you progress through your week keep these experiences fresh in your mind and in your intentions.*

Our biggest fear in life is that
we will not be able to cope.
Think about it.

Any fear you encounter is related to
your concern that if indeed this situation
transpires—you will not be able to handle
your reactions.

As you heal your inner teen and strengthen
your relationship with your Higher Power
you will develop a confidence in your ability
to grieve which ensures your ability to cope.

REFER TO THE "DAILY CHECK-IN SHEETS"
AND THE "7-DAY REVIEW"
FOUND IN THE APPENDIX TO LOG YOUR
EXPERIENCE.

Tenth Module—
Inner Adolescent

Rebellion Versus Passivity

We do not want our 15-17-year-old within running our life—but we sure do want to learn how to listen to that voice, for this is the aspect of us who monitors our truth and integrity. Any violation—be it self-imposed or from another—will result in this inner self rebelling against our inner adult and wreaking havoc until we right that wrong, speak our truth, and come back into faith with ourselves"

YOUR INNER ADOLESCENT (Ages 15-17)

Y OU HAVE JUST finished working with the dynamic of getting comfortable with your discomfort. Now it is time to begin to integrate a new vibration of energy into your day-to-day life. You begin to discover ways to expand each fiber of your being so your body can hold an increased frequency of light. You have started to step more and more into your Future Self and have begun to co-mingle with an empowered, new image.

In this upcoming module, you will build on this newfound knowledge...you will be given the opportunity to refine this new image. You will draw from what you experienced as an adolescent and begin to carve out and define a stronger identity. Some of you will accomplish this by actively rebelling against all you have ever known. Suddenly, what you had been able to tolerate in many areas of your life will somehow emerge as unacceptable. Tolerance for anything that even suggests a lack of authenticity can be unbearable. You may find yourself feeling more harsh than usual. You may even appear cocky to those in your life who have watched you change and grow but have never before experienced the person they are about to now encounter.

With respect to your program, this adolescent within may be the one who is rebelling against your moving closer to accomplishing your goals. If this inner self does not understand your purpose and does not buy into the fact that it is a step towards your individuality, it will protest with great sabotage. You may project that rebellion out onto others or you might derail with an inner rebellion which stops you cold in your tracks. The source of this rebellion, this unrest, this non-negotiable need to speak your truth and to stand in your authenticity originates from your experiences in adolescence when you were between the ages of fifteen and seventeen. How satisfied you feel in intimate relationships, how secure you feel with the person you have become and the amount of rebellion you feel within yourself and with others are issues rooted in the fifteen-to-seventeen-year-old self.

Developmental Tasks of the Fifteen-To-Seventeen-Year-Old

As we reached mid-adolescence, rebellion became essential if we were to move into the final stage of development—preparing for our place in the adult world. We began to settle down in terms of our sexual feelings. We started "going steady." As couples, we still paired within groups, as the group provided the base for identification, but we were beginning to learn the skills necessary to establish a long-term relationship—although, for an adolescent, long-term usually meant from six weeks to six months.

Peer acceptance became more important than parental acceptance. Even though we wanted to sprout our wings, we still needed to feel the safety of home. Of course, we never would have said that. We behaved more rebellious than we were. It was a time when we began to define a self outside of the family. To be different than our parents meant to be separate from them. We defined that self by separating from our parents and family and by struggling self-consciously to be different. That was what growing up involved.

This stage of development was similar to the toddler stage because we again experimented with setting limits and establishing boundaries. Whatever our Adult Self has difficulty saying no to, our fifteen-to-seventeen-year-old will rebel against through behavior. When the Adult Self is able to set limits and say no, this adolescent within rebels less. Until then, this part of self will continue to rebel. We are rebelling against things which feel unsafe or unfair…and things which threaten to compromise our individual nature.

Developing a unique sense of self was the primary task in this developmental stage. Rebellion was and still is a response to anything which threatens this definition. This inner teenager will act up to be separate and different. If you are around someone who tries to control you and "make you over in their image," this part of you will rebel. This is the part of you who holds your individuality as the prime importance and anything which threatens it will butt up against its wrath. This was evident in the angry adolescent voice I had to work with before I could clear the path to go to Washington DC and continue with my work. Underneath her wrath, however, was the wound of the younger, more vulnerable self who was being protected by the armored adolescent. This part of us is the gatekeeper to our pain and unless we can gain enough courage to confront it, we will never earn the trust needed for these parts to reveal themselves with the confidence that they can now be healed.

Standing Up For Yourself—*The* barometer for how much we stand up for ourselves is evident in those moments when we feel betrayed. Most often, when we examine these feelings more closely, we can detect the exact moment when we sold ourselves out. Long before another betrays us, we have most often betrayed ourselves. They have given us signs of their untrustworthiness, but we chose to ignore them.

Standing up for yourself simply means that you are astute enough to identify your truth and then have enough courage to speak it. Working with this stage will give you an opportunity to examine the points where you sell yourself out and project your self-betrayal onto the person you empowered to betray you.

Being Caught Up In An Active State Of Rebellion Or Passivity— Rebelling when you were an adolescent was essential if you were to move into the final stage of development—preparing for your place in the adult world. There may have been many reasons this rebellion did not occur. In order to rebel there had to be someone you cared enough about to rebel against, and there had to be a structure against which you could safely rebel. The degree to which you were allowed to rebel will determine the degree to which you were able to define yourself as separate from your caretakers. If you were restricted from this feat you may have become passive and instead projected your rebellious nature onto others. You may have externalized this feeling by attracting those who would act out your rebellion for you.

Needing To Be Right—Another expression of this stage of development in your adult life is when you find yourself becoming righteously indignant about some cause or issue. Your ego may be invested in being seen as the expert—your self-esteem may be intertwined with assuming if you are a grown up then you know what is best. You may find yourself fighting battles you don't even care about just so you can prove the other person wrong. If this rings true, it is time for you to ask your inner adolescent who he or she is really angry at and what truth has not been spoken which now needs to be expressed?

Defining And Owning Your Uniqueness—This stage and focus invites you to clearly define for yourself the difference between being selfish and being self-caring; between having a healthy self-esteem and a nauseating sense of self-importance; between being conceited and holding an "earned appreciation" for your uniqueness. Now I understand in some circles to even claim you are unique is a step towards relapse, but having a solid connection with your true source, while at the same time having an appreciation for your unique expression of that source, can be a sign of maturity. As you learn to appreciate your unique characteristics without being attached to them, you can further appreciate and revere the uniqueness of others.

How These Patterns May Be Carried Into Adulthood

So how does all of this material filter into your adult life? The pattern exhibited in adulthood which relates to this stage of development is found in your need to hold onto an identity or at least to establish one. This is the part of you who does not want to be the same as everyone else—who will rebel against the mundane—who, through their very beingness, will challenge others to stretch beyond their comfort zone. This is the part of you who will harshly set limits or let others know what you like and dislike. If you feel angry or betrayed, it is your adolescent who is responding to a perceived betrayal. If you feel repressed, there is most likely an inner adolescent who fears to butt up against someone he or she perceives to be in authority, and this part of you does not like it! In order to operate in sync with this part of self, the adult part of you needs to meet the challenges of holding your authenticity. Anything which emerges that is less than this pursuit will be met with the rage of your inner adolescent.

This rage or depression can emerge at any point in your journey. You may find yourself rebelling against those in your life who held the notion you would not succeed. You may find yourself feeling righteously indignant about injustices which relate to some unspoken aspect of your inner self. This is when you will begin to shed the old ways and defiantly carve out a new you...to break away from any external structure which has been used as a false source of identity. You may find yourself breaking away from your role of wife/husband, or a negative self-image such as being "no good", or too fat or too thin, or not smart enough, educated enough or any and all of the above. As an adult, you may feel rebellious against any external structure which has served as a point of reference for the old you as you then replace it with a more current and refined point of reference for the new you.

This is the step where your true signature is put on any endeavor or relationship...where the idea or the job becomes "yours!" This is when you become settled in your role with others. You have more comfort at being who you are and in allowing the rest of the world to accept or reject you. Your reference point for self-worth is no longer externally projected; it is now internalized and based on the process of self-referencing.

Potential Spiritual Lesson

So what may the potential spiritual lesson look like? The answer to this would be found in exploring when in the history of the Soul you experienced a rebellion or betrayal with respect to your Higher Source. Have you turned away from God and betrayed your inner knowingness only to then blame the Higher Source for abandoning you? Have you failed to set the appropriate limits for yourself spiritually and then blamed it on the organization to which you belonged?

The lessons related to this stage of development and which would be reflected in your pursuit of mastery have to do with any area of your life where you do not stand in your truth. You may have achieved some mastery or completed a goal and now, all of a sudden, fear that new expectations will be put upon you from some unknown source.

A REVIEW OF HOW TASKS FROM THIS STAGE OF DEVELOPMENT EMERGE AS GOALS IN ADULTHOOD WITH RESPECT TO SPECIFIC AREAS OF CONCERN:

Body Image—*Physical Body*—We have come to terms with our health, our disease, our size, and age. This is when we make peace with the person we have become and with what we have done in the past which compromised our physical bodies.

_____1. I know exercising is good for me, but it is such a fad, I refuse to do it.

_____2. Even though certain foods do not agree with me, I eat them anyway.

_____3. I eat, drink or addict when I am angry.

_____4. I don't like to relax, it makes me too nervous.

9. Self-Image—*Emotional Body*—We become even more brazen and confident with who we are and how we feel about ourselves. Our self-esteem becomes internally, rather than externally, referenced. We have carved out a sense of self and we become more specific about who we are and what we want to do. During this step we are able to move into speaking our truth with great confidence…although our truth is still expanding and evolving, we are comfortable with this inconsistency and feel little need to defend our right to change our mind.

_____1. I don't really know what I like or dislike.

_____2. I like to shock others with my ideas of what is important.

_____3. I am very determined about what I want to accomplish in my life.

_____4. I find other people's opinions about me irrelevant.

10. Belief systems—*Mental Body*—

_____1. I speak what I think no matter what anyone else says.

_____2. I like to say things that shock others.

_____3. My thoughts may be inconsistent, but I figure at least they are mine.

_____4. If someone disagrees with me I will defend my view to the end!

11. Spirituality—*Spiritual Body*—(Spiritual Path or Recovery Program)

We begin to understand we can find a "unique" sense of self through our spiritual identification—it is a structure against which that inner self rebels as we continue to define our own unique thread of spiritual belief.

_____1. I am determined to speak my truth, even if it gets me into trouble.

_____2. I enjoy testing my spiritual beliefs out on others.

_____3. I enjoy shocking others with my unique spiritual beliefs.

_____4. I enjoy a good argument about spirituality.

As Related To Your First Contact In A Recovery Program For Addictions

When we start a recovery program our inner teen will wreak havoc with the structure. No other aspect of our self will rebel against the doctrines as much as this one will. The adolescent also projects out any responsibility for the addiction and takes the position that the only problem was that he or she got "busted." "I can control my use any time I want to—I just don't want to."

_____1. I think what they talk about in these meetings is stupid!

_____2. If I just wouldn't have gotten caught I wouldn't have to be here.

_____3. I feel so restless here—"they" want me to be like everyone else.

_____4. If I am honest with how much I used loved ones will leave.

12. Family and Intimate Relationships—In our family relationships we are now more brazen and risky with speaking our truth and being real…despite the possibility of losing them. The same is true in our primary relationship…we have to speak our truth irrespective of the risk because to remain in the relationship in a non-authentic manner is intolerable.

_____1. Even though my family and I disagree I speak up nonetheless.

_____2. Even if I agree, I like to disagree with someone just for the fun of it.

_____3. I find myself in situations where my values are unique and stand out.

_____4. I would rather keep my feelings to myself than risk losing a close friend.

13. Sexuality and Passion—Sufficiently design our own unique sexuality based organically on that which matches our innate wisdom and integrity. See our sexual expression not only as an expression of the universal energy but also as a partner to the source of our creative energy. We learn how to manage that energy and channel it productively.

_____1. I like to experiment with sexual alternatives even if they offend others.

_____2. I have creative talents but do not express them.

_____3. I find my sexual values are unique and often stand out.

_____4. I am a person with great passion and will compromise it for nothing.

14. Prosperity and Abundance—With respect to manifesting abundance we become more willing to risk everything for the chance to do what we love and hope the money follows. We are unwilling to "prostitute" ourselves anymore. We have to stay true to our own unique passion and path and see the money and prosperity coming in from this source.

_____1. I spend money on items that most others would not.

_____2. I don't like spending time on anything that doesn't fit with who I am.

_____3. I refuse to spend money on items which are harmful to the planet.

_____4. I purchase only those things which reflect my individual spirit.

15. Job, Career or Climb on the Corporate Ladder—We begin to rebel against the external or corporate structure…carving out a position for self that is respected and draws on the specific talents of us as an individual. If there is no room for this in the corporate system then the rebellion takes the form of unrest as we gather support

to confront the unhealthy parts of the corporate system or as an employee we would quit or get fired.

_____1. I am determined to speak my mind—even if it gets me into trouble.

_____2. Even if I agree, I like to disagree with my co-workers, just for fun.

_____3. I enjoy testing company rules.

_____4. I have strange ideas and I enjoy shocking others with them. *As you peruse the above material, contemplate how the issues of this developmental stage interface with your daily life and perhaps reflect the issues and lessons of your Soul. Then turn your focus to your body and to your quadriceps which are the muscles that carry the essence of this stage of development because they are bold and powerful—operating behind the scenes and yet essential to the overall movement and agility of our entire physical being.*

WORKING WITH THE QUADRICEPS MUSCLE WHICH CORRELATES TO THIS STAGE OF DEVELOPMENT

The muscle group which correlates to this stage of development most profoundly is the quadriceps. These muscles are the most active muscles when it comes to monitoring movement and mobility and transporting us, via our bodies, from one place to another. They are also the part of our body which is brassy and throws our weight around in a commanding, sometimes over-confident way. They are extensions of the hips which, for women, are the gateway to the heart of their femininity. They protect or receive. For men, the quadriceps are used to thrust and penetrate—not only in love-making but in any endeavor.

This week, as you bring your focus to the different areas of emotional challenge carried over from your inner adolescent, consciously give your body permission to release the unexpressed energy related to feeling power and control, rebellion and passivity. Reflect on this time in your life which invited you to flex your muscles in your own individuality and to carve out a sense of self as you mastered the technique of inflated grandiosity.

Quadriceps Muscle Meditation: *I invite you right now, however, to bring your focus to your quadriceps. Breathe into these muscles and ask them to reveal any issues of false rebellion and overconfidence which no longer serves you. Listen and record your responses. Learn to understand the language of your body and it will always reveal your most beneficial next step.*

THE CHAKRA CENTER WHICH CORRELATES TO THIS STAGE OF DEVELOPMENT IS THE THIRD EYE AREA.

Your sixth energy center is located at the center of your forehead in your third eye area. It is the center of your higher vision; associated with your pituitary gland, it offers a balance to the whole system. By focusing on this area and energizing it with the color of indigo, you can begin to draw to you everything you need to fulfill you in this lifetime. This energy center is associated with your adolescent within, your fifteen-to-seventeen-year-old. This is the part of self who can speak your truth if you will listen. An adolescent sees things as they are and comments with honesty to those who will listen. It is a time when you are carving out a sense of self and finding your true identity—spiritually, emotionally, physically and mentally.

Third-Eye Chakra Meditation: *Take a moment to bring your focus to your third eye area. Imagine a ball of energy rotating and being infused with the brilliant color of magenta. Allow this energy to spin out any issues related to feeling rebellious or passive as you become more comfortable with your new authentic vibration of adolescence. See your Angels now touching the location of your sixth chakra as they use their angel dust to calm any discomforts, fears, and anxieties, and assuage all doubts as you become more and more comfortable in your new physical form. When you feel complete take another deep breath, open your eyes and record what you experienced.*

To bring closure to this week's work reflect once again on how your cherished saboteur™ emerges with respect to your feeling rebellious or complacent. What has your Adult Self learned which will now assist it in responding to the needs of this wounded self so the tendency to sabotage can be dissolved? Once you have given this the mental attention it needs close your eyes and proceed.

Closing Meditation: *See the fifteen-to-seventeen-year-old in front of you. Ask what is needed in order for this wounded one to feel safe. Respond to that need and then invite this inner child to reside in the center of the sacred chamber of your heart where he/she will be safe. Fill your heart center with the golden light of love and the healing light of the violet flame. Then bring your attention to the center of your head and ask that the master cell is re-activated with this new DNA vibration of autonomy and self-definition. Feel the energy pulsating through your body as it travels down your spinal cord to your creator cell where this same intention is decreed. Take a deep breath and ask that every cell in your body now holds this new DNA patterning and that the quadriceps— which have resonated with the disturbance of rebellion or complacency— can now relax, align and harmonize. Take a deep breath and record your experience in your journal. As you progress through your week keep these experiences fresh in your mind and in your intentions.*

REFER TO THE "DAILY CHECK-IN SHEETS" AND THE "7-DAY REVIEW" FOUND IN THE APPENDIX TO LOG YOUR EXPERIENCE.

Eleventh Module—
Young Inner Adult

Mediocrity Versus Mastery

When you experience your challenges as lessons instead of burdens, true mastery occurs. You become a student of your life instead of a victim of it.

YOUNG INNER ADULT (17-21)

THIS LAST PHASE of your program invites you to take all you have learned and begin to claim it and practice it until it becomes the real you. There will be times, as you take this experience into your day-to-day world, you will feel as though you are acting as if you are someone you are not. This simply is giving space and recognition to all of those parts of you who have not embraced the new you as easily as it has the core you. This process will be on-going. You have a new point of reference—a new blueprint which you can systematically apply to any endeavor of your choice.

You begin by examining how you can best take this new point of reference into your day-to-day life. You will be able to experiment with how you now want to modify the components of this program—your daily check-ins, your commitment to a goal, your need to process issues as needed, and your connection to a support group which nourishes your continued evolution. Your blueprint for how you integrate these new learned skills and habits into your day-to-day life can be better understood by examining how you originally accomplished this task between the ages of seventeen to twenty-one because this was the first time you encountered such a task. To understand this dynamic more fully, let's examine these final developmental tasks with a little more depth.

DEVELOPMENTAL TASKS FROM AGES SEVENTEEN TO TWENTY-ONE

How effectively you run your life—how responsible you are with respect to the daily habits which enable you to manage your life in a productive manner; your relationship to the masculine and feminine traits within you and your relationship to your internalized value system are all related to what you learned or did not learn during the last years of your official childhood. These years are the years when you are supposed to have the opportunity to practice being an adult while still living in the safety of your family.

Between the ages of seventeen and twenty-one, you began to be treated as an adult. Learning how to be responsible and manage your life were important issues. You began to relate to others more maturely. You learned how to provide and fend for yourself as you prepared for college, got married, or found a job and moved into an independent living situation. Goals became more concrete as you began to discover what you wanted from life and made plans to achieve those goals.

At least that is how it was supposed to be! Some of you moved away from home but remained dependent emotionally, perhaps even financially on your parents. Others moved right from the home of your parents to the home of your wife or husband and never had an opportunity to experience autonomy in the adult world. Yet others moved out even before this time—unprepared for the adult world— but thrown into the mix with what you had on your back and in your "tool chest." You had to fend for yourself and act as if you were competent long before your time.

Irrespective of what your transition was into adulthood, the patterns learned and habits developed from this time will set the stage for how you master carrying your achievements into your day-to-day life in a meaningful and productive manner.

You will begin to explore how you want to use all you have learned from this structure to enhance your life. What habits have you developed over the course of your life which you can now incorporate on an on-going basis? What have you integrated? What is still left to be resolved? Each time you apply this structure to an endeavor you will learn more about yourself and flush out the blocks which prohibit you from, not only experiencing your joy but also, from sustaining it.

You will be invited to examine the origin and effectiveness of those values. The buzzword for this stage of development is *evaluation*. The more comfortable you are with reviewing and examining your life and then making the appropriate adjustments, the more successful you will be with your continued evolution and growth. You will look at your personality through the lens of the masculine and feminine within you and explore how these principles have or have not been integrated into your day-to-day life. You will be invited to evaluate your satisfaction with respect to your career, your relationships, your passions and your productivity.

You will have an opportunity to recall past dreams; to evaluate the realization of those dreams and to revise and recommit to new dreams. You will also be given the support to look at your life from a holistic angle—how integrated are your spiritual values into your day-to-day activities? How congruent are your thoughts on your feelings and your actions? What have you learned about your body and your relationship with your body since the beginning of this program that is useful? How have you internalized what you have learned? How can you now set new goals and commit to new aspirations? Keep all of these questions in mind as you ponder the themes for this stage of development.

Examining Your Values—Values are what give your life meaning. You develop your value system based on what you observe from those around you. Family, friends, and society at large play a huge role in your value development. You learn about the roles of men and women from what you observe. You learn the value of money; of integrity and honesty from what you observe. You develop a work ethic and a blueprint for your relationships all by what you observe and then weave into your own unique formula for living. You are invited to ponder all of these values for yourself and determine which ones now support the new you and which values need to be revised?

Focus first on your relationships. Look at the relationships you have in your life. How many people in your life are acquaintances? How many would you call good friends? How do you define a meaningful friendship? What do you value in your friendships? Look at your intimate relationships—and ponder what is valuable about them. What aspects of each relationship support your authentic self and which relationships require you to be a version of who you really are? What do you want to do with this new awareness? Take the time to ponder your relationships—notice how much courage it takes to be honest and to hold the truth of the quality of the relationships you have attracted into your life. What do your relationships say about you? How do they mirror your own strengths and challenges?

How you respond to these questions will be most influenced by the relationship you had with your same-sexed parent because it is from this parent you learned what it meant to be an adult as a man or a woman. To have made this transition successfully would have required that you had a meaningful relationship with your same-sexed parent. It would have been necessary to have seen traits in your same-sexed parent which you wanted to emulate. The development of your masculine and feminine sides would have been most influenced by what you observed of the men and women involved in your life at that time. Teachers, clergy, bosses, and mentors all would have played a positive or challenging role in the person you became.

Your ability to weave the creative aspects with the side of you who can take that creativity and mold it into action originated with the models you had. How did the males in your life take action? How did the females express their creative talents? Were there mentors in your life who successfully tapped into their creativity and were able to express this creativity in the world in a meaningful way? Most of us are strong in one area but have challenges in the other. It will be useful to explore more fully the masculine and feminine within you and the degree to which they dance with ease.

Career Satisfaction—You will also want to turn your eye to how you make your living. In some ways, it does not matter what you do, but rather, how you do it. How do you feel about the ways you work in the world which enable you to provide for yourself? Do you provide for yourself? Have you always had to provide for yourself or have you been taken care of by others? What are your independent abilities? In what areas of your life are you interdependent? How do you feel about this? If you had to define a work ethic—what would yours be? How do you find value in what you do?

What you discover is going to relate directly back again to what you observed and the models, positive and negative, you had for this integration. The value of examining these traits is that you then have a starting point from which you can begin your work. You cannot determine who you want to be until you are clear about whom you do not want to be. Part of becoming a functional and productive adult—one who has mastered integrating a higher value into the day-to-day activities—is one who can muster up the courage for such self-reflection. If you can engage in this kind of perpetual self-inventory without shame or guilt, then you are constantly in a position to modify and re-commit to a never-ending evolution of your highest form. You become a student of your life instead of a victim to it.

The Maturation of your Spiritual Intent—The most promising component of this journey is the invitation to consciously integrate your spiritual aspirations into your day-to-day activities. The entire thrust of this material has been to provide you with a structure which can assist you in developing the habit of integrating your spiritual practice into your daily life. Taking all you have now learned involves successfully weaving your spiritual values into the way you live your life on a day-to-day basis. Examining the following will assist you in this endeavor. How do you integrate your spiritual principles into the manner in which you treat your physical form? How do you weave it into your daily thoughts? What belief systems have been altered? Use these questions to assist you in your self-examination.

There is more and more support for living a spiritual life in a physical body. More and more individuals are finding ways to integrate their belief in a Higher Source into the actions they take on a daily basis. Is it helpful to examine your day-to-day life through this lens? What do you value spiritually? How do you integrate those values into how you treat others, how you treat yourself, how you treat your body, and what do you want to do about this?

Evaluating Your Achievements and Setting New Goals—In this final aspect of your exploration you begin to look back and ahead…you are encouraged to look through the eyes of the newly, empowered self, feeling pride for what you have accomplished and intrigue and excitement about what you can now set your sights on. How can you set new goals? How can you establish a new vision for who you want to become next? Have you become the person you wanted to become? How does this new you compare to who you hoped you would be by this time in your journey? How do you feel about this? What are your disappointments and what aspects of your journey thus far make you feel proud?

Completing a leg of any journey always invites evaluation and recommitment. Acknowledging what you have accomplished while at the same time being able to set new goals is what keeps this whole process of living an adventure. When we stop setting new goals, we cease to make use of the time we have on this planet and in this body. Your progress can be defined only by you and your higher source— but when we feel we have no more to learn—we don't. We send a signal to our body that the time has come for us to begin the journey back home.

It is my belief that when we cease learning, we begin dying. Some make their transition immediately—others take years to pull their energy from these forms and to transition back to the spiritual realm. Where are you on this journey? What are your new sights…new goals…new aspirations? How can you take the structure you have been invested in and give birth to a new way of living your life with feeling, non-addictively?

How These Patterns May Be Carried Into Adulthood

So what is the purpose of all of these questions? How does all of this material fit into what you learned as a young adult? The same questions you have been invited to explore above are the same issues you had when you were in the developmental stage of seventeen to twenty-one. How prepared you are and how willing you are to be involved in a constant evaluation of your life originates from what you experienced at that time in your life for this stage of development marked the first time you made a major transition—the transition into the adult world.

This stage of development and adult patterns developed, reflect the manner in which you shift from being a novice to being seasoned. You will see this represented in your present level of achievement with respect to your accomplishments—but the integration of this will be revealed in the ease with which you participate in this on-going evaluation. This transition prepares you for entry into any refinement phase where true mastery can be maintained.

Potential Spiritual Lesson

So how does this material interface with what your Soul may be here to learn? Know that this is not the first time you have had to practice this transition into mastery. Just like serenity, mastery is not a fixed state. It is a stance in life and in life's situations which you achieve, lose, revise and once again attain.

It is living, moment-to-moment, in the process of grief as you feel the anxiety of impending change; attempt to hold onto the old; use your anger and dissatisfaction to break free; allow yourself the luxury of standing naked in the void and then integrating the new vibration with ease. Each experience in life invites you to integrate more fully the vibration of joy. The manner in which you choose to do so will vary according to the layer you are focusing on at that time. Nothing is constant. Everything is ever-changing and each new day offers a new opportunity to be who you want and know you can be.

A REVIEW OF HOW TASKS FROM THIS STAGE OF DEVELOPMENT EMERGE AS GOALS IN ADULTHOOD WITH RESPECT TO SPECIFIC AREAS OF CONCERN:

1. Body Image—*Physical Body*—Peace has been made with our physical forms and we can now maintain a presence and a connection without guilt or shame. There is a confidence we can cope emotionally and still stay present. In our exercise program, we have reached our goal and have the skills to maintain it and integrate exercise into our daily lives with ease.

_____1. I wish I accepted my body just the way it is, but I don't.

_____2. I try to eat in a healthy and responsible way but am not good at it.

_____3. I would like to exercise at least 3—5 times a week, but I don't.

_____4. I want to feel more comfortable in my body than I do now.

2. Self-Image—*Emotional Body*—We are ready to step into our day-to-day world with authenticity and confidence. Our self-esteem is based on this authenticity and we have developed a

support system to mirror this. Our belief system is quite formed and integrated with who we are in such a way that we feel no need to defend or challenge...it just is. There is mastery of definition with respect to what we believe, and we feel comfortable exposing our belief system.

_____1. I like to hang around others who think and act as I do.

_____2. I wish I could feel authentic—but most of the time I don't.

_____3. I find it difficult to be honest about what I really feel or think.

_____4. I don't feel comfortable exposing who I am and how I feel.

3. Belief systems—*Mental Body*—As we enter adulthood we begin to stretch our capacity to think for ourselves without reactivity. We begin to recognize that not all individuals think the same, but we are comfortable with being around others who think as we think and those who see the world differently.

_____1. My thoughts are not very well formed and are ever-evolving.

_____2. I have no idea what I want to be when I grow up.

_____3. My behavior seldom matches how I think.

_____4. I get uncomfortable expressing my thoughts.

4. Spirituality—*Spiritual Body*—(Spiritual Path or Recovery Program)—At this juncture we can find a purpose through the external structure provided by a spiritual group or dogma by relying on the belief system to define the deeper meaning of life and by giving this part of self a way in which to participate in the world with deliberate purpose.

_____1. I continue to feel uncomfortable with what I believe.

_____2. I feel conflicted when speaking to others about my spiritual beliefs when I know their beliefs are different than my own.

_____3. I am uneasy about the spiritual choices I make in my day-to-day life.

_____4. I can't accept other's beliefs which are different than my own.

5. Family and Intimate Relationships—Having mastered

communication and compassion, we are now able to experience authentic and vital relationships with those we love. They are not always peaceful or without tension, but they are real and laced with a commitment to obtain and maintain an integrity which promotes trust and growth.

_____1. Many of my relationships are not based on mutual trust and appreciation.

_____2. I do not do very well with differences in my relationships with others.

_____3. When someone challenges me I have a hard time defending myself.

_____4. I am uncomfortable with others who "agree to disagree."

6. Sexuality and Passion—These energies mix confidence and trust with a willingness to produce from this connection within. We can experience our creativity as God-given and therefore a source of the light which gets expressed through our creative endeavors. We can even experience our sexuality as being an extension of the universal energy and engage in our sexual encounters with this level of sacredness.

_____1. I don't believe sexuality can be an extension of the Universal Source.

_____2. Sexuality is sacred, but I don't find many partners who feel the same way.

_____3. If my creative projects are challenged, I feel they have little worth.

_____4. I know I am passionate about life but am afraid to express it.

7. Prosperity and Abundance—By this time we have mastered the lessons of abundance and live with a belief that needs and wants will be met with ease and without effort.

_____1. I believe abundance is a direct extension of the Universal energy.

_____2. I feel abundant in my life but know there is room for improvement.

_____3. I do what I love—I just wish the money would follow.

_____4. When I look at the world I wish I saw more abundance and prosperity.

8. Job, Career or Climb on the Corporate Ladder—Having rebelled against work that did not match our true mission, we begin to successfully establish our creative lifework that uses our divinely inspired talents and offers our unique gift to the world.

_____1. I wish I enjoyed what I do for a living, but I don't.

_____2. I don't know what I want to do when I grow up.

_____3. If an evaluation challenges my self-image I feel deflated.

_____4. If I had more training I could go into business for myself.

As you peruse the above material, contemplate how the issues of this developmental stage interface with your daily life and perhaps reflect the issues and lessons of your Soul. Then turn your focus to your body and to your shoulders—the muscles which carry the essence of this stage of development because they hold the tension of the world.

Working With The Shoulder Muscle Which Correlates To This Stage Of Development

The area of the body which most often carries the energy related to this stage is your shoulders because this area of your body holds the tension of the world. Our shoulders rear up when we feel stressed—tighten when we feel at risk. When you begin to work with this muscle group and strengthen it and flex it, you will dislodge any issues this area may have housed.

This week, as you bring your focus to the different areas of emotional challenge carried over from your young adult years, consciously give your body permission to release the unexpressed energy related to these issues.

Shoulder Muscle Meditation: *I invite you right now, however, to bring your focus to your shoulder area. Breathe into it and ask your shoulder muscles to reveal any issues they may have held for you. Listen and record your responses. Learn to understand the language of your body and it will always reveal your most beneficial next step.*

The Chakra Center Which Correlates To This Stage Of Development Is The Crown Chakra

The Seventh Chakra is your spiritual center and can be found at the very top of the crown of your head. It correlates to the pineal gland. Energizing this center with the color of crystal white or violet strengthens your connection to spirit, to your Higher Power or to God as you understand him, her or it. This center relates to the issues and tasks of your young, inner adult. Your seventeen to twenty-one-year-old is the part of you who negotiates your inner needs with the outer world. It is this part of self who is responsible and responsive. It is he or she who can guide you in making your connection with Spirit and help you balance the needs of the human self with the desires of the spiritual self. It is this part of you who evolves into the Adult Self—who works with spirit to assist your discovery of the true reason for your being on this planet. The Soul task that may be associated with this energy center may involve examining your history of how you have expressed your spirituality in the real world and the success with which you have integrated your spiritual values into your day-to-day life.

Crown Chakra Meditation: Take a moment to bring your focus to the top of your head or that area known as your crown chakra. Imagine a ball of energy rotating as it is infused with the brilliant color of golden light which transmutes all fear and worry and replaces it with the confidence of someone who trusts their inner knowingness, feels connected to their Higher Guidance, and is aware of and present in their body. Allow this energy center to spin out any issues related to feeling doubt or fear of moving into the world with the talents and skills of your new vibration of young adulthood. See your Angels now touching the location of your seventh chakra as they use their angel dust to calm any discomforts, fears, and anxieties and assuage all doubts as you become more and more confident in your adulthood. When you feel complete, take another deep breath, open your eyes and record what you experienced.

Closing Meditation: To bring closure to this work, once again, take a moment to consider how your cherished saboteur™ emerges with respect to your entering into the adult world. What has your Adult Self learned which will now assist it in responding to the needs of this wounded self so the tendency to sabotage can be dissolved? Once you have given this the mental attention it needs, close your eyes and proceed.

See the seventeen to twenty-one-year-old in front of you. Ask what is needed in order for this wounded one to feel safe. Respond to that need and then invite this young inner adult to reside in the center of the sacred chamber of your heart where he/she will be safe. Fill your heart center with the golden light of love and the healing light of the violet flame. Then bring your attention to the center of your head and ask that the master cell is re-activated with this new DNA vibration of mastery and assurance...

that your connection to your Higher Guidance and your awareness of your body and your inner world ensure success and a willingness to excel. Feel the energy pulsating through your body as it travels down your spinal cord to your creator cell where this same intention is decreed. Take a deep breath and ask that every cell in your body now holds this new DNA patterning and that the shoulder muscles resonate with holding their own—confident you are equipped to deal with life's challenges and make the most of its gifts. Take a deep breath and record your experience in your journal. As you progress through your week, keep these experiences fresh in your mind and in your intentions.

REFER TO THE "DAILY CHECK-IN SHEETS" AND THE "7-DAY REVIEW" FOUND IN THE APPENDIX TO LOG YOUR EXPERIENCE.

Twelfth Module—
Keep Moving Forward

We are engaged in one of the five stages of grief every minute of every day. If we are not anxious, we are busy trying to control—bargaining with life and trying to fix whatever we determine is not right. If we are not fixing, bargaining or controlling, we are angry or agitated things are not going our way. If we are not angry we feel flat, sad or depressed. All other times we feel peace

GRIEF AND BEYOND

MOVING FORWARD IN your growth, as well as your exercise program, requires a willingness to grieve anything which stands in your way of success. Below is an article which describes this process—and an overview of the five stages of grief we each tend to move through as we deal with our day-to-day life. The exercises which follow put this process into action and escort you through it step-by-step. I have included a Ten-Step Formula which follows allows you to take this one step further and apply everything you have learned in this program to one single issue.

As you take what you have learned into the daily practice of living, you will realize that it is more than a one-time program. What you have developed is a lifestyle which can ensure your success in any area you choose. What you have developed is the formula for a way of life. It has prepared you to not only consciously aerobically exercise—but also consciously live! When you call on the assistance of your Angels, Teachers, and Guides and apply the knowledge you now have regarding the ways you can befriend and work with your cherished saboteur™, you will be empowered to confront and resolve any obstacle to your success.

Befriending the process of grief is one of the most effective methods to live your life non-addictively with feeling and grace. As you will see it is a process which will benefit you in your daily life on an on-going basis—because—as you will see—there is not one minute of your day you are not engaged in at least one of its five stages.

METHODS TO PROCESS YOUR GRIEF

This section offers you a series of processes you can use to begin working with your own grief. The formula offers you the structure—these suggestions provide the process for working through your tumultuous emotions. As you become more familiar with these stages you naturally begin to find your own methods for befriending this process.

You come to understand that embracing the difficult feelings by having the courage to breathe into them expands your capacity to experience your pleasure, passion, and joy. You begin to appreciate that you are constantly on a teeter-totter between love and fear with everything else falling somewhere in between. Life itself becomes as entertaining as a board game—where you land reflects where you need to go next.

Processes for Anxiety, Panic, and Denial

1. Make a list of the ways you act out to keep yourself from feeling the panic or discomfort of your loss...in other words, ways you have kept, you keep, or you get yourself back into denial! This will help you begin to recognize the beginning pangs of loss.
2. Take a piece of paper and draw a picture which symbolizes your anxiety. This gets these feelings out—gives them form.
3. Dialogue with your anxiety—ask who inside holds it and what that part of you needs from you. Breathe through the anxiety and see where it leads you. This creates a relationship to your anxiety so you can respond to it instead of collapse into it.

Processes for Bargaining

1. Write briefly about how you feel you are bargaining with "showing up" for your life. What might this reveal about the pain of potential losses that are inevitable as you step forth into your empowered self? What part of you benefits from the sabotaging of the success of your goals? Who suffers and battles with a sense of failure? How does your Co-Dependent Bargain™ interface in this relationship?
2. What in your life no longer fits, and how are you trying to keep yourself from facing this fact? Again, the Co-Dependent Bargain™ is the contract we made with a parental figure or with God where we agreed to do something in exchange for feeling safe and protected. These agreements follow us into adulthood and into every relationship we have. The problem is that the other party is either unaware of this agreement or unable or unwilling to live up to this agreement so we end up feeling

betrayed and full of rage when faced with the fact that our bargain was not kept. Sometimes we even extend this contract to ourselves as we make deals with our destructive or addictive behavior—convincing ourselves that we can control or manage our out-of-control behavior. This shows up in our day-to-day life when we bargain with our agreements and make false promises to ourselves and others which, when we do not follow through, erodes our self-esteem.

3. With the above In mind, identify your Co-Dependent Bargain™...

    _____, (addressing those with whom you made/make the contract)

    I will _____ (The sacrifice, compromise you are willing to make) If only you will _____. (What you hope to get in return)

    How does your co-dependent bargain™ impact your day-to-day life? Do you see yourself living out this bargain as a way to manipulate yourself and others? How would your life change if you gave up the bargain and came into your true empowerment? What would happen if you coped successfully with your life and took responsibility for yourself by giving up the temptation to feel like a victim? Take time to really think that process through because it holds unlimited possibilities for evolvement.

4. Draw a picture which represents your anger. Use this as a way to discharge your discomfort and to identify your pain. Give it form!

Processes for Dissolving Anger

1. Journal Process—Respond to the following questions to explore the fabric of your anger. Once completed, you will be ready to do the "weeding out" process. What is your unspoken truth? To whom does it need to be told? What holds you back from doing so? What do you fear will happen if you speak

your truth? Are you willing to cope with those possible consequences? If not, what are you willing to cope with? How far can you go right now to speak your truth, and where do you have to be mindful and protecting of yourself? Don't push if you are not yet ready to push. Forced labor seldom results in a productive birth.

2. "Weeding Out" Process—I originally came across this exercise in a book written in the 80's by Sondra Ray. Since then I have used this or a version of it in a multitude of ways, and it never fails to weed out my saboteurs and those within me who resist change. Instructions: Write "I am angry" in column one followed by your immediate response in column two. Continue until you can write "I am angry" in both columns with vim and vigor!! Use more paper if necessary.

Example:

1. I am angry.	1. But they did the best they could.
2.	2.
3.	3.
4.	4.
5.	5.
6.	6.
7.	7.
8.	8.
9.	9.
10. "I AM ANGRY!	10. "I AM ANGRY!"

What to do about the anger which will emerge at the moment? We have anger which is stored and anger which erupts—the following are suggestions which can be applied to both.

First, surround yourself with light and ask that any anger expressed be encased in the light and sent directly to the higher source to be transformed. This will seal it so that its energy will not bleed out into other areas.

Then, when you feel in alignment to do so, use any of the following techniques to express your anger and to get it out.

1. Write and/or do mirror work (deals with the mental and emotional bodies).

2. Beat on pillows—throw a tantrum, stomp—do any physical activity which gets the emotion out of the body (emotional body).

3. Do the silent scream—screaming in a car (emotional body).

4. Exercise to make the energy manageable (note: aerobic exercise, such as jogging, etc. reduces current anger, anaerobic exercise, such as yoga, swimming etc. reaches anger that is more deeply rooted in the muscular fibers.)

5. Create an inner dialogue where you listen to your inner child's anger as the Adult Self. Allow it, you do not have to change it or fix it. You just have to help him or her discharge it responsibly so it does not bleed into inappropriate acting out in day-to-day life.

6. Make a list of critical statements you say to yourself on a regular basis—now review the list and make an affirmation you can use to negate your critical statement.

7. Make a list of your personal gripes, pet peeves, and those behaviors which irk you most when you see them exhibited in others. Then review the list—how do you see yourself exhibiting those same behaviors—or if you cannot relate to that angle—are they doing something you do not allow yourself to do so it mirrors a shadow side to you? If so, how do you feel about that?

Processes for Releasing Despair

1. Write letters to those who you feel have betrayed, neglected or wounded you. Let them know that you, as the adult, are now

willing to take responsibility for the feelings of the wounded selves who have felt victimized by their actions. Forgive them so you can move on and become empowered enough to take responsibility for your younger self's fear and pain.

2. When you feel ready—write another letter to the parts within you who are ready to let go—welcome them home and make your amends and vow to them to keep them safe. Know that it is the Adult Self who needs to be responsible for this promise— but you can always bring in the angels or guardians to tend to your wounded self's needs. Just make sure the needs are addressed by a nurturing party.

3. Take a moment and write the truth of your loss—let your inner child—the aspect of your Soul or the wounded Adult Self state in **BOLD PRINT** his or her truth which needs to be told.-

4. Then, write a letter to the person to whom this truth needs to be stated. It is not necessary to send this letter. The method simply gives you a way to get the emotions discharged so your Adult Self can determine the most appropriate action to be taken.

Process of Release And Forgiveness

The following ritual was given to me by a Hawaiian Elder named Josie. It is but one way to orchestrate a formal forgiveness. Please feel free to use or create your own as well.

Hawaiian Forgiveness Ritual—Ho'oponopono

Forgive me _____ If I have hurt you

In any way, shape or form, In thought, word or deed, In any time, any place, Past, present or future Forgive Me.

And I, _____forgive you For hurting me

In any way, shape or form, In thought, word or deed, In any time, any place, Past, present or future

I forgive you!

And may the creator of all things Forgive us both:

All Ho'oponopono It is done…So be it!

This ritual can be said between you and another, between you and your body, between you and your inner child, between your Spirit and your Personality.

It is also a common practice to ceremoniously take any notes, pictures or expressions of your grief and burn them. It cleanses and frees the emotions and symbolically transforms the energy of your pain so you can send its essence back to the Divine Light for healing.

I then take the ashes of my process and go into Mother Nature to make an offering. As I do this I express my gratitude for all I have learned and re-affirm my vows to sustain the new vibration of joy I have claimed by having the courage to grieve. You are now ready to complete this Soul Steps process with ceremonies that bring closure and reverence to what you have just accomplished.

LAST THREE DAYS
CEREMONIAL CLOSING

Endings are just beginnings turned backward. You have completed what you began. You showed up. You deserve to celebrate and this celebration will hold the seeds of what you have created. It will nourish your entire psyche. Over the next few days, you will do ceremonies which will then enable you to design a plan of celebration that compliments the new you and rewards your success. You will be encouraged to splurge a little—not in the old, self-destructive way— but rather in a new and more nurturing way.

...However, first things first...

DAY ONE: *"Applying What You Have Learned"*

To bring completion to the intensity of this structure it will be useful to walk through the stages of grief which accompany any ending...the five stages of grief you studied just last week in your program. This activity will give you an opportunity to experience the stages of grief in action as they help you bridge from the external structure created for you to an internal structure which will serve you the rest of your life.

Each stage of grief holds the polar vibrations of wanting to restrict and hold on and wanting to expand and let go. Each stage presents the challenge to identify the fearful aspect of you—the residue of your wounded self who tends to hold on—and help him or her to build trust in the part of you who is capable of moving forward— your *once-future-and-now-present-self.*

It may help to envision this challenge as though you are on a teeter-totter and both parts of you are vying for control and power. The trick is for the expanded, more confident part of you, your *once-future-and-now-present-self,* to wedge itself into the middle of the teeter-totter. Once there, he or she can offer comfort to the fearful one until that part of you feels safe enough to trust and let go.

Keep this teeter-totter metaphor in mind as you move through each of the following stages of grief. It will assist your *once-future-but-now-present-self* in walking your wounded ones to a state of release, trust, and acceptance.

Keep in mind it is common to want to jump right into celebration without acknowledging the feelings associated with an ending. This, however, can sabotage what you have gained and you can lose ground. If you bear with this ending process that illustrates how you grieve a completion of something you will be more equipped to fully experience the rewards of a celebration well-deserved.

STAGE ONE—From Anxiety to Excitement

The first emotion you might notice as you complete the structure of this program is a twinge of anxiousness. The structure provided for you has offered a safety net. You may now feel a bit nervous about this safety net dissolving and anxious about sustaining the momentum you have set in motion. *Give yourself permission to acknowledge these feelings and record them in your journal.*

The polar opposite of your anxiety is excitement. Entertain, for a moment, the fact that anxiety operates on the same vibrational frequency as excitement. Often our sense of anticipation gets eclipsed by a more fearful and anxious part and we fail to recognize there is actually excitement about taking what we have learned and applying it. It is exhilarating, at least to one part of us, to engage in something new. It mimics a graduation of sorts.

Trust that you are ready to integrate all you have learned in a more harmonious way and will be able to sustain the new patterns you have acquired. Claim the part of you who is excited and you will be able to nurture the aspect of you who holds the fear.

Activity—Write in your journal your response to what you have just read. How does it relate to you? How can you comfort your fears and seize your excitement so you can launch into the next stage of grief which will help you mold your regimen into a lifetime pattern?

STAGE TWO—Bargaining Your Way Into A New Regimen

For the past several months you have worked with the structure created for you through this manual. Bargaining or trying to hold on to that intensity is an outgrowth of your fear that you have not sufficiently internalized the structure of the new patterns to sustain a reliable shift in your behavior. You most likely will not be perfect in this endeavor. The antidote for this fear is going through the process of modifying your program in such a way that it is structured enough to be used daily yet fluid enough to accommodate the alterations needed in response to the demands of your day-to-day life. In other words, ease up! Trust yourself and your connection to your Higher Beings and you will not fail.

What will help, however, is to channel all you have learned into the development of a daily regimen which will nourish your well-being on an on-going basis. Leave room for modification and alteration. It is human nature to get bored with routine. If you find this to be true, then add variety to your workouts and invent new ways to connect with your Angels and Guides. It is part of human life to get thrown off course because of the demands of your daily life. Go easy on yourself. Stay connected to your Higher Self and Guardians and show up each day with a renewed commitment to be the best you can be. Leave the rest to God and your Angels.

Hopefully the last 90 days have given you a taste for how much better your life works when you take the time each day to flex the muscles of your body and make your connection to your Teachers, Angels, Guides, and Higher Self. Weaving this into a daily practice will enrich every other moment of your day and devising a plan on how to manage this weave will help you anchor it into your day-to-day life.

Meditation—Again come back to the metaphor of the teeter-totter. Give form to the part of you who wants to be overly rigid in this structure for fear you will not follow through or perhaps its opposite, who wants to abandon all structure. The antidote for this rigidity is balance. Your once-future-but-now-present-self is now the one who brings balance to this activity and helps the more fearful one who either wants to abandon all structure or be overly rigid settle down and operate more realistically.

STATE THREE—ANGER

Anger is easy to manage if you keep in mind that anger is simply truth unspoken. As you move into your day-to-day program capitalize all you have learned about speaking your truth. Consciously establish a barometer which reflects the first stirrings of irritation. These are a strong indicator that you have not spoken your truth in some area of your life and are engaging in an act of self-betrayal. If you train yourself to notice the early signs of this self-betrayal it will be easy to rectify the situation and come back into integrity.

Integrity is when you are operating harmoniously and there is a flow of your higher, more spiritual instincts and the physical activities anchored in daily living. A continuum of distress ranges from the first signs of discomfort to out-and-out rage at the discrepancy between your spiritual and human selves. If you sensitize yourself to these signs you will be more equipped to deal with them in their early stages. The tool which most effectively assists you in monitoring this is establishing the habit of taking what is called a daily inventory. In Twelve Step programs, this is the Tenth step. It helps keep you current with your own internal infractions…interactions which left you feeling compromised…undelivered communications which can gather dust and create a windfall of disaster.

Activity—Taking a daily inventory is simply taking the time— perhaps during your exercise—to review the events of the last 24-hours and to assess if there is anything or any interaction which is left unfinished. If so, what is it and what needs to be done about it? Watch for signs of anger and discomfort—when detected, ask what truth has not been spoken. Speak your truth to yourself and others and you will be able to keep the flow between you and your Higher Teachers fluid and nourishing.

STAGE FOUR—Despair And Sadness

The myth associated with this stage actually has to do with the fear that you will not know how to cope with the void left when there is no longer a pre-designed structure in place dictating each move. You can experience the fear that once this structure is over you will not have the self-discipline to continue your new habits. Again, this is where a daily connection with our Higher Self and Angels can assist. They can do for us what we can sometimes not do for ourselves. Show up for your exercise and connect with your Higher Teachers, and trust in self will continue to expand. Use your Healing Team to balance out this teeter-totter and you will always come back to a sense of harmony and safety.

If you do get off track know that each day offers a new opportunity, and remember; if you just stop and pray, the connection between you and your Higher Self will be restored. Breathe… breathe…breathe… If you feel empty close your eyes and fill yourself with divine light. If

you need a one-liner to break a collapse—try reciting to yourself…
"God's love resolves this situation here and now…" Repeat it over
and over and over again and I guarantee it will never fail to raise your
vibration and pull you out of the spiral in which you may periodically
find yourself engaged.

STAGE FIVE—Acceptance And Re-Investment

Once you have acknowledged the four stages above, you will be
ready to embrace and celebrate what you have internalized because the
trust in self will be restored. Revel in it. Re-invest in it. Know you will
never again be the same. If you step from the heart of your Soul; revere
your body; embrace your emotions; befriend your mind and trust that
it works on your behalf you will forever be empowered to continually
re-invent yourself as you perpetually expand into a neverending new
you!

This completes the wind down for day one. Again, take a deep
breath and ready yourself for the activities of day two.

DAY TWO: *"Revering your Mind, Body, Heart, and Soul"*

Today you will de-fragment your mind, create a bathing ritual
for your body, a safe haven for your wounded ones and experience a
massage for your Soul. It is the day to tend to the four aspects of your
psyche and pay the proper respect.

De-Fragmenting the Computer of Your Mind

After an intense regimen such as the one you have just completed
it is helpful to organize all of the input your brain has received. The
fragments linger in the wings and organization will bring focus to
your next step. So how do you do this? You do it by sending waves
of sound through your entire being. Strange to think that humming
could re-calibrate the electrical circuitry of your mind buttoning does
just that. Try it right now.

*Meditation—Take a deep breath and then bring your focus to the
center of your being and begin to hum. Feel the vibration run up and down*

*your body. Let the sound of the tone get fuller as it fills your entire chest…
then extend that vibration through your whole body…keep doing this until
your body is tingling with this new vibration. Envision your brain as a
computer screen and see all of the fragments of information vibrationally
organize themselves synchronizing themselves in a geometric fashion.*

*Stay with this imagery and watch as your mind quiets and your focus
sharpens. Imagine that the core issues which have emerged during this
process get sorted out into three categories. Bring your guidance in and
allow them to show you the headings of your three categories. Then write
them down in your journal.*

Trust that over the next month or so you will begin to see how
every glitch you encounter fits into these three categories. Each of
us has approximately three core issues which seem to be the defining
parameters of our life. Each time we learn how to manage one level of
the core issue another level emerges. Once we understand this matrix
and the context of our growth we are in a position to capitalize on it—
study our responses to these issues and become a student instead of a
victim to the challenges of our pain.

THE BATHING RITUAL FOR YOUR PHYSICAL FORM

Once you have befriended your mind you are ready to honor your
physical form. During this process you have learned how to revere
your body and stay conscious of its needs. You have witnessed how
your body serves you—if and when you develop a partnership with it.
Submerge your body now in a tub of bath water which is infused with
your favorite bath beads, bubbles or scents shows your body you are
willing to express your gratitude.

But first, you want to help your body shed what is no longer useful
to it. One way to do this is to do a salt scrub.

*Activity—Take your favorite lotion and heat it for 20 seconds in the
microwave—once it is warmed up stir in enough salt granules, you can use
regular table salt, to create a paste-like substance. Place the mixture on the
side of the tub.*

Run a bath and fill the water with whatever scents, bubble bath or beads you choose. Stand in the tub and begin to rub the salt mixture over your whole body until your entire physical form has been cleansed and any old skin has been gently scrubbed off.

When you feel you have had enough, sit down in the water and enjoy the silkiness of your skin. Yes, even if you are a man, your skin will still love this. It is snake-like in that each time you do this ritual you have the opportunity to shed the old you and step out of that tub in a new physical form. Once you have rinsed the salt off your skin you may want to empty the tub and rinse off in the shower. As you do so, imagine that the droplets of water are crystal balls of light which now seal your physical form with protection and love.

The more ceremonious you make this ritual the more rewards you will reap from it. Let your inhibitions be rinsed away as you treat your body as reverently as the way you would like to be treated. Set this intention and its vibration will carry you into the rest of your life magnifying this desired response.

CREATING A SAFE HAVEN FOR YOUR WOUNDED ONES

You have just spent a significant time getting to know the little ones within who need your comfort, compassion, and love. Now, you want to create a safe haven beyond your heart where they can reside and forever feel safe. Each of your wounded ones will benefit from systematically being placed in a safe haven with a protective Angel or animal totem which can always be by its side.

Activity and Meditation—Take time now to make a list in your journal of the wounded selves you discovered over the last 90 days. Create a safe place for each one and then ask who they would like to have by their side to protect and entertain them. Once you have your list compiled close your eyes and move each one into their own room—giving them the freedom to decorate it the way he or she wishes to decorate. Record your experience in your journal.

These rooms exist in the mind's eye and can be drawn into your inner work anytime your wounded ones slip back onto center stage and are in need of assistance.

Learning to Honor Your Cherished Saboteur™

Honoring the part of you who has been the culprit derailing you from your ultimate goal is a challenge. If you learned anything from this process, hopefully, it was the fact that those aspects of you who sabotage you do so out of the false belief that they are protecting you and keeping you out of harm's way. If you see beyond their pain you will be able to capitalize on their efforts to sabotage, knowing that once you address their concerns you will be aligned and able to proceed without fear. Trust your cherished saboteur™ and value its efforts to notify you that you are in harm's way. Partner with this part of you in a positive way and adjust your direction accordingly.

Activity—Sit for a moment and write your cherished saboteur™ a letter of appreciation. Devise a plan for how you can listen to its warnings and capitalize on its efforts to keep you safe.

Giving Your Soul

Your Soul is massaged when it is drenched in the vibration of the divine light.

Meditation—Bring your focus to the center of your master cell which resides in the center of your pineal gland in the center of your head. Envision a new, higher frequency of energy being infused in the center of that cell. Imagine that the very DNA of your master cell is infused with this new frequency. This master cell frequency is then sent to the center of your creator cell which resides at the base of your spinal column. Once this frequency of energy is anchored at both points envision it vibrating up and down the spinal column—its vibration being carried out to every cell within your body. Imagine the energetic undulation of this vibration relaxing the essence of your very center. This sensation then extends through your entire physical form and on out to the etheric body which exists approximately three-to-five feet beyond the boundaries of your physical body. Bathe each Chakra with this energetic vibrational frequency which will allow it to harmoniously spin at the exact speed which is most conducive to its supporting your entire being. Each body has now been tended to and you are ready to create your final ceremony and celebration.

DAY THREE: *"The Ceremony and Celebration"*

You can either use this day as the day you create and participate in this ritual or you can use it to design the events for a later date. Your ceremony should seal this experience and your celebration should honor it.

THE CEREMONY:

1. Begin by selecting an Angel card which brings forth a message and theme for this work. Record its message in your journal.

2. Come into meditation and call in your Healing Team. Acknowledge each one and thank them for all of their support. Interact with your Healing Team in whatever way feels right for you. Sometimes they have gifts to offer you. Sometimes you have offerings for them. Trust what comes forward and respond accordingly. Once you feel complete record your experience in your journal.

3. Extend your daily inventory established earlier to now include a daily connection with your key supporters. Ask them for guidance on how you can keep your relationships with them active and vital on a daily basis. Notice which members of your Healing Team will participate on a daily basis and which ones will be called in only on occasion. Record your findings in your journal.

4. Next, retrieve the letter you wrote at the beginning of your program. Read it out loud and respond accordingly. When it feels appropriate, decide if you would like to burn this letter now as a way to release and cleanse its essence. This will help to reclaim the transmuted energy in a positive and useful manner. Record your experience in your journal.

5. Add whatever else feels appropriate to you which would bring ceremony to this ending.

THE CELEBRATION

Now comes the good part. Gather all of your selves for this activity and meditation because it involves taking an inventory of what each one would like to do to celebrate their successes.

Activity—Make an actual list of each part of you who wants to participate in this celebration and besides the name record how it would like to celebrate. Then step back and review your list and apply the following meditation to each suggestion.

Meditation—Breathe into the highest part of you and assess if this suggestion would benefit your entire being. Would any aspect of this suggestion put any part of you in a position of compromise? For instance, a young inner child might want to celebrate by going and having cake and ice cream. This activity might respond to the needs of this younger self but it could put in jeopardy all you have attained with respect to your body. What is required in this case is mediation. Come back on your teeter-totter and work with these two extremes until both needs can be met...the needs of your inner child and the needs of your body. It is this art of mediation and compromise which will bring forth resolution and harmony and assist you in designing the celebration which supports all aspects of you.

Activity—Once you have designed the components of your celebration—bring forth the part of you who can now take these plans and implement them. Structure your celebration. Write it down in black and white and determine when these events will take place.

Be as creative a possible—but more importantly—allow yourself to enjoy what you have earned and definitely now deserve.

EPILOGUE: *Message from your Future Self*

"You have arrived. Look at me—position yourself in front of a mirror and look directly into your eyes and see me—I am the part of you who carries the seed for your Divinity. I hold in my arms those within you who are afraid and lonely and without faith. See me... embody me...love me...for I am you."

Now take a moment and respond. Write a letter to your Future

Self. Create that connection. Empower this part of you so he or she can attract you to the most Divine Essence you can manifest.

Dear Future Self ....

In Closing ... The journey never ends.

To assist you in carrying what you have accomplished in your Soul Steps Program into the rest of your life I am including supplemental material on "Helping your Inner Child Grieve" and am providing an overview of my signature, Seven-Layer Healing Process, which integrates inner child work with energy tapping.

Both of these processes will hopefully support your ability to continue to use this process as a way to more successfully live your life.

For complete instructions on how to master the Seven-Layer Healing Process refer to my book, Share the Gift which presents this process in full.

SUPPLEMENTAL MATERIAL

Our Underlying Fear—
The Fear We Will Not Be Cope

Y OU HAVE JUST given birth to your Future Self and defined and worked with your own definition of mastery. In the material that follows you will have the opportunity to deepen your work. The thread you pull to proceed is a thread that is universal to all—the underlying fear that we will be unable to cope. Our mastery is thwarted and the manifestations of our desires blocked because of an underlying fear we will not be able to survive if we lose something or someone we are unprepared to live without. The object of our feared loss is unique to each of us, but its undercurrent permeates every dream—every hope—every disappointment.

Take a moment to think of those times in your own life when you were most distraught. Tune into the anxiety of that stress. What is its source? What is at stake? What do fear you may lose? What do you envision would happen if you were faced with such a loss? What are those people, places, or things in your life about which you might hear yourself say, "If I ever lost_____, I would never survive."

When you can identify your greatest fear you can begin to address the first time you felt that fear. For most it began at the exact moment we first experienced the world as unsafe, when we first lost trust in our environment, when we first feared we would not be able to cope.

THE BEGINNING

Whether remembered or not, there was that moment in your life when you first felt a loss of safety. The circumstances may not be the same as another, but the impact was the same—you froze. That moment in time is what Hal Bennett in his book, Follow your Bliss refers to as the *essential wound*. It was at that exact moment when you first feared you would be unable to cope. You feared you might not survive. It was then that your life, even if you did not know it, began to not work. That moment followed you into adulthood and has been sabotaging your efforts to succeed ever since.

Whether it's a career that never gets off the ground, a relationship that never appears, or an exercise program to which one can never quite commit, it is easy to give up when met with defeat. Many lose hope in their ability to manifest what they desire. Intentions are set. Prayers and affirmations are offered, and yet, many continue to experience struggle in attaining their goals.

To understand the mechanics of this self-sabotage you have to adjust your kaleidoscopic lens a bit to grasp that we do not get what we want through wishes, intentions, prayers, or affirmations. In fact, we don't actually get what we want at all. We get *what our most fragile self feels* about what we want!

According to the universal principle called the *law of attraction*, the energetic magnet that attracts what we desire is *how we feel* about what we desire. The desire is merely the context. It is the substance of the intention we set; the wish and hope we affirm. However, what draws that which we desire into our experience is the *tone* with which we deliver our intention. It depends on how accepting we are of our self and how deserving we feel about our desire. If we feel good about ourselves and feel worthy of our desires, there is no resistance, no block to our allowing our dreams to manifest. But when we don't feel good about the person we are our dreams get eclipsed by our unworthiness.

Our unworthiness is based on the fear we are not good enough to succeed. We may shoot out arrows of intent or desire, but they get shot down by the weight of our doubts, fears, and shame—all of which are related to negative beliefs we developed as a child. Those beliefs became the cornerstone of our self-esteem, and our self-esteem determines the feeling tone or vibrational energy we send out to our world and to the universe.

All things are energy, thoughts, and feelings as well. What we think and feel emits a vibrational frequency which then magnetically attracts its vibrational match. Every desire begins with a thought. We think it. We want it. We begin to dream about it. If the feelings associated with that desire are pure, without hindrance, we will allow the desire to manifest and appear in our physical world with acceptance and ease. If, however, the desire gets high-jacked by unconscious Fears and doubts, the universe will respond in kind by sending back the exact match for the desire. And often it is laced with this fear and doubt.

Those feelings of unworthiness, that followed us from childhood and resulted in a form of vibrational resistance, thwart our mastery. This resistance fuels our inner child's need to sabotage. The impact of this sabotage is most evident in the on-going conversation we are having in our own mind. It is the emotion associated with this constant chatter that gets transmitted to the universe and ultimately attracts into our experience things that match the vibrational frequency of that resistance. So literally, again, what we feel we attract!

Now we were not born with resistance. We extended into this life from the vibration of the pure positive energy of our non-physical self which vibrationally exists in an energy field of unconditional love. Some call this energy field, or this non-physical reality, God, the Divine Matrix, the Vortex, All-That-Is or Spirit. The essence of us that exists in this non-physical reality is referred to as our Inner Being, Divine Self, God-Self, Holy Christ Self, or Higher Self. However you refer to these energy fields, it is from that non-physical dimension that we extend when we take on the density of physical form. Our non-physical self vibrates at a higher vibrational frequency than our physical self.

This again is significant because according to the law of attraction, everything is vibrational—everything is energy. *But the "frequency of vibration" of all things varies.* The energy in the physical dimension *vibrates* at a significantly lower frequency than that of the non-physical one. In fact, the energy vibration slows down to such a degree that this very alignment with the physical realm results in a form of spiritual amnesia. So even though we are not separate from this all-loving, Inner or Higher Self, we ultimately lose conscious contact with it and experience it as such.

This Inner Self is the source of our authenticity. Connection to it is what allows us to feel whole, complete. Those of us who are on a spiritual path dedicate much of our life to attaining and then sustaining this connection. A disconnection from our source of authenticity results in our feeling anxious and alone. This loss is perhaps the source of all of the other losses we experience. This disconnection leads to our feeling despair, anger, shame, and grief as we progressively exchange the connection we feel to our authentic self for a connection sought from others in our physical world.

As you have seen in the previous material this exchange and ultimate loss of our connection to our authentic self slowly occurs during the first six years of our life during which time our brains are operating at the theta level. The minute we are born, and perhaps even while in the womb, we begin to download, without discretion, every impression of our physical world. We begin to establish the very fabric of the person we are to become, based on the introjections of parents, teachers, the media, and society as a whole.

We are, in effect, progressively disconnecting from Source energy while simultaneously experiencing the process of socialization. Like a computer, our subconscious mind is being programmed. We are downloading the instruction manual on how to fit in and how to be like everyone else. These ingested beliefs are infused with feelings and expectations which ultimately become the operating system from which we *attract*. The degree of tension associated with each of these responses determines the density of the vibrational energy which, in turn, dictates the speed with which we are able to manifest our desires—the heavier our emotional state the slower our manifestation.

Over time this disconnection from our authenticity leads to the loss of our sense of self and our ability to accept ourselves as the person we are. This disconnection from our Higher Self and the ultimate loss of our authentic self are the underlying core of every loss we need to grieve.

Our self-acceptance becomes anchored in how others treat us. We lose sight of the person we are. We become the person we are expected to be. Every experience magnetized after that serves to verify this inherited set of beliefs which, for better or worse, reflects the values of others but defies the essence of our true and authentic self. The very things we struggle to attract and invest in attracting hold a value for us based on these beliefs and expectations embedded in our subconscious programming since childhood. They are based on the disconnection from our authentic self and motivated by the impending feeling that we are not acceptable, and therefore not worthy, just the way we are.

GENERAL THOUGHTS ON THE PROCESS OF GRIEF

We all grieve. Much of the time we are not even aware we are grieving. We associate grief with a major loss such as that of a loved one or the loss of our security when we lose our house or a job. But as you will see in this material, it is my experience that we are in one of the five stages of grief all the time. Every major feeling we have fits into one of the stages of grief. Grief is a way we let go. Grief is a way we expand. Grief is a way we grow. We are constantly dealing with the evolution of change, and change requires that we let go of what was and embrace what is unfolding and emerging. It is the process of the ebb and flow of living life itself.

In this section, whether you are dealing with the loss of a loved one through death or divorce; the loss of a possession of comfort such as a house or even a car; the loss of a pet, or a hobby that has provided comfort, companionship, and support; the loss experienced physically with an injury, an accident, or the process of aging itself; or even the loss of a wallet, a cell phone, or an item of sentimental value; you will go through the five stages of grief. If those emotional reactions are not in some way resolved they will get stuck in your body and come back to haunt you physically, emotionally, or mentally. So, needless to say, it is in your best interest to fully understand the process of grief so you can embrace it, resolve it, and grow from it. My hope is that this following material will help you do just that!

But to do so it is essential that you get comfortable with grief. To do so, it is useful to have a fuller understanding of grief because most cultures do not embrace grief. They support a more stoic approach to loss and encourage the "buck up and bear it," philosophy. In the long run, that approach does not work. That approach did not work when we were children. It does not work when we confront loss as an adult, and when dealing with multidimensional grief from other times and places it doesn't work.

As children, we did not have the emotional maturity and capacity to process the intense emotions of grief. And if you choose to explore other realms and other lifetimes you will most often find that the fragment of your Soul did not have a choice either. But today, now, in this time and space, you do have a choice. And today, in this evolution of our growth you have ample support and technique to deal with grief. So my hope, in addressing grief more fully here, is that I will be offering you that choice and hopefully, you will be inspired to, and equipped to deal with your grief irrespective of its source.

So let's begin at the beginning.

Grief results from the stress response to fight, flee, or freeze. When we experience trauma as a child our efforts to resolve these moments of stress get interrupted. Instead, we get locked into the stress response and spend much of our life bouncing amidst situations to which we react. As we have already discussed the psychological community is now referring to this response to our world as a complex form of "post-traumatic stress disorder", or simply PTSD. What is relevant for this grief overview is that when PTS, which originated in childhood, is coupled with a major loss in adulthood, the coping mechanisms of the past trauma will dictate the response to the current crisis at hand. In fact, even if we have not suffered from PTS, most experience at least some residual, childhood grief that has not been resolved.

Research now suggests that the essential wound we encounter the first time we experience the world as unsafe establishes the blueprint with which we will deal with loss throughout our lives. The context and intensity of our unresolved loss may differ. However, the commonality is that the lack of resolution is based on the conscious, or unconscious, fear that we will not be able to cope if we confront the depth of intense feeling associated with loss. What few realize, and what most cultures do not support, is the fact that *learning to embrace the process of grief is the antidote for our fear that we will be unable to cope.* Learning how to process grief is the most promising way to live a fulfilling life because it enables us to truly live life without fear.

Most of us are somewhat familiar with grief. We have experienced loss. We relate to grief as a process that must be endured, but only when there is a *major* loss, a measurable loss, one that has a beginning and an end.

However, as I suggested earlier, grief is a predictable process we experience on a regular basis in response to the many challenges we face each day. These commonly accepted stages of grief are experienced in response to even the little moments of loss—minute losses— like the momentary loss of self-esteem we feel when we do not live up to our own potential, or the loss of trust we might feel when a friend does not live up to our expectations. We can even experience grief when we fail to achieve a "personal best" in some desired endeavor. Without realizing it, we progress through the five predictable stages of grief even in response to these minor infractions.

Often, the process takes as little as ten minutes. But irrespective of how long it takes, we do progress through the same stages of feelings one experiences when confronted with a major loss. We feel anxious, (stage one—denial, panic, anxiety) which is mitigated by a desire to fix, control, or change the situation, (stage two—bargaining). When this fails, we feel anger and irritation, (stage three—anger). When we are exhausted by our anger, we begin to let go. We collapse into the truth of the loss and feel the deep despair, (stage four—despair). If we are lucky, with time, we do resign ourselves to the loss. We accept the loss. And, depending on the severity of the loss, we do reinvest and move on, (stage five—acceptance and resolution).

But many are not that lucky. An individual can get stuck in any one of these five stages of grief. If one's PTS is triggered, he or she can ruminate about the situation for days. If this occurs then, irrespective of the nature of the loss, the individual will continue to get retriggered at the stage of grief he or she was unable to resolve in the first place. This person simply goes from one triggering experience to the next, forever caught in a state or reactivity, experiencing few moments of peace and calm. Anxiety-ridden and overly active in co-dependent behavior, he or she can approach the world with rage and anger, or suffer from depression and despair.

Nonetheless, whether our childhood trauma was severe or not, most of us find we are living in a society in which unresolved grief has become an epidemic. The current economic situation continued threats of terrorism, and relentless wars coupled with current stresses of daily life leave us afraid and confused—triggering childhood wounds and adult doubts about our ability to cope. We are thrown into the stages of grief as we express our unresolved anxiety, confusion, often are expressed through compulsive and addictive behaviors.

We may eat too much; drink, drug or smoke too much; love, shop, work, gamble, or worry too much. But we live out of fear rather than faith—compulsion rather than choice—isolation rather than unity, as we long to feel safe and secure. But there is little human security. Whatever excessive behavior we choose, it simply serves to numb the fear of the unknown, the pain of our grief.

Millions are pharmaceutically treated for depression, anxiety disorders, and post-traumatic stress. Each of these ailments has its roots in unresolved grief. When our grief is not processed, the lingering feelings of loss accumulate. They erode our hope and often lead to rage and despair. When faced with a major loss, these unresolved feelings roar deep within and exacerbate the current crisis.

The depth of emotion can become a source of fear—fear that we will not cope.

And there is some truth to this possibility. The underlying effects of our grief get stored in our body, morph into physical ailments, and become a steady source of emotional, physical, mental, and spiritual, decline. The emotions may get numbed by our addictions, but our grief does not go away. It lays dormant, threatening to resurface with a vengeance, demanding the attention it deserves.

Yes, it is my experience that grief is deserving of our attention? It is deserving because these five stages of emotion are a natural response to living our life fully. It is deserving because dealing with the contrast and the resolution of that contrast is what invites our Soul to grow. It inspires us to work with our inner children so they can be safe. It relieves our body of storing the unexpressed emotions related to the perpetual loss we feel from just being human in this unpredictable world. And it allows us to live non-addictively, free to embrace, without fear, all that life has to offer.

Why?

Because if we have the tools to grieve we have the ability to cope. And, again, our biggest fear when confronting loss is that we will not cope. When we trust our ability to cope with whatever life brings us we have no need to fear what life brings us. And life certainly brings us experiences that will challenge, and inspire. But life also offers a myriad of opportunities to be triumphant.

So what's the first step to dealing with your grief? You first have to acknowledge it. You begin to identify the challenges of loss by recognizing those moments when, in response to challenging emotions, you restrict and contract. That very response shows you where you are out of alignment with your Higher Self or Inner Being with respect to something in your life. You are out of alignment with your most illuminated self. In response to some unexpected experience in your life, you have collapsed into an old fear and your job is to explore and resolve the exact source of that collapse. If you understand the five stages of grief we have a starting point for that exploration because every challenging emotion you encounter can be categorized as one of these five stages of grief. And every contrasting feeling, when resolved, holds the opportunity for expansion and growth.

When we experience loss, it is indicative of our attachment to someone or something. The attachment itself can be healthy and fluid—the resolution of its loss expanding and illuminating. When we lose someone we love or lose something of great value, our feelings of grief are a testament to how much that someone or something truly meant to us. It is a sign that we allowed ourselves to love, to be attached, to care. To grieve is to be alive. Grieving is a way we let go and allow a new form of the relationship or situation to emerge. That is the promise of the fifth stage of grief. We accept the loss of what was. We open up for a new form of connection to unfold and take its place. This is even true when we lose something of sentimental value, an object that we would prefer not to live without. Perhaps it is a piece of jewelry passed on as a family heirloom. It can even be that favorite pen or a book given to us by a special friend. What is the new form of a loss such as this? It is letting go with grace. It is finding a way to release and let go. That is indeed the final stage of grieving anything lost. Finding the grace to accept and let go so we can emotionally move on, and be filled with what life has to offer when we are not holding on to something that is gone.

As I look back on the experiences I have had with all of the moments of grief I have felt during this lifetime, I feel a sense of fulfillment. Being able to breathe through the grief and get to the place where I felt completion enabled me to stay connected to my Creator, to my Inner Being, my Higher Self. That connection enabled me to get out of my way and let the situation of loss morph into its next evolution. Trusting the process of grief empowered me to love without fear. That trust is what enabled me to stay connected to those I lost, during and after, their passing, in profound ways. My life is richer because I do not fear love. It is richer because I do not fear attachment. It is richer because I do not fear emotion.

When you can stay connected to your spiritual source, ask for, and receive, insight regarding the higher purpose of even your momentary losses, and fearlessly embrace the process of grief, you can rest assured you will be able to successfully live life unafraid to love. You will re-establish your trust in being able to cope. You will come to have faith in your ability to breathe through the anxiety, embrace the momentary anger, disillusionment, and despair, and with grace, return to a state of resolution and acceptance involved in everyday losses. When you can grieve, you can live life without hesitation. When you can grieve, you can nestle safely in the comfort of the arms of your Higher Power and feel bigger than your fears.

It is said there are two predominant states of emotion—love and fear. We are either feeling afraid or feeling love. Every other emotion falls somewhere in between. We cannot feel love and fear at the same time.

What can you do when you slip from the safety and comfort of trusting your Higher Power into the depths of fear that you will not survive? You guessed it! You can embrace the process of grief.

But to embrace grief, you have to understand grief in a more practical and non-intimidating way. To do so it is important to fully comprehend and accept that *you are already in a constant state of grief.* Let me give you a simple example. Although you might not realize it, as was suggested earlier, you can experience the five stages of grief every time you miss a phone call. Well, at least every time you miss a phone call you wanted to receive. Picture for a moment those times you've heard your cell phone ring but could not get to it in time. You hurriedly dropped what you were doing but to no avail. You got there too late. The caller had hung up.

What was your response?

Whether identified as such or not, it was most often the first stage of grief—denial. This was followed by the tension and anxiety related to what you perceive you have missed. You may find yourself pushing 'call back,' but with no luck. The caller is leaving you a message or has gone on to another call. What happens then? You feel frustrated. You try to manage the situation by calling again. And this cat-and-mouse game can go on for several minutes.

Have you ever talked to your phone as if you are talking to the person trying to reach you? "Pick up! Pick Up," you command. In today's world, you most likely send a text message commanding a response. That's when you slip into the second stage of grief. You find yourself bargaining with the dead phone as you hear yourself plea,"Just, pick up! I'm here—just callback!" But inevitably the other person has shut off the phone, or is engaged and cannot connect. What do you feel when "managing the situation" does not work? Most often you experience anger and disappointment, and sometimes sadness and despair.

The feelings may be mild. But they are the feelings of grief nonetheless. The sadness does give way to the knowledge that the person will indeed call back, or the call comes through and you breathe a sigh of relief for the need has been met. However, you come to terms with this incident; a resolution does ensue.

You first experienced disbelief that you had missed the call. This disbelief covered up the initial anxiety (stage one) which got denied as you tried to manage the situation (stage two). When this did not work, you most likely felt irritation or even anger (stage three), which then gave way to despair (stage four). And then, ultimately, you resigned yourself (stage five) to the fact that the person would indeed call back. In a period of several minutes, you experienced the five stages of grief. If you recognize these steps, you move through them and do not get stuck. The more you befriend this process, the more moments of contentment you will experience.

So I encourage you to have the courage to befriend this process. Learn as much from this material as you can, then seize the opportunity of your loss to learn more elsewhere. Relate to grief as a way to manage and resolve all of life's challenges and disappointments. Don't deny it. Treat grief as a friend. Learn how to breathe through your anxiety, let go, and give up your attempts to control the outcomes of situations over which you have no control. Give yourself permission to beat on a pillow, scream in the mirror, or throw a tantrum in the safety of your own home, as you rid yourself of the energy of your anger. Learn how to befriend the void and emptiness of your despair, so that place within you can be cleansed and prepared for you to bring in something new. Find that serene point of reference, then make that your goal to constantly process whatever keeps you from sustaining a sense of calm and peace. Experience life. Stay present for life by identifying the stages of grief. Your comfort with grief is a sign that you are not afraid to live. It is a sign you have the courage to love. If you are willing to actively engage in the process of grief, if you know how to graciously move through those stages, you will have a method by which you can deal with whatever life hands you. And life does hand you challenges. It hands us all challenges. Part of the human experience is to bump up against the glitches in our daily life.

But if you can become comfortable with the process of grief, you can live fearlessly with the assurance that you will indeed be able to cope. If you can cope, you can love and live from your heart. If you can cope, you can succeed!

HEALING AND BEYOND— DEALING WITH FIVE STAGES OF GRIEF

No matter how good you are, you are going to have to deal with life's challenges. You are going to get stuck in traffic jams. Friends are going to disappoint you. Things are not going to turn out as you had hoped. You are going to collapse into old family roles or simply have "bad days." The Energy Therapies will help you address both current and past issues of losses and equip you to live life non-addictively without fear.

USING EFT TAPPING TO GRIEVE CURRENT LOSSES

Traditional tapping is most effective for dealing with current losses because you are addressing the emotions of the present. Interactive Tapping™ targets the underlying feelings that can emerge whenever we go through a real or perceived loss. In this next section, you are addressing those losses that are happening in your life now. It is necessary to neutralize the intense emotion that accompanies your present-day loss because that, in essence, is your dealing with that first, essential Layer of the healing process which is "Empowering your Adult Self."

STAGE ONE: PANIC, DENIAL, ANXIETY

Discussion: When we experience a real or perceived loss our first response to that loss is panic. We either go into the fight or flight response, or we freeze, shut down, deny, and go into a state of shock, (called psychic numbing). We want to deny the truth of the challenge.

Embracing the loss would leave us too raw. The anxiety is the tension we feel in the pit of our stomach when we try to imagine life without this attachment. It is the response we feel when something has been ripped from our very core. We become panic-stricken. We can even experience a psychological split because we cannot endure the pain. Some even get aggressive and hostile, others become depressed.

And of course, there is always the option to compulsively or addictively act out. As was discussed in the previous section, addictively medicating our grief quiets the tumultuous feelings of grief sometimes for decades.

Ultimately, we even lose sight of the original loss. We simply experience a restlessness quieted by our addictive or destructive behavior. Eventually, we either die of the addiction or find ourselves in recovery. If we make it into recovery, the unresolved loss is waiting for us. We begin the journey through the stages of grief—the bargaining, anger, and despair. But now there is the grief of the time lost as we ran from our grief. Those feelings also need to be addressed and processed if we are to ever come to a resolution.

Focus Questions: Use these following thought-provoking questions to identify how you feel.

1. *How have you dealt with the anxiety regarding the given situation upon which you now want to focus?*

2. *Have you channeled your tension related to your loss into work?*

3. *Did you deflect your attention to another person, or activity—implode and become riddled with depression—or perhaps consumed with shame and guilt over your regrets.*

4. *Did you numb out with process addictions by excessively eating, smoking, exercising, compulsively spending, or gambling?*

5. *If any or all of the above are true how long ago did the actual loss you need to address occur?*

6. *Take a moment to really ponder how you have dealt with your tension and anxiety. How you have avoided the feelings you felt you could not bear.*

7. *Bring your focus back to that moment when you first realized this challenge. Notice how you managed the anxiety that accompanied this experience.*
8. *Notice where in your body you held your anxiety?*
9. *Record your thoughts and feelings in your journal.*

Suggested Exercise: Draw your Anxiety

You might want to further your exploration by drawing a picture of your anxiety. This gives your psyche an alternative way to express this tension. You will then be better able to neutralize your challenging emotions with tapping as you introduce the possibility of feeling something new, which in turn, can morph into your conviction to embrace the feelings of this stage of grief.

EFT for Anxiety

While tapping on your karate point state the following:

Even though I felt anxious in this situation, and I can feel it in the pit of my stomach, the back of my neck, or in the stress, I hold in my shoulders, I love myself fully and completely.

Even though I feel great anxiety with respect to the perceived loss, I now choose to work with this fear, release it from my body, so I can begin to resolve this grief.

Even though I am experiencing great anxiety about this situation, I choose to believe I am in the arms of my Higher Power and, with that support, I choose to begin to let go.

Now tap on your endpoints. Refer to the graph if necessary.

Neutralizing the Negative

Eyebrow: Really feel anxious ... feel it in my stomach, shoulders, or neck...

Corner of the eye: Cannot imagine surviving this loss ... Under the eye: Really frightened regarding this loss ... Upper Lip: Am afraid I won't survive ...

Lower Lip: What if I don't survive ... Collarbone: So frightened I won't survive ...

Under the arm: Just want this fear to go away ... want it out of my body and Soul...

Chest bone: So afraid I won't survive ...

Rib: This anxiety has been with me for so long... Wrist: Will it ever go away?

Head: Just want this fear gone ... out of my body and soul ...

Moving from the Possibility of Change to Conviction ...

Eyebrow: Maybe if I bury myself in the arms of my Higher Power ... Corner of the eye: Maybe I can let go and Let God ...

Under the eye: Please Higher Power fill this void ...

Upper Lip: Help me move beyond this gut-wrenching loss and fear ... Lower Lip: Just want to feel safe and believe I can cope ... Collarbone: Maybe with help, I can survive ...

Rib: Maybe I can find the support from above and within

Wrist: I can connect with my inner child and then give this anxiety to God

Under the arm: I choose now to turn this over ...

Chest bone: I choose to surrender to my Higher Power and God ... Head: I am strong enough ... I can survive.

If you feel a shift in energy enough to move on, then do so. If not, continue to tap until you feel some relief. Feel free to adjust the words as you like.

As long as you are tapping, even if you say nothing, your body will begin to let go and relax. Your goal is to move out of your anxious place. It is also at this juncture that I might go to YouTube and play that EMDR Celestial video. When I do this I simply let my eyes move back and forth without saying a word. I have found this practice to also be effective in moving me out of the anxious state. If you have experienced the exercises of TRE® or any kind of breathing technique you might want to try these as well. Irrespective of which method you use, the goal with each of these stages of grief is to always move out of the reactivity back to a state of peace and calm.

STAGE TWO: BARGAINING

Discussion—When we can no longer tolerate the rawness of the loss we try to regain some sense of control by focusing on how we can change or fix the circumstances. Even though our attempts fail, the activity allows us to discharge some of the energy which gets stuck. These attempts are called the bargaining phase because we start making agreements with our self and with the object of our loss. We try to bargain with the circumstances of the loss. In a frantic manner, we try to manage the situation to ward off the inevitable pain.

Focus Questions: Respond to the following questions:

1. *How did you try to make this situation better?*
2. *What did you do behaviorally to try to change this situation or ignore this situation to pretend it did not exist?*
3. *This was your attempt to bargain with these circumstances. Did it work? If not, did you try something else or did you collapse into your anger or despair?*
4. *Is there anything about which you feel regret? If so, try to describe the circumstances and the accompanying feelings. This can be the source of much of your grief. It is important to flush those feelings out and address them.*

Suggested Exercises: Attempts to Manage the Loss

If it feels useful to do so, explore the deeper meaning of your attempts to manage the loss. Determine who inside feels such a need to change this situation. Who finds your present circumstances so intolerable? What motivates you to change, fix, or control, this situation in your adult world. You will find this motivation can be entirely different than what you experienced as a child. If you separate these two motivations and focus now on the adult's need to bargain, the process will be more effective. The inner child's feelings and need to bargain and control will be addressed in the next section. For now, use the tapping sequences to begin to manage your own need to manage.

EFT for the Bargaining Stage

> *Tap on your karate point while stating the phrases below. Customize these to fit your needs.*
>
> *Even though I tried but failed to control, fix, or change, this situation (imagine it in your mind's eye), I love myself fully and completely.*
>
> *Even though I have put great effort into changing this situation to no avail, and have exhausted myself in my attempts, I love myself fully and completely and am willing to tap this need to control away.*
>
> *Even though I have tried so very hard, I now realize it is not my place to alter this situation, and I love myself enough to choose instead to detach and let the outcome go.*

Use the following samples to begin your neutralization process. Add your own phrases accordingly but continue to tap around the endpoints saying your reminder phrase until you have neutralized the negative, introduced the possibility of change, and feel conviction with respect to your new stance.

Neutralizing the Negative

> *Eyebrow: Really tried so very hard …*
>
> *Corner of the eye: Am exhausted with my attempts … Under the eye: Just wish I could let it go …*
>
> *Upper lip: But fight this need to control and fix … Lower lip: It is so in my nature to jump in … Collarbone: Wish I could just let go and let God …*
>
> *Under the arm: But this need to do something takes over … Chest bone: And I just don't seem to be able to let it go … Rib: Feel too much anxiety to let go…*

Wrist: Hard to give up the hope ... Head: Wish I could relax and let it go ...

Moving from the Possibility of Change to Conviction ...

Eyebrow: Maybe I can begin to try something new ... Corner of the eye: Maybe I can tap instead of reacting...

Under the eye: Maybe what I can change is the way I respond ... Upper lip: Maybe I don't always have to be the one ...

Lower lip: I am going to tap until I can let go ... Collarbone: Tap myself through the need to respond ... Under the arm: I can choose to not control ...

Chest bone: I can deal with the panic, and let it go ... Rib: I have a new way of coping ...

Wrist: I really want to respond in a new way ... Head: I feel strong and secure in my ability to let go!

Again, use whatever method necessary to move from the tension of your need to control to a release and a letting go.

STAGE THREE—ANGER

Discussion— Anger seeps in once we realize our bargaining is not going to work or we simply feel angry and agitated at the loss of our cherished situation. This is often expressed as crankiness or being critical of everything around us. The irritation enables us to discharge some of the energy of the anger but keeps us from totally letting go of an attachment that can no longer exist.

But part of us does not want to let go. We feel angry that we even have to let go. We do not want to feel the loss. Often our anger is covert and even misdirected. It may be expressed at our self for blowing it. *"It's not nice to be angry."* We can feel shame or guilt for feeling angry. On the other hand, we may project our anger onto another–blaming that person for everything under the sun. Either way, the anger is not resolved. This criticalness or complaining does reduce the tension, but it does so without ever actually severing the tie to that which we lost. The transition from our blame/shame frame of mind occurs when we can no longer suppress it, and our feelings seep out in rage.

This rage is often raw and unfiltered. It fuels our courage, whether willingly or unwillingly, to embrace the depth of grief which accompanies our loss. Sometimes it is done with great volume because we don't know how to speak it without volume. Use the following focus questions to help you find your truth and prepare yourself to speak it.

Focus Questions: Respond to the following questions in your journal:

1. *Take a moment to think about your loss. Determine when and how you experience or have experienced the irritation or anger at this stage of your grief.*
2. *Do, or did, you recall feeling irritated at anything/everything around you? If so, that is covert anger.*
3. *Do, or did, you feel righteous—vindictive—aggressive? This is an expression of overt anger—misdirected anger.*
4. *Do, or did, you have a shorter temper with others–with yourself—with the circumstances in your life? This is an example of generalized anger.*
5. *Do, or did, you feel like you wanted revenge? This is an example of revenge anger.*

All forms of anger are valid and need to be expressed. If it feels safe, use the following exercises to revisit that rage and anger now.

Suggested Exercises: Transmuting the Energy of Anger

Pick and choose which of the following methods appeal to you. However, I do recommend that you always begin with the first one. Sealing your anger before you release it is just the responsible thing to do. Otherwise, the disruptive energy spews out into the universe and coagulates with another vibrational rage as well. This is why some are reluctant to express the anger–they don't want to put that energy out into the world. But if you take responsibility for working with it in a transformative way this does not happen. It is just energy that is recycled and transmuted for another higher use. So again, I recommend you always begin with creating protection around you and the release of your anger.

1. Creating Protection—First, so that you can always feel safe, close your eyes and imagine that you surround yourself with that bubble light. Sometimes I call in an Angel or a Master or Loved One to assist. Then, ask that your anger is being encased in this Light and that as you express it the anger be transmuted in Violet Light, then be sent directly to the Great Central Sun to be transformed. This will seal your anger so that its energy does not bleed out into other areas. When you feel complete and secure proceed with any or all of the following exercises.

2. The Silent Scream—aka—Whisper Yelling—To do the silent scream you can take a pillow and simply scream into it. Scream by opening your mouth but blocking the volume from coming out. It releases the frustration without alarming anyone around you.

3. The Private Scream—If you really need to release the volume of your anger then this method is an option. Scream in a car or in the woods where you will not be heard.

4. Throwing a tantrum—This is a wonderful exercise or activity that enables you to jump up and down, flailing your arms around and making grunting noises, or yelling "No," to what you are releasing and then ultimately yelling "Yes," to that which you wish to attract. This resets the central nervous system immediately. Animals do this naturally when they have been stressed by a life-threatening experience. In fact, TRE© is founded on this principle so it definitely works!

5. Exercising—This releases the energy and makes it more manageable.

    (Note: aerobic exercise, such as jogging, etc., reduces current anger, anaerobic exercise, such as yoga, swimming, etc. reaches anger that is more deeply rooted in the muscular fibers.)

6. Meditation—Using the breathing techniques you were introduced to in the last section, let yourself relax and go into a meditative state. When you tap you can hold this image in your mind's eye as well. That combination augments this method even more.

7. *Journal Writing*—I recommend when you record your responses in a journal that you use it for stream-of-consciousness writing, recording without censure whatever thoughts and feelings come to mind. By the time you have finished your inner work, you will have a rich collection of the feelings you identified, experienced, resolved, and healed. It will be similar to having a photo album that documents your inner journey.

8. *Drawing*—Drawing your pain accesses your creativity and lets you give form to the feelings of anger. Describing the voice of the angry self with words can be limiting; drawing often gives you a richer symbolic means of expression.

9. *Mirror Work*—Mirror work involves sitting in front of a mirror and having a dialogue with your angry self. It allows you to see for yourself how your shoulders slump or the mannerisms present when you express your anger. Tapping on your endpoints while you look at yourself in the mirror can accelerate this technique. You do not have to say anything, although you can, it is not necessary. Just observe and tap and see where it takes you. Looking at your own image in a mirror is also one of the most effective ways of finding that higher, more evolved part of yourself. By facing yourself eye to eye, you can look beyond your physical deficiencies and see the wise, Inner Being within you. The tapping below will also help you get started, but again, draw on any resource you may have acquired on your way to spiritual fitness and health.

EFT for Anger

Tap on your karate point while stating the phrases below. Customize these to fit your needs.

Even though I felt/feel rage (anger, revenge, etc.) in this situation (imagine it in your mind's eye), I love myself fully and completely." Continue with tapping around the points saying your reminder phrase until you feel flat.)

Even though I felt righteous and wanted revenge in this situation, I know it was my wounded one, and I want to be able to respond instead of collapsing into the pain."

Even though I felt anger inside but did not dare to express it for fear of retaliation, I want to neutralize that feeling, so I can speak my truth and let go.

Now tap on the endpoint to begin to resolve the energy of your anger and your rage. If it gets too intense always opt to seek support. Call a practitioner, schedule an appointment with someone you trust and give yourself the assistance you deserve.

Neutralizing the Negative

Eyebrow: All of this rage....

Corner of the eye: ... this anger and rage...

Under the eye: ... really uncomfortable with the feelings of anger.
Upper lip: But I feel so violated and betrayed.

Lower lip: Isn't it wrong to feel this much rage? Collarbone: It's not okay to feel such anger ... Under the arm: ... better stuff it again...

Chest bone: ... but it won't be pushed back down. Rib: So uncomfortable with this rage ...

Wrist: ...and yet it won't go away...

Head: All of this anger... can't silence that voice... it's too late.

Moving from the Possibility of Change to Conviction ...

Eyebrow: But maybe I can tap it away

Corner of the eye: I can give myself permission to speak my truth...

Under the eye: I choose to speak my truth while I tap it away...

Upper lip: It sure has not worked to push it down...

Lower lip: I need to figure out a new way ...

Collarbone: Perhaps if I tap while I vent to my Inner Being Under the arm: I will finally be able to speak my truth.

Chest bone: ... and then I will invite my inner child to do the same. Rib: Somewhere in time, this truth needs to be stated and heard.

Wrist: If not now, when?

Head: If I want to be real I have to be able to speak what I feel.

Truly embrace the energy of your anger. Remember, this is the force that will let you move on and allow the new form of the relationship to that which you lost to unfold. When you speak your truth, you free yourself from the denial. You free yourself to be real.

When we can truly, and honestly, embrace our anger, the volume diminishes. We speak our truth authentically which opens the door to great sadness. We admit how angry we are with our loss. The anger ultimately severs the hope that we can alter the reality of the loss. This surrender brings relief. We are finally free to stand in the void of the emptiness left by our loss as we collapse into the next stage of grief– the sadness, and the despair.

STAGE FOUR—DESPAIR

Discussion: After allowing the severing of your hope there is usually an exhaustion–an emotional and physical exhaustion. It takes energy to hold on to those feelings of loss. Despair over this situation can feel like complete hopelessness—sadness—numbness. Despair is that experience of apathy and of giving up which leads to a sense of surrender. But most often the surrender begins with that apathy of complete hopelessness.

You will feel tired and worn out. You will need to sleep a great deal and let the reality of this loss settle into your psyche. You are readjusting to life without this challenge. Many mistake despair for depression. In reality, it is the exact opposite. Although the two feeling states feel the same their function is quite different.

Depression is a result of stuffing down feelings we feel unable to cope. It is the equivalent to stuffing socks into a bag until it is bulging. The emotions are suppressed, cramped together, and ultimately become toxic to the body and soul. Despair, on the other hand, is experienced when we have the courage to feel the sadness appropriate to the loss of something that we valued. It is the emptiness, the void—a void that cannot be filled until it is felt.

Feeling your despair is embracing it. It is standing in the center of the space once filled with the object of your loss and allowing yourself to confront the bareness of its absence. It is the last stage of letting go of the physical way you have related to what you are now losing. Once you can endure that emptiness, and let go of the attachment to relating to your loss, the space can be filled with a new vibration.

How do you do this? You simply breathe through it. Allow the void to be embraced. From this allowance comes the resurgence of something new. For this re-emergence to occur, you have to put a form to and embrace your despair. Use the focus questions below to assist you.

Focus Questions: Respond to the following questions:

1. What is one of your favorite, most loving, moments or experiences related to the object of your loss?
2. Describe this memory in as much detail as possible? Focusing on this memory recreates the vibration of attachment from which you will draw when you begin to allow the new form of relationship to emerge. *For instance, when I had to grieve no longer being able to run for exercise because my knee gave out I had to let myself really acknowledge the joy I felt when running. I revisited every race I had run and every trail I had experienced.*
3. What is it you will truly miss about this object of your loss?
4. How will your daily life be affected?
5. Imagine you are standing in an empty room. Allow yourself to really feel the absence of everything related to the object of your loss. Imagine no stimulation–no distraction–no mementos that hold the memory of this loss. It is gone. Truly see how

it feels to be without that which you lost. *Facing the relevance running held for me—really admitting that running had enabled me to cope and had kept me balanced and in connection with my Higher Self was riveting. It made me realize the true depth of the loss. And when I faced that truth-that running was indeed the primary avenue of release and connection I had to grieve before I could replace it with something new. In fact, I even had to admit I was grieving! For a while, I just felt the apathy and despair but had not identified it as being connected to not being able to run anymore. Only when I identified that I was grieving was I able to embrace those feelings and move on. Completing the suggested exercise below was one of the methods I used to accomplish the task.*

6. When you have answered the above questions then go on to the suggested exercise and let yourself admit and speak your truth.

Suggested Exercise: Letter to Your Loss

Write a letter to the object of your loss. Tell him, her, or it, all that you are going to miss about no longer having this object be part of your life. If you were involved with this object of your loss on a daily basis then speak about the void that you must now face. Say what you were perhaps unable to admit or even realize as long as there was not this void. If it is a pet or a person you have lost through death or divorce, say what you may not even have known you felt when your loved one was around. Put it all down on paper.

When we write our feelings out like this, we get the energy of the feelings out of our body. We externalize the feelings thus bringing them from the unconscious to the conscious mind. The feelings are then more stimulated and present in the energetic meridian system, and therefore, more susceptible to being neutralized and released with our tapping.

Each of the focus questions and journal exercises above will assist you in embracing your despair more fully. The more you allow that emptiness to be there the more room you will have to allow the relationship to morph into a new form and the more benefit you will get from your tapping sequences.

EFT for Despair

> *Tap on your karate point while stating the phrases below. Customize these to fit your needs.*
>
> *"Even though I felt/feel sad, despair, or hopeless in this situation (imagine it in your mind's eye) I love myself fully and completely."*
>
> *"Even though this sadness is more than I can bear, it feels good to finally acknowledge the truth, to be honest with myself so I can begin to heal.*
>
> *"So even though this truth has been buried for a very long time, it feels so relieving to lance his wound, so my inner child and I can begin to heal."*
>
> *Continue with tapping around the points saying your reminder phrase until you feel flat or have very little emotional charge. Then proceed to the reminder phrases.*

Neutralizing the Negative

> *Eyebrow: So much sadness...*
>
> *Corner of the eye: Have run from it for many years...*
>
> *Under the eye: Not sure how to feel ...*
>
> *Upper lip: I have cut off from this truth for so long... Lower lip: The sadness, the despair, the emptiness is so big...*
>
> *Collarbone: Will I ever be able to move beyond it and really heal? Under the arm: I feel so alone, what if I do not survive?*
>
> *Chest bone: I am not sure I can tolerate this much emptiness... Rib: No wonder I did not feel safe.*
>
> *Wrist: This loneliness is almost more than I can bear. Head: What if I don't survive?*

Moving from the Possibility of Change to Conviction …

Eyebrow: But I am not alone, not like before.

Corner of the eye: I do have a support system …

Under the eye: My inner child and I can survive.

Upper lip: I want to draw on all of the resources I have gathered along the way.

Lower lip: I have done a lot of work on myself.

Collarbone: I have a lot to offer my wounded one from my past.
Under the arm: Together we will neutralize the pain, return to safety, and heal.

Chest bone: I have come a very long way on this journey…

Rib: I am not alone…

Wrist: I have my Higher Self–inner child and I can release and let go.

Head: It truly is time to let go to let God handle this, so we can heal.

Again, draw from whatever methods you have at hand to assist you in embracing the depth of this void and despair. When you feel ready to move on then go to that stage where you feel some relief.

STAGE FIVE—Resolution And Acceptance

Discussion: This stage is when you resolve the grief related to your current loss. You are ready to allow a new form of attachment to unfold. You have embraced each stage of your loss, and have dealt with the void. You are now ready to replenish with something new–to replace the old form of attachment with a new form, a form as of yet, unknown.

This final stage is when your Adult Self gets to make peace with the loss because you have dealt with the feelings of the immediate loss. The loss is replaced with a feeling of wholeness, of being complete. You are finally safe to bring in something new. Trust in self, and your Higher

Power can be restored. The healing of the residual losses endured by your inner child will soon begin.

But first, you want to complete this process with your Adult Self. This completion comes when you sense you are ready to address the higher purpose of your loss. You are ready to go into meditation with your Healing Team and inquire about the purpose of your loss. You are receptive to asking how the resolution of your loss can benefit you spiritually and contribute to the expansion of your Soul.

When we address our healing in such a way, we move from being a victim of our loss to being a student of it. We recognize the spiritual significance of this loss. We begin to understand that having embraced the stages of grief so courageously, and having accepted our loss so authentically, opened our hearts. It expands our consciousness and enables us to see our life without this object of our loss differently.

In dealing with the loss of a loved one you may come to understand more and more that there truly is no loss. You may have experienced signs or visitations–those extraordinary experiences that give you the inclination that your loved one has not gone far. You can begin to comprehend that there is merely a change in the form of the relationship.

But this all begins when we are ready for the higher purpose of our pain to be revealed. The following exercise will help move you in this direction. However, this pursuit is one that will continue indefinitely. It has been over thirty years since my father passed away, and I continue to learn from the relationship we have today. The evolution is truly endless.

Focus Questions: Respond to the following questions.

1. *Take a moment to picture the source of your loss in your mind's eye. What's it like to tune into the vibration of your heart?*

2. *How was your heart attached to that which you lost?*

3. *How did you respond to the loss at the time of its occurrence?*

4. *Ask who inside felt such grief and what does he or she need from you now? How do you want to respond to this pain and loss? Comfort*

your little one and assure him or her that you are going to assist in resolving the hurt, the sadness, the anger, and despair. But now is not the time. Now you need to step away from the depth of the loss and look at the loss through the eyes of your elevated self.

You may want to return to the breathing exercises in which you bridged from your Adult Self to your higher self. It is from this expanded state of consciousness that you can begin to address questions of this higher, spiritual nature. When, as adults, we have an understanding of the higher purpose of our pain we are in a much better position to later assist our more fragile inner child in dealing with his or her original experience of the loss of safety and love.

Suggested Exercise: I am willing to see the bigger picture of my Loss"

1. *Now imagine you are standing before your Guardians and your Higher Self.*
2. *Ask about the higher purpose of this loss.*
3. *What was it your Soul may have wanted you to experience in dealing with this loss?*
4. *What was its purpose? What were its promise and reward?*
5. *Record your responses to this interaction with your Healing Team. Include your thoughts about this higher, more spiritual perspective on your recent loss? How are you now different than you were before enduring and resolving this loss? How have you grown?*

EFT for Acceptance and Resolution: Meditative Tapping to Rewire the Brain

Meditation tapping is very powerful in that it augments the vibrational intensity of anything you are affirming or intending. The text for this meditation is based on the principles of the "law of attraction". Keep this in mind as you begin to redirect your attention to a new form of connection with the object of your loss. When you do this you will be creating a new vibrational resonance. This vibration or buzz is what will attract the new object or experience into your life. The buzz is usually felt as a tingling all over your body, or a surge of energy up your spine.

According to quantum physicists, this surge, buzz, vibration, signals that the neurons in your brain are firing the neurotransmitters that support the emotional response or vibrational response to the affirmations included in this meditation. According to the Teachings of Abraham, if you hold this "buzz" for 17 seconds it energetically takes the vibrational form needed to be launched as a desire. If you hold it for 68 seconds, your DNA begins to replicate the picture and attract its vibrational match.

Tap on the endpoints while you recite this following meditation as an affirmation and an intention setting tool.

I am now ready to fully let go and allow this new evolution to occur. I have honored my attachment to that which I have lost. I really am ready to expand my consciousness–to vibrationally merge with my Higher Self–for it is from that vibrational point I can create an attachment after that which I lost. There does not have to be a void–a loss. The vibrational connection has merely changed. I can expand enough to connect and recreate in a new way. I now have the courage to do just that.

You may want to add variations to this meditative tapping sequence, but those words should give you the idea of what you are trying to accomplish. When you feel that connection is secure, proceed to your last tapping sequence for processing the grief of your Adult Self which will prepare you to address the unresolved grief of your inner child. There may be other momentary flashes of anxiety, anger, or despair. But you have given yourself a model for breathing through those responses to your grief to the point where you will never be a victim of your multidimensional loss again.

You have freed up the energy you had tied up in your multidimensional grief. You can now work with the residue of your past; learn about your inner child's pain, bring him or her home. You can now assure those parts of you that they can be free to feel their feelings. You will not abandon them in their pain. You will get the help you need, pray for the guidance required, so you can assist them in letting go and feeling safe. Your current loss inspired this healing so you can finally learn how to live your life without fear.

HELPING THE INNER CHILD GRIEVE— WITH INTERACTIVE TAPPING™ SEQUENCES

Inevitably, when we suffer a loss as an adult, the residue of the past comes to haunt us. I remember what occurred when, as an adult, I lost my first pet. A plethora of unresolved grief erupted. It felt as though I were crying every tear I had ever repressed. The floodgates opened. The depth of feeling overwhelmed and frightened me. Luckily I had a talented counselor who helped me navigate through the rocky terrain of my unresolved childhood losses that had been triggered.

In my case, not only did my childhood grief emerge. The multi-dimensional grief of the history of my Soul seemed to collide with events in my present life. I found myself engulfed in a grief for which I had no context. With time the story revealed itself to me as the story of Antoinette. The same tools and methods I have shared in this book and used to heal that multidimensional bleed-through can be applied to processing grief from any dimension and time.

How Past And Present Collide

Again, your essential wound occurred at the precise moment you realized you were not safe. You went into a panic and experienced terror you would not survive. This moment is the origin of your Post Traumatic Stress Disorder. It is this underlying trauma that gets reactivated whenever we experience any loss for which we must grieve. Symptoms of our PTS get activated anytime we experience a situation in our day-to-day life that resonates at all with the original neglect, judgment, shame, or abuse. The unresolved feelings related to this first experience of loss determine how we navigate through the feelings of the current losses irrespective of their intensity. They are the source of our loss of trust. They are the origin of our fear we will be unable to cope.

As I stated in the general overview of grief, all feelings encountered as a human being can be linked in some way to the five stages of grief. When we help our inner child process the unresolved emotions of childhood—whether they are labeled as loss or not—we begin to build a relationship with him or her that restores the trust. This restoration is necessary for dealing with the present-day loss because the intensity of your loss as an adult is fueled by the unresolved emotions you experienced as a child.

In the previous section, you dealt with the immediate feelings of loss–those related directly to recent losses experienced in your life as an adult. In this next section, you begin to dig deeper into those unresolved issues from your past–those issues which fuel your current response to life in ways you can only now begin to recognize and resolve.

Keep in mind what the inner child is grieving is the original loss of safety. If there were an actual loss, such as the death of a parent, or the trauma of a divorce, these situations would need to be targeted more specifically. But for now, you are just working with the residue of the loss of safety that is most likely getting triggered any time there is an experience in your current life that feels unsafe. For a deeper healing that is more age-specific, I recommend you obtain a copy of *The Inner Child Workbook*. Each developmental stage includes a section with instructions on how to help that particular inner child grieve. It can most easily be purchased through Amazon.com.

STAGE ONE: DENIAL: "THE INITIAL AND CURRENT RESPONSE TO THE LOSS"

To reiterate, because we were too young to endure the panic and survive, we went into shock and experienced a numbing denial of the truth. Our body stored this pain in our electrical circuitry, and we developed what is called *Chronic Post Traumatic Stress Disorder.* Some of us dissociated and went into that dark hole previously referenced. Our emotional system simply shut down.

If, as an adult, you experience a lack of affect, or it seems as though emotional expressiveness is missing, it is a sign that your inner child split off because he or she could not endure the pain. Sandra Ingerman's book, *Soul Retrieval,* refers to this as "Soul Loss." Her book covers this subject in much more detail than I am prepared to address in this material, but *Soul Retrieval* is certainly a worthwhile read and can also be purchased through amazon.com.

These next two exercises will assist you in identifying the possible Soul loss your inner child experienced that is now resurfacing in response to your current loss.

Exercise: Ponder your current loss. When you bring focus to the feelings, you are now revisiting try to recall the first remembered experience when you felt a similar set of emotions. Follow the thread of your emotions. Let that tension escort you back to that first remembered experience. Don't force it, just trust whatever thoughts or images emerge. This will give you an idea of the essential wound that may have been triggered. Then record your thoughts in your journal.

Exercise: Now take this experience one step further. When you experienced or re-experienced, this loss, and you did, or perhaps do not, have the mechanisms to cope, the energy is diverted. Think for a moment how you may have diverted your attention from this set of feelings related to your current loss.

Usually, we react with some excessive behavior. In fact, it is most likely in this arena your addictive behaviors emerged. So, think for a moment, how you cut off from the feelings with which you could not cope. Did you ignore them? Did you compulsively or addictively act out? Take a moment to make a list of the ways you acted out (and perhaps still do) to keep yourself from feeling the panic or discomfort of your loss. In other words, write down ways you have kept or keep yourself in denial! Record any thoughts you might have on this list in your journal.

Exercise: Take a plain piece of paper. Draw a great big garbage bag in the center of the page. It can be something as simple as what's featured here. Now write in the center of that garbage bag all the thoughts, feelings, and events, associated with your anxiety, denial, and panic. Include everything from your perspective, as well as from your inner child's perspective, that you want to tap on and ultimately release. Once done, have this garbage bag sitting in front of you. As you tap, know that your psyche is neutralizing everything you have put in that bag. The procedure is called, "bundling the baggage." It was developed by EFT Master Lindsay Kinney and is very effective in the processing of feelings associated with one subject. Everything that is written down and symbolically placed in the bag is neutralized by your psyche as you tap on the respective points of release.

A Note on Tapping for the Inner Child—The tapping process I will be facilitating for each stage of your inner child's grief uses the same three setup phrases to identify the unresolved feelings that would inhibit your inner child's ability to grieve. Creating an affirmation for the acceptance of the way in which your inner child coped is one of the first steps in winning the trust of your inner child. It is acknowledging the inner child's response to his or her situation while neutralizing any judgment you, as the adult, might have about the manner in which you, as a child, coped. This acceptance establishes the platform to begin to heal. For example, an inner child setup would look like this: "Even though as a child I was unable to cope and withdrew, I love myself and this little one fully and completely. I know this was the best she could do." The setup phrase states the obvious but does so in a way that accepts the inner child did the best job she or he could.

The sequences are then again divided into two, progressive sections. You first neutralize the negative thoughts and feelings your inner child had at the time of the loss. Sometimes you are speaking to the inner child, in which case you will be using the pronoun, "you." And sometimes, when using the pronoun, "I", you are giving your inner child a voice. I suggest you stay with each series of the sequences until you feel an energetic shift that signifies your inner child is ready to move to the next round. However, be patient. Often this is the first time your inner child has been able to speak his or her true feelings about the trauma and fear experienced in childhood.

Also, though it is important to give your little one the room to vent, it is equally important to do so while you are tapping. Remember, tapping sends the electrical impulse through your body to untie the knot of tension experienced when you target these unresolved feelings. It is the tapping itself that ensures the feelings are being neutralized. To vent with no recourse for dissolution can lead to your ruminating and feeling retriggered all over again with no reprieve or resolve.

The second set of sequences introduces the possibility of change. This shift in the focus of the tapping softens the psyche and invites your inner child to consider the possibility that it is safe to trust the Inner Adult. This is a new concept for your inner child. He or she is not used to feeling accepted and allowed to speak. The last statements of tapping should leave you feeling strong and energized. They should reflect the shift in your inner child from fear to trust. Use the statements I have provided as an example but definitely customize your own sequences as well. Only you know exactly what needs to be targeted with respect to your childhood experience. Once this shift is accomplished, the two of you will be ready to progressively proceed through each of the respective stages of grief.

Tapping for your Inner Child's Anxiety

Now allow the feelings and thoughts you dislodged in the first part of this discussion to be infused with the words I have provided as you continuously tap on your karate endpoint stating each of the following setup statements at least three times:

Even though I felt anxious in this situation—and as a child I know I have felt this anxiety before—I can feel it in the pit of my stomach, the back of my neck, or in the stress, I hold in my shoulders, I love myself fully and completely.

Even though this has triggered many memories of previous losses, I now choose to work with this fear, release it from my body, so I can begin to resolve this residual grief of my inner child.

Even though I am experiencing great anxiety about this situation, I choose to believe I am in the arms of my Higher Power and, with that support, I choose, as the Adult Self, to begin to help my inner child express and release his or her fear.

Neutralizing the Negative for your Inner Child ...

(Start out speaking as the adult...)

> *Eyebrow: Really feel anxious ... feel it in my stomach, shoulders, or neck.*
>
> *Corner of the eye: He/she believes the loss cannot be survived...*
> *Under the eye: Really frightened regarding this loss ...*
> *Upper lip: Afraid he or she won't survive ...*

(Now switch to the voice of the Inner Child ...)

> *Lower lip: What if "I" don't survive ... Collarbone: So frightened I won't survive ... Under the arm: Just want this fear to go away ... Chest bone: So afraid I won't survive ...*
>
> *Rib: I'm too young to feel this afraid. Wrist: Will it ever go away?*
> *Head: This anxiety has been with me for so long...*

Moving from the Possibility of Change to Conviction ...

> *Eye: Maybe if I bury myself in the arms of my Adult Self... Corner of the eye: Maybe I can let go and feel safe ... Under the eye: Please help me fill this emptiness ...*
>
> *Upper lip: Help me move beyond this gut-wrenching loss and fear ... Lower lip: Just want to feel safe ...*
>
> *Collarbone: Maybe with help, I can survive ... Rib: Maybe I can find the support to feel safe.*
>
> *Wrist: I want to connect with my Adult Self and then let this fear go. Under the arm: I want to trust ...*
>
> *Chest bone: I want to trust my Adult Self...*
>
> *Head: I am hoping he or she is trustworthy enough to help me survive.*

Keep tapping until you really feel the energetic shift of releasing and letting go. Customize your own reminder phrases so you can address the unique way your inner child may be experiencing this stage of grief.

STAGE TWO: THE INNER CHILD'S BARGAIN: "MAKING DEALS TO MANAGE THE LOSS WHICH WAS MITIGATED BY YOUR CO-DEPENDENT BARGAIN™"

Again, the Co-Dependent Bargain™ is the contract we made as a child with a parental figure, or with God, in which we agreed to do something in hopes of being lovable enough to warrant their willingness to keep us safe. The problem is that the other party was either unaware of this agreement or unable or unwilling to live up to this agreement. Consequently, we ended up feeling betrayed and full of rage when confronted with the fact that our bargain was not kept.

As adults, we integrate the shame of this failure into our self–talk, and it becomes the basis of our internal critic and our projected, judgmental self. The culprit who perpetuates this self-talk and protects us with mal-adaptive coping mechanisms is what I referred to previously as our *cherished saboteur*™.

Exercise: Lets now work with that bargain. This bargain was directed to the parent you were hoping would protect–the parent with whom, as a child, you were compromising and bargaining with in hopes of winning the approval needed to feel safe. Fill in the blanks according to what feels right.

Example: Mommy, I will be a good little girl, and do everything you ask, if only you will love me enough to stop hitting me so I can feel safe. Customize it to your inner child's experience and reality.

Your Co-Dependent Bargain™_____, (*the parent with whom you are making the bargain) I will _____ (the agreement you tried to make–i.e.e, "I will be perfect; I will be good") if only you will (what we hoped to get in return) "keep me safe, you will love and protect me."_____.*

Write your Co-Dependent Bargain™ *out:*

Now bundle the baggage of all of your attempts to manage the situation over which you had no control... write in the center of that garbage bag all the thoughts, feelings, and events, associated with your attempts to bargain with your loss of safety as a child, the ways in which you compromised yourself in hopes of returning to a state of safety and peace. Include everything you can recall from your inner child's perspective, that you want to tap on and ultimately release.

Tapping for Bargaining Stage

Tap on your karate point while stating the phrases below. Customize these to fit your needs.

Even though I tried but failed to control, fix, or change, this situation (imagine it in your mind's eye), I love myself fully and completely.

Even though I tried very hard to change this situation I was just a little kid. But it is so nice to feel that my Adult Self loves me anyway. There really wasn't anything I could do.

So even though I did try so very, very hard, I now realize it was not my place to alter this situation. I was too young. It is so comforting to now know that my Adult Self loves me enough to detach and accept the outcome of what it was.

(PLEASE NOTE: If, as the adult, this does not resonate, return to the tapping sequences to clear yourself of the distraction and unwillingness to be present for the healing of your inner child. If you are still carrying judgment about how you, as a child, handled this situation then this needs to be neutralized with your tapping before you can be an effective agent of change for this fragile one within you.)

Next, use the following examples to begin your neutralization process. Add your own phrases accordingly, but continue to tap around the endpoints saying your reminder phrase until you have neutralized the negative, introduced the possibility of change, and feel conviction with respect to your new stance.

Neutralizing the Negative for your Inner Child

Eyebrow: Really tried so very hard …
Corner of the eye: Am exhausted with my attempts …
Under the eye: Just want to let it go …

Upper lip: But fight this need to control and fix ... Lower lip: It is so in my nature to jump in ... Collarbone: Wish I could just let go ...

Under the arm: But this need to do something took over ... Chest bone: And I just didn't seem to be able to let it go ... Rib: Felt too much anxiety to let go...

Wrist: Hard to give up the hope ...

Head: Wish I could have relaxed and let it go ...

Moving from the Possibility of Change to the Inner Child's Conviction ...

Eyebrow: Maybe I can now begin to try something new ...

Corner of the eye: Maybe I can turn to my Adult Self instead of feeling so scared.

Under the eye: Maybe what I can change is the way I respond ...
Upper lip: Maybe I don't always have to be the one ...

Lower lip: Maybe my Adult Self can be in charge ...

Collarbone: Maybe my Adult Self can help me move through the need to respond ...

Under the arm: I can give up control ...

Chest bone: I can tolerate this panic and let it go ...

Rib: I can let my Adult Self show me a new way of coping ...
Wrist: I really want to respond in a new way ...

Head: I feel strong and secure in my ability to trust and to let go!

Keep tapping until you really feel the energetic shift of releasing and letting go. Customize your own reminder phrases so you can address the unique way you may experience this stage of grief.

Exercise: Designing a Nurturing Statement—To heal this bargain your Adult Self needs to design a nurturing statement that counters the compromise–a loving statement his compromising, wounded one needs to hear in order to give up the bargain. Design that statement now.

An example of Adult Self speaking to an inner child – "*Honey, you do not have to do anything other than be yourself. I love you and promise not to ever hurt you. You are safe with me, and deserve all the love and protection I can, and am willing to give.*"

Now come up with your own statement that fits your unique co-dependent bargain™. Record it in your journal.

Once you have your statement, tap on the endpoints as you imagine saying this statement to your inner child. Keep saying it over and over until you feel a connection has been made. Let the healing of these words really sink into the inner child's awareness. State it slowly and with heart. You are anchoring this new belief system into the inner child's experience. The tapping neutralizes your inner child's doubt and fear while progressively reinforcing his or her willingness to believe and trust.

Exercise—This exercise overrides the old belief system housed in the codependent bargain and replaces it with a new way of thinking based on the trust that has been restored to you and your inner child. In essence, this proclamation is what the Adult Self can now say to the inner child that is believable once this bargain has been dissolved and trust has been restored.

Read each proclamation separately while repeatedly tapping on the endpoints. Read it first from the Adult Self to your inner child, and then, as your inner child, to your Adult Self. Customize the words if it feels right to do so.

Proclamation for the Adult Self: I, _____, (state your name) AM WORTHY OF YOUR TRUST. YOU ARE A CHILD OF THE UNIVERSE AND DESERVE TO BE PROTECTED AT ALL TIMES. IT IS MY JOB AND MY HONOR TO LOVE YOU AND TO KEEP YOU SAFE. AND I PROMISE THAT IF I AM NOT PERFECT, AND IF THERE ARE MOMENTS WHEN I FLOUNDER AND DO NOT FOLLOW THROUGH, I WILL HOLD MYSELF ACCOUNTABLE. I WILL ASSURE YOU IT WAS NOT YOUR FAULT, AND TOGETHER, WE WILL COME BACK INTO THE LIGHT WHERE WE CAN HEAL.

Proclamation for the inner child: I, _____, (state your name) AM WORTHY OF YOUR LOVE. I AM A TRUE CHILD OF THE UNIVERSE. I CAN TRUST YOU, MY ADULT SELF. I NOW BELIEVE I DESERVE TO BE PROTECTED AT ALL TIMES, AND I TRUST THAT YOU WILL KEEP ME SAFE. I UNDERSTAND THERE MAY BE TIMES WHEN THIS IS NOT THE CASE, BUT I BELIEVE YOU WHEN YOU SAY THAT YOU WILL NOT ABANDON ME. YOU WILL NOT BLAME ME. INSTEAD, YOU WILL ACKNOWLEDGE YOUR MISTAKE AND TELL ME YOU ARE SORRY SO THAT TOGETHER WE CAN HEAL AND TRUST.

It is this kind of dialogue you and your inner child need to have to enable the two of you to deal with the more intimidating feelings of anger and rage.

STAGE THREE—Anger "The Unspoken Truth"

Anger seeped into our inner child's experience when the denial and bargaining no longer worked. It was anger at the loss, agitation at the loss. But for most that anger could not be expressed. It had to be camouflaged or repressed and ultimately became the source of our negative self-image. As you read in the overview of the development of the inner child's pain, it is easier to collapse into shame and believes there is something wrong with us then to hold the anger at our parents for not being strong enough to love us in the way we deserved. Making it our fault gives us the false impression that there is something we can do to impact a situation about which we feel totally helpless.

If we were not muted and silenced then the anger was most likely discharged through more overt behaviors such as hyperactivity, or the development of Attention Deficient Disorders. Those behaviors let off steam, but the underlying feelings are never addressed. Few children are ever truly able to embrace the full essence of their anger. Even as adults many of us continue to be afraid of our own anger and mute its expression.

Instead, we continue with our truth remaining unspoken. But the truth was that we did suffer a loss. And if we are ever to feel safe again that little part of us needs to acknowledge the truth of that loss, the gut-wrenching truth that he or she did not feel safe or protected.

Much of the anger you experience in your inner work is anger fueled by memories of loss experienced before you had the knowledge and tools to cope with it. The emotion was an instinctive response to feeling unsafe. What went unexpressed got lodged in the tissues of your body. And it remains there as an energy block (or, as Gary Craig, founder of EFT calls it, an energetic disturbance) until it can be physically released.

The thought of releasing anger is frightening for most people. The fear is that the anger will be endless. The fear is that if we take the cap off of our latent anger, we will not cope. But anger can be released, and it can be released in a constructive and beneficial way. To ensure this occurs I always recommend you begin your anger work with the same simple exercise you did when working with the anger of your present-day self.

Exercise: Creating Protection—To create the safety you and your inner child deserve, begin by closing your eyes and imagining that you are surrounded by a bubble of Light. Set the intention with the universe that your anger be encased in this Light. Ask that your anger is transmuted with a violet flame. And finally, request that the energy of your anger be sent directly into the Great Central Sun to be transformed. This practice will seal your anger so that its energy does not bleed out into other areas.

When we truly trace the threads of our anger we most often discover that the anger comes back to our being angry at ourselves for not saying no. We may even feel anger related to regrets about which we now feel shame. This anger is toxic–to us, and to all those around us.

However, when we responsibly express our anger we soon come to understand that the unresolved anger emerging is the residue from the grief of the past. The child within us did not have the option to deal with the emotions in any other way. We begin to realize that it is this level of unrest from the unexpressed anger of our inner child that keeps us from resolving our grief and moving into another form of a relationship with our current losses. But now that the anger has been identified it can be released and resolved.

The first step to flushing out the anger is to weed out all of the negating statements that block this anger from being realized. The following exercise will help you do this.

Exercise: Anger Exercise—Using your dominant hand, write in the first column, "I am angry." In column two, using your least dominant hand, write your immediate response. *See the example below.* The experience of going back and forth with these statements dislodges the self-talk that originated from your inner child's old belief systems. It also flushes out the responses that perhaps you as an adult have adopted as a way to continue the denial of these feelings.

The purpose of this exercise is to continue writing in the columns until you can righteously own the anger of your inner child. Your inner child most likely had a right to be angry. If you own it, when you do your tapping, the energy of that anger will be sufficiently stimulated in the electrical circuitry of your body so it can be neutralized. Try to continue until you can write, I am Angry," in both columns with no resistance.

Example:

I am angry.	1. But they did the best they could.
I am angry.	2. But it's not her fault she died.
3.	3.
4.	4.
5.	5.
6.	6.
7.	7.
8.	8.
9.	9.
10. "I AM ANGRY!"	10. "I AM ANGRY!"

Once done, bundle the baggage of your anger. I usually just draw the bag over the columns as a way of throwing them in one big bag. Then have your list in front of you when you do this round of tapping. Your psyche will automatically neutralize the anger on all levels available. You will also be able to use what you have written as your reminder phrases. You can do the few rounds I have provided, but then please tap using your own words. It will make your experience much richer.

Tapping for your Inner Child's Anger

Begin by tapping on the karate point for the setup statements.

Then continue by tapping on each of the endpoints.

Even though I feel rage (anger, revenge, etc.) that I was left alone and felt so afraid, I want to finally feel safe and protected by my Adult Self; I want to trust that I can express these feelings and still be loved.

Even though I later felt righteous as an adolescent and my anger did enable me to survive, I know that anger was an expression of my hurt. I know it was triggered by this current loss, but it reminded me so much of when I had no power and felt so alone. But I'm not alone now. I want to trust enough to say what I felt—safe enough to speak my truth.

So even though I felt anger inside, I did not dare to express it. I feared retaliation. I was powerless and at risk. But that was then—not now. Now, I want to neutralize those feelings. I want to trust my Adult Self to keep me safe while I finally speak my truth. I want to let go of this pain and be able to trust enough to feel joy. I feared retaliation, but that was then and this is now.

Neutralizing the Negative

Eyebrow: All of this rage …

Corner of the eye: …this anger and rage …

Under the eye: …really uncomfortable with these feelings of anger. Upper lip: But felt so abandoned and alone, so violated and betrayed. Lower lip: It felt unsafe and wrong to feel this much rage.

Collarbone: It was not okay to feel such anger.

Under the arm: So I stuffed my feelings and pushed them back down... ...

Chest bone: But now it won't be pushed back down ... Rib: Even though it is so uncomfortable ...

Wrist: ... it won't go away ...

Head: All of this anger... can't silence that voice... it's too late ... no matter how afraid I feel.

Moving from the Possibility of Change to Conviction ...

Eyebrow: So maybe I can give myself permission to speak my truth. Corner of the eye: I want to find my courage ...

Under the eye: ... to speak my truth while I tap with my adult ... Upper lip: It sure has not worked to push it down ...

Lower lip: I need to figure out a new way ... Collarbone: Perhaps if I tap while I vent ...

Under the arm: I will finally be able to speak my truth ...

Chest bone: ...with the protection of my Adult Self...

Rib: Somewhere in time, this truth needs to be stated and heard. Wrist: If not now, when?

Head: If not with my Adult Self, then who else can I trust, where else can I turn?

The inner Child finally speaks his or her truth!

Eyebrow: I am angry!!!!

Corner of the eye: I didn't deserve what I got. Under the eye: I deserved to feel loved.

Lower lip: I deserved to feel safe. Collarbone: It was them not me!

Under the arm: I am no longer willing to take the blame ... Chest bone: ...to feel shame about the person I am!

Rib: I am lovable!

Wrist: I did not deserve what I got...

Head: I can finally say that out loud and feel confident my words will be heard. I can trust and will still be loved!

Again, customize these statements and keep tapping on the endpoints until the anger is released and the inner child finally feels he or she has been heard and is still loved. Only then can the two of you, inner child and Adult Self, be free to move into the emptiness of the loss and, once and for all, acknowledge the void so it can be filled with love and light.

However, if there is still an edge to your anger, the following exercises will serve to rid your body of the energy. Some of these exercises are aimed at dislodging the inner child's anger. Some are simply to move the energy out of your body so you can let it go.

Additional Methods to Release Anger

I am again including these following methods to deal with the anger of your inner child. Remember to always begin with the first one. Sealing your anger before you release it is just the responsible thing to do. Otherwise, the disruptive energy spews out into the universe and coagulates with another vibrational rage as well. This is why some are reluctant to express the anger–they don't want to put that energy out into the world. But if you take responsibility for working with it in a transformative way this does not happen. It is just energy that is recycled and transmuted for another higher use. So again, I recommend you always begin with creating protection around you and the release of your anger.

1. Creating Protection—First, so that you and your inner child can always feel safe close, your eyes and imagine that you surround yourself with that bubble light. Sometimes I call in an Angel or a Master or Loved One to assist. Then, ask that your anger is being encased in this Light and that as you express it the anger be transmuted in violet flame then be sent directly to the Great Central Sun to be transformed. This will seal your anger so that its energy does not bleed out into other areas. When you feel

complete and secure proceed with any or all of the following exercises.

2. The Silent Scream—aka—Whisper Yelling—To do this you can take a pillow and simply scream into it. Scream by opening your mouth but blocking the volume from coming out. It releases the frustration without alarming anyone around you.

3. The Private Scream—If you really need to release the volume of your anger then this method is an option. Scream in a car or in the woods where you will not be heard.

4. Throwing a tantrum—This is a wonderful exercise or activity that enables you to jump up and down, flailing your arms around and making grunting noises, or yelling "No," to what you are releasing and then ultimately yelling "Yes," to what you are want to attract. This resets the central nervous system immediately. Animals do this naturally when they have been stressed by a life-threatening experience. In fact, TRE© is founded on this principle so it definitely works.

5. Exercising—This releases the energy and makes it more manageable.

   (Note: aerobic exercise, such as jogging, etc., reduces current anger, anaerobic exercise, such as yoga, swimming, etc. reaches anger that is more deeply rooted in the muscular fibers.)

6. Meditation—Using the breathing techniques you were introduced to in the last section, relax and go into a meditative state. Then invite your inner child into your mind's eye and listen to your inner child's anger. Allow it; you do not have to change it or fix it. You just have to help him or her discharge it responsibly so it does not bleed into inappropriate acting out in your day-to-day life. This is useful if the tapping did not quite address the depth of your inner child's rage. You can tap as you hold this image in your mind's eye as well. That combination augments this method even more.

7. *Journal Writing*—I recommend when you record your responses in a journal that you use it for stream-of-consciousness writing,

recording without censure whatever thoughts and feelings come to mind. By the time you have finished your inner work, you will have a rich collection of the feelings you identified, experienced, resolved, and healed. It will be similar to having a photo album that documents your inner journey.

8. *Verbal and Written Dialogues*—Dialoguing is a tool that involves talking to the different parts within you; orchestrating an inter-action so that a healing can occur. It can be done verbally, when you are actually stating the feelings of the different parts involved in the exercise, or it can be done by writing the responses of each character. When you are dialoguing between the Adult Self and a younger inner child, again, I suggest you use your least-dominant hand to write your inner child's responses. It was difficult, as a child, to master the skill of writing. Sentences were shorter, words more direct. By using your least-dominant hand, you will find that this experience is recreated. The more mature response of the Adult Self is experienced by using the hand you are most accustomed to using. This is true when you are dialoguing with the inner child about his or her anger. Ask questions.

9. *Drawing*—Drawing your pain unleashing your inner child's your creativity and lets you give form to the feelings and the different internal characters without using words. Describing the voice of the critical self with words can be limiting; drawing often gives you a richer symbolic means of expression.

10. *Mirror Work*—Mirror work involves sitting in front of a mirror and having a dialogue with your younger selves in order to observe the body and facial movements that accompany these parts within. It allows you to see for yourself how your shoulders slump when you speak from your child self, or how you wince when you express your inner child's fear. It also helps you see more clearly your physical demeanor from your adult point of view. Looking at yourself in a mirror is also one of the most effective ways of finding that higher, more evolved part of

you. By facing yourself eye to eye, you can look beyond your physical deficiencies and see the wise, Inner Being within you.

Once you feel the energetic shift of this younger one within you, and you can sense he or she has let go, you are ready to move on to the next stage.

STAGE FOUR—THE INNER CHILD'S DESPAIR "STANDING IN THE VOID"

When our inner child has finally been allowed to speak the truth, he or she collapses into the arms of the Adult Self in complete exhaustion. The truth has been acknowledged and contained. The despair in childhood was masked by shyness, lethargy, fear to engage, often mistaken for "quietness." But usually, that quietness was a loss of trust and a fear of retaliation if the true self was revealed. To truly embrace the source of our loss at such a young age would have put us at too much risk—the risk of not surviving the fear—risk of being exposed and punished—the risk of being shamed, blamed, or humiliated.

So the despair for the inner child is more of an expression of the loneliness and the abandonment he or she felt at having to be so cut off from what was really felt. It was in response to the loss of the real self. As you saw in the overview of childhood grief, this stage of grief touches the loss of the real self, the angst felt in having to compromise the person we were in order to strive for the safety we needed to survive. The antidote for this despair is for you as the Adult Self to assure the inner child that you have indeed evolved to a place where this is no longer true. It is welcoming the inner child back to his or her true essence, accepting him or her for the unique individual he or she truly is. It is done by validating the inner child's truth as was done in stage three and now allowing the inner child to tolerate the loss of your support.

Exercise: Experiencing and Releasing Despair

1. Write a letter to the younger parts of you who have had to let go. Welcome them into your force field, into a relationship with your Higher Guidance and the part of you who can tolerate this loss. This letter serves as a way to gather those parts of you that had to be sacrificed and banished in order for the inner child to survive. Acknowledging them by assuring their feelings will be heard, their needs met, makes this release more complete.

2. Take another piece of paper, write a second letter and let the inner child speak. Use your least-dominant hand so the true feelings of the younger self can bypass the conscious mind and be spoken with honesty and truth.

Now write down all of your words, phrases, and pictures that capture the despair of your inner child. Let him or her draw the sadness, the emptiness, then throw all that you want to neutralize into your bag and bundle the despair so you can help your inner child healing.

Tapping for your Inner Child's Despair

Begin by tapping on the karate point for the setup statements.

Then continue by tapping on each of the endpoints.

Even though I felt so much sadness, despair, and hopelessness back then I know it is now safe to let it go.

Even though this sadness has felt as though it were more than I can bear, it feels so good to finally acknowledge the truth, to be honest with my Adult Self, so together we can begin to heal.

So even though this truth has been buried for a very long time, it feels so relieving to lance this wound, to trust my Adult Self enough to open that door so ultimately we can begin to heal.

Continue with tapping around on the endpoints saying your reminder phrases until your feelings are neutralized and you can experience the courage to let go.

Neutralizing the Negative

> *Eyebrow: So much sadness ...*
>
> *Corner of the eye: Have tried to run from it but failed ...*
>
> *Under the eye: Not sure how to feel ...*
>
> *Upper lip: I have been cut off from this truth for so long ... Lower lip: The sadness, the despair, the emptiness, is so big ...*
>
> *Collarbone: Never thought I would be able to move beyond it and really heal?*
>
> *Under the arm: Thought I was so alone like I would not survive? Chest bone: It was so hard to tolerate that much emptiness ... Rib: No wonder I did not feel safe.*
>
> *Wrist: That loneliness is almost more than I can bear. Head: Can hardly believe I survived.*

Moving from the Possibility of Change to Conviction ...

> *Eyebrow: But I am not alone, not like before.*
>
> *Corner of the eye: I do have a support system ...*
>
> *Under the eye: I am getting stronger. I do trust my Adult Self and know he or she can help me let go.*
>
> *Upper lip: I want to trust all of the resources he or she has gathered along the way.*
>
> *Lower lip: My Adult Self has done a lot of work since then ... Collarbone: ... there's a lot to offer that can help me heal.*
>
> *Under the arm: Together we can neutralize the pain. I can feel safe enough to stand in the pain ... I will not be standing alone.*
>
> *Chest bone: We have come a very long way on this journey... Rib: I am not alone ... This is now, not then.*
>
> *Wrist: I can release and let go.*
>
> *Head: It truly is time to let go, to let God handle this so that we can heal.*

Exercise: The Inner Child's Truth about the Despair!

1. Go into a meditation and invite your inner child to write his or her pain of the void. Do so with your least-dominant hand so the true essence of that younger self can emerge.

2. Then picture yourself as the adult holding the inner child in your arms or having your inner child sit near you enough to feel safe. Quiet yourself and be present enough to support this vulnerable one's admission of how alone he or she really felt.

3. Tap on your endpoints while you are listening. If that is too cumbersome invite your inner child to write down the truth of the despair then imagine he or she reads it as you tap and neutralize the deeper levels of the pain.

Keep tapping until you really feel the energetic shift of releasing and letting go. Customize your own reminder phrases so you can address the unique way you may experience this stage of grief.

STAGE FIVE—ACCEPTANCE AND RESOLUTION "LETTING GO AND MOVING ON"

Acceptance and resolution of our loss mean we have processed the first four stages of grief. We have addressed the residue of our essential wound–this loss triggered in our inner child–loss felt when, as a child, we felt powerless and feared we would not survive. All of that grief has now been addressed and resolved.

The following tapping sequence will anchor this new reality into your force field and that force field of your inner child as well. This tapping meditation that follows is a wonderful way to wrap up the final stage of grief. With your inner child in your arms, you can now proceed on the journey of exploring the different realms of consciousness that enable you to pierce the veil between your physical world and the world of the unseen. But perhaps more importantly, you are now equipped to live your life with feelings, non-addictively, with the confidence that there is nothing with which you cannot cope. Your trust in self is an asset, that not only benefits you, but benefits all those in the world, and actually humanity itself.

Tapping for Acceptance and Resolution

Begin by tapping on the karate point for the setup statements. Then continue by tapping on each of the endpoints. This will anchor in this positive affirmation. Again, keep doing tapping rounds until you feel the "buzz." Hold the energy of this affirmation for 17 seconds as it takes form; then for another 68 seconds so the DNA can begin to replicate this new picture and attract its vibrational match.

Even though my inner child's grief got triggered in response to my recent loss, and he or she held this memory of not being safe, we have been reunited in trust and love. It IS safe to release all cellular memory of our grief, both present and past alike. We CAN now rewrite that cellular memory. With confidence, we know that we are loved by our Higher Source (God, Higher Power, etc.) enough to feel safe and to recommit.

So even though it has taken us a while to make peace, I am so grateful we navigated through this grief. I have finally found my way home, have reunited with my inner child, and am now ready to live a life beyond fear knowing I will be able to cope.

So even though this has been a long time coming, we have finally healed enough to allow ourselves to expand and attract.

Continue with tapping around the endpoints saying your reminder phrases until you feel flat or neutral.

Neutralizing the Residue of the Negative Eyebrow: This has taken a very long time.

> *Corner of the eye: Sometimes it felt as though I would never find the strength!*
>
> *Under the eye: So many months for me … Upper lip: And years of my inner child!*
>
> *Lower lip: Wish I could have healed before… and not wasted so much time.*
>
> *Collarbone: I wish we could have embarked on this journey before. Under the arm: Really wish I could have found peace at an earlier time.*

Chest bone: Wish it had not taken the loss of my loved one... Rib: ... But I can now envision another level of this situation...

Wrist: And the truth is I needed the current loss to flush out the old wounds...

Head: ... and that wounded one that really needed to be healed.

Moving from the Possibility of Change to Conviction...

Eyebrow: I really could not know what I did not know...

Corner of the eye: Each stage of grief was valid in its own way...

Under the eye: I would not have had the compassion any earlier...

Upper lip: and without compassion, I could not have healed my inner child.

Lower lip: I want to focus on the fact that the time has finally come...

Collarbone: I could not know what I did not know ...

Under the arm: I did the best I could with the resources I had at the time.

Chest bone: I am just glad the time has finally arrived ...

Rib: We are now united, and the healing is done.

Wrist: My inner child and I are finally ready to move on. Head: We are united, have let go, and I can now expand.

The last task of grieving involves forgiveness. What are you forgiving? Everything! You are ceremonialzing your forgiveness of your loved one for leaving you. Your inner child forgives you for taking so long to rescue him or her. Perhaps your inner child even forgives those who wronged him or her. And you forgive your higher guidance, understanding you were not a victim of this loss. And last but not least, you are asking your body to forgive you for its having to bear the brunt of your unresolved feelings and stress until you were truly ready to do for yourself what your body had been doing for you all these years.

The Hawaiian Forgiveness Ritual was given to me by a Hawaiian

Elder named Josie. It is but one way to orchestrate a formal forgiveness. The shorter version is more popular and is included below. But I like to use this longer version when I am sealing a piece of work around grief. I use the shorter version for dissolving stress at the moment. Please feel free to use or create your own as well.

Exercise: Hawaiian Forgiveness Ritual—Ho'oponopono

Simply put, Ho'oponopono is based on the knowledge that anything that happens to you or that you perceive—the entire world where you live—is your own creation and thus, it is entirely your responsibility–a hundred percent, no exceptions. Your boss is a tyrant–it's your responsibility. Your children are not good students— it's your responsibility.

There are wars and you are feeling bad because you are a good person, a pacifist? The war is your responsibility. You see that children around the world are hungry and malnourished, if not starving? Their want is your responsibility. There are no exceptions. The world is your world. It is your creation. As Dr. Hew Len points out– "Didn't you notice that whenever you experience a problem, you are there?"

It's your responsibility doesn't mean it's your fault, it means that you are responsible for healing yourself to heal whatever or whoever it is that appears to you as a problem.

It might sound crazy or just plain metaphorical, that the world is your creation. But if you look carefully, you will realize that whatever you call the world and perceive as the world is your world, it is the projection of your own mind. If you go to a party you can see how in the same place, with the same light, the same people, the same food, drink, music, and atmosphere, some will enjoy themselves while others will be bored. Some will be over-enthusiastic and some depressed, some will be talkative, and others will be silent. The "out there" for every one of them seems the same, but if one was to connect their brains to machines immediately, it would show how different areas of the brain would come alive, how different the perceptions there are from one person to the next. So even if they apparently share it, the "out there" is not the same for them, let alone their inner world, their emotions.

How do you heal yourself with Ho'oponopono? Three steps: by

recognizing that whatever comes to you is your creation, the outcome of bad memories buried in your mind; by regretting whatever errors of the body, speech, and mind, caused those bad memories; and by requesting Divine Intelligence within yourself to release those memories, to set you free. Then, of course, you say Thank You. So what does that all really mean? It means that what you heal is your response to any of the issues in your world about which you have strong feelings. Dr. Hew Len healed a whole psych ward just by simply holding the files of the patients in his hands and saying the prayer on *his reactions* to their histories. His disgust or fear regarding their circumstances is what he asked to be released. And it worked. It took him four years but he healed every patient and the entire ward was closed! So I invite you to work with it in the same way. Heal your reactions to the world and you heal the world! Heal your reactions to loved ones and you heal your loved ones.

You do so by reciting the prayer. Below is the long version … I recite this while tapping on the endpoints. It augments the clearing and neutralizes anything I might be holding on to in the unconscious.

FORGIVE ME _____

If I have hurt you

In any way, shape or form, In thought, word or deed,

At any time, any place, Past, present or future

FORGIVE ME.

AND I, _____ FORGIVE YOU

For hurting me

In any way, shape or form, In thought, word or deed, At any time, any place,

Past, present or future I FORGIVE YOU!

AND MAY THE CREATOR OF ALL THINGS FORGIVE US BOTH: ALL HO'OPONOPONO

IT IS DONE... SO BE IT!

This prayer can be said between you and another, between you and your body, between you and your inner child, between your Spirit and your Personality. It can be said to the one you have lost as a way to resolving their passing and a way to release the attachment so you both can move on.

The shorter, more popular version is simply: I'm Sorry...Please Forgive Me I love you...Thank You.

I repeat this over and over while tapping on my endpoints. Another one-liner I use to reduce the stress and anxiety before it even gets to stages two, three and four, is, **"God' love resolves this situation, (these feelings of loss) here and now."** Again, I say that repeatedly as I tap on the endpoints until the gut-wrenching feelings of loss subside.

The losses of your life have been acknowledged, processed, and released. The residual grief triggered in your childhood has been addressed. You have learned how to relate to your fragile one in a new and more profound way. Being able to embrace those parts within you that feel more vulnerable ensures that you will be able to respond to your fears instead of collapsing into, and reacting to, them.

In this next section, I introduce you to my signature *Seven-Layer Healing Process.* The sequential layers evolved in response to a personal healing session I did with of my inner seventeen-year-old. When I processed the multidimensional bleed-through about which you have just read I did not know about tapping or EFT. In the following section, I introduce you to that method of healing. Processing Antoinette's story helped me deal with intimacy and intimate relationships and even helped in expanding my career. What it did not dissolve was my issue around money. As you will see in the next section the need to dissolve that block again centered on Dad's nervous breakdown. That piece of inner work inspired me to use tapping to teach my inner child the laws of the universe and ultimately gave birth to my signature method of energy therapy now known as interactive tapping™.

Again, to fully learn this process step-by-step I suggest you explore my *Share the Gift* eBook which can be obtained on my website which again is www.EFTForYourInnerChild.com. The printed version and the Kindle book can also be purchased through amazon.com. That material thoroughly addresses the inner child sabotage from a spiritual perspective and targets four major issues of concern about attracting: intimate relationships, abundance, right livelihood, and reciprocal partnerships.

But the following overview will introduce you to the concepts of my *Seven-Layer Healing Process* and give you a bird's eye view of how this sequential process works.

The Seven-Layer Healing Process

THE INSPIRATION-THE PROCESS

L IKE MOST THINGS, the "mother of intervention" is need. This model is no exception.

My Inspiration for the Birth of my *Seven-Layer Healing Process*

Below is a letter written and emailed to the founder of EFT, Gary Craig, on 11/17/06. It was written after my first organic tapping experience which became the foundation for the merger of my inner child expertise with the innovative techniques of the new energy therapy called EFT. It further evolved into my signature method of energy therapy I then coined, Interactive Tapping™, which ultimately wove into my *Seven-Layer Healing Process* that is the cornerstone of every consult I conduct.

Dear Gary,

I just had the most profound experience with EFT. My name is Cathryn Taylor. I am the author of *The Inner Child Workbook*, which was first published in 1991 and is considered one of the classics in the "inner child" field. For the past twenty years, I have been working with this concept and instructing others on how to identify and resolve their inner child's conflicts. Several years ago I came across your EFT techniques. Since then I have been applying them to addictive behaviors and teaching clients how to use EFT to mitigate their anxieties.

But today was a real milestone.

For the past several months, I have been facilitating a new series called "Teaching Your Inner Child the Law of Attraction." The series was inspired by the movie, *The Secret*. As is usually the case, we teach what we need to learn. When we attract more Light, we illuminate that shadow self who vibrates at a lower frequency. The very act of teaching this subject uncovered my last "cherished saboteur™" (my coined phrase for the part of us whose actions are intended to keep us safe, but whose impact keeps us from getting what we want).

"She" had been acting up ever since I taught my first class. I came to discover that this little one is my inner 17-year-old that is stuck in a moment of time when, just as she was ready to leave for college, her hero (my father) had a nervous breakdown. That part of me has been frozen and held captive at that moment ever since. It became apparent today that according to the belief system of my inner adolescent, any time I truly wanted to step into my mastery and manifest abundance, she assumed it would require "leaving" my father. This perceived reality triggered her fear which compelled her to addictively act out or compulsively distract. Her perceived threat eclipsed my passion and sabotaged my ability to succeed. No matter how healthy I got in all areas of my life, there always remained this shadow part of me that sabotaged my success. This distraction sustained her loyalty to her father but resulted in my experiencing an underlying and unidentified state of anxiety and despair.

Today is the day that I finally put it all together. By teaching this inner adolescent how to do EFT, I brought her into my mind's eye and invited her not only to learn the principles of *The Secret* but to also learn how to cope with her grief over Dad's breakdown. I had used EFT to deal with emotional disturbances, but I had never combined tapping with my inner child meditations to go back in time to actually teach that frozen part of me how to tackle the gut-wrenching emotions of helplessness, fear, anger, embarrassment, and utter despair. That part of me was never able to cope with the fact that she could not save her father from his emotional demise. His breakdown had somehow become her failure and that failure translated into her not being able to fully succeed without feeling as though she were abandoning him. It is amazing to me how a part of us can stay so incredibly loyal to the parent who does not cope with his or her own life. Afraid to surpass and abandon that parent, many of us sustain one area of our lives that remains dysfunctional.

Inner child work is based on externalizing the old wound, giving it a face, and then interacting with that part to make it feel safe. The model is a magical way of empowering our most competent Adult Self while simultaneously being able to acknowledge and respond to our more frightened parts. It is a way to "repairent" ourselves. It is a way to "right" old wrongs, to retrain the brain to expect something new— something healthy and life-giving.

But today a miraculous shift occurred when I actually stepped back in time and taught my inner teen how to neutralize the frightening feelings of the time. By combining EFT and guided inner child meditations I was able to go back to that frozen time in math class when she looked at the clock and knew at that exact moment her father was getting electric shock treatments to eradicate his pain. Having identified with him to such a degree she wondered how long it would be before the same would be necessary for her. She had no idea how she could possibly deal with her life any differently. If he couldn't cope then how could she?

I had been running from that moment, and that question, ever since.

But today I was finally able to help her find relief. Today I was able to set her, as well as myself, free. Faith was restored, and I am now able to step into the mastery I have worked so hard to achieve. I had done many meditations, but nothing had completed, dissolved, or neutralized, the pain of that moment. This combination finally did just that. EFT is a brilliant method to neutralize the pain of our inner child's past. Thank you for bringing it to the world and for being so dedicated to teaching others how to use this tool to heal.

CATHRYN TAYLOR, MA, MFT, LADC
November 17th, 2006

Bringing It All Together

And that was the birth of this method of healing. Again, the relationship-based sequences morphed into my interactive Tapping™ technique which ultimately became the basis for my signature *Seven-Layer Healing Process*—the backbone of every piece of work I do with another. I truly believe and have experienced, that combining the context of my inner child expertise with the energetic interventions of EFT provides perhaps one of the most empowering avenues for working with those parts within you that sabotage your best efforts to succeed.

As is evident in all of my writing, the heart of my model is that the healing agent for the old wound, which results in your sabotaging behavior, is the interaction between your wounded one and a part within you who can respond with compassion, love, and care. However, in order to achieve this healing, you must develop a soothing inner voice which can respond to the wounds and needs of this younger self.

Unfortunately, this interaction is often eclipsed by the stress we feel in our day-to-day life. Instead, as we witnessed in working with the grief of our Adult Self and inner child, we collapse into the wound and react to the current situation from the outdated coping mechanisms of our more primitive self. in my world, this is referred to as the inner child or a fragment of your Soul.

This dynamic was further substantiated when recently I was introduced to a series on the New Brain Science+. *As I referenced in the previous section when I listened to the* New Brain Series, *hosted by Ruth Buczynski, Ph.D. of the* National Institute for the Application of Behavioral Medicine, *I was inspired to expand my Seven–Layer Healing Process. I already knew in 2006, when I first developed this healing process, that* tapping, in itself, rewired the brain in that it positions a negative experience with a positive one. But *infusing it with the basic tenets of this new science makes it even more effective. By simply adding the very language the brain understands one can more effectively promote sustainability of growth by building new, positive, neuropathways in the brain.*

This is essential in facilitating the movement of new paradigms from the short-term memory of your brain to its long-term storage. So before we

can even begin to discuss the first layer of healing, which
your Adult Self, it will be useful to review the new bra
Once you have some basic understanding of these new dis
be more equipped to understand and implement the Seven __.., ..*Healing*
Process.

How the Brain Works

As Dr. Richard Hanson , again the guest speaker on the New Brain Science webinar and author *of the* Buddha's Brain, *and* Hardwiring Happiness, *explains that, when discussing how the brain works, it is important to note that our negative reactivity originates in the amygdala, or lower brain, which ignites our fight, flight, or freeze, response. In order for change to occur new experiences need to be lodged in the hippocampus where it can be stored as a long-term memory. The prefrontal cortex, or the Higher Brain, whose* basic activity is considered to be the orchestration of thoughts and actions in accordance with internal goals, can *then draw on this new experience from the hippocampus and use it to determine new behaviors. In short, stress responses can be changed and new behaviors sustained when new experiences are lodged in the hippocampus and are accessible to the prefrontal cortex.*

But in order to do this, we **have to learn how to retrain the brain to hold positive experiences.**

A major contribution of this recent discovery is the fact that this is not our natural state. In fact, it is quite the opposite. It is more common to default to the short-term memory of the amygdala which is hardwired to detect everything as a threat which keeps us in a perpetual state of stress.

This is a proven fact. Neuroscientists did indeed discover that our brain is not only hardwired to deal with stress—it is hardwired to look for negativity and focus on anything perceived to be a threat.

In fact, when our brain registers that one of our basic needs such as safety, satisfaction, and connection, is not met, it fires up the fight, flight, or freeze, response as a way for us to survive.

This knee-jerk response is anchored in the first layer of the brain, and it served our ancestors very well, for a very long time. It enabled them to determine if an object was a rock or a lion, and if it was a lion, they had the adrenalin to respond. The stress was short-term. If he or she survived then this outburst was followed by the return to a recovery state. This enabled the organism to refuel, renew, and repair—which, in essence, enabled mankind to survive.

Today, the threat of being eaten by a lion has been replaced with modern-day threats, such as the rejection experienced through the insult or abuse of a friend or lover; the fears of making ends meet; the inability to find a life-supporting job, or even the general unrest that is ever-present in the air! Our lower brain, the amygdala, is hardwired with all of these cues and our present-day psyche goes about finding experiences in life which confirm that this "need to be on alert" is indeed warranted if we are to survive. The result is chronic stress and the impact is failure and shame. *So, in today's world, this survival mechanism creates a challenge and that challenge occurs in two ways.*

The first way is the one which was just mentioned—those threats that are being perpetually triggered keep us in a sustained state of fight or flight, which results in anxiety and despair. We can also freeze and become immobile, which keeps us in a state of dissociation—disconnected from ourselves and others in our world.

But the second, more insidious, way this presents a challenge is that these threats trigger those deeper fears that have been pushed down in our unconscious from childhood and lurk, undetected, in our psyche. These fears run deep, often have no name or face, but interrupt our ability to live a peaceful and productive life. In other words, in an attempt to survive, our brain is actually hardwired to continually keep us on alert and reinforce these unconscious fears and suspicions for which we are forced to find a context. We fidget around trying to find a reason for this fear because we believe if we find "the" reason we will be able to resolve it and return to a state of peace and calm.

We are not aware of the fact that our brain is constantly searching for things for us to fear. Unaware we are hardwired to feel this way most of us assume it is our deficiency, our maladaptive way of relating to the circumstances of our life. We feel shame and inadequacy because we anxiously and inappropriately respond to life with the assumption that it is our inability to cope.

The Brain's Evolution

Over the past six-hundred million years our brain has evolved in three stages: the brain stem, the subcortical region that includes the hippocampus, and then the third, and most recent stage, the cortex, which sits on top.

On the webinar, Dr. Hanson stated, "Our three basic human needs, safety, satisfaction, and connection, are managed by overarching brain systems aimed to avoid harm, approach awards, and attach to others. The brain stem manages the ongoing survival/ maintenance of the body. The subcortical region includes the hypothalamus, the thalamus, the basal ganglia, the hippocampus, and the amygdala, and regulates the stress response. The human prefrontal cortex, which has roughly tripled in volume over the last three million years of evolution, is the seat of judgment and helps us regulate our attention, feelings, and desires.

So, long story short, any animal—whether it is a fruit fly or a human being–needs to be safe and avoid harm, needs to be satisfied and therefore approach rewards, and needs to, in one way or another, connect with others of its kind. When there is a basic sense of safety, satisfaction, and connection, the brain defaults to the responsive mode."

Dr. Hanson calls this the "green zone"." But when we default to what he refers to as the "red zone", the body burns resources faster than it takes them in. In terms of avoiding, approaching, and attaching, the mind is colored with a sense of fear, frustration, and heartache. In modern life, we are exposed to an on-going mild stress that Dr. Hanson refers to as the "pink zone". There is very little time to recover. Our nervous system never gets a chance to fully reset. We internalize this distress and *assume it is the result of our own dysfunction. We assume we are doing something wrong—that it is our fault.*

So the "red zone" tears us down, and the "green zone" builds us. But most of us exist in the "pink zone "where our brain is hardwired to be in a state of floating anxiety and fear. We are unaware of the source so we never know how to discharge the adrenalin of the stress. We get caught in a state of self-blame and self-recrimination. *And the field of psychology supports this perception. With all of its diagnoses, disorders, and maladaptive behaviors that field has inadvertently supported this annihilation of the trust in self by labeling everything as maladaptive and neurotic.*

Now *I believe this is huge because what this has essentially done is support the idea that unworthiness!*

Well, newsflash! It's not your fault.

In truth, it is your very nature to be suspicious and non-trusting. Your brain always defaults to negativity. It is hardwired to do so. So you have the capacity to respond positively, but this response has to be fostered, and it has to override the very nature of defensive reactivity.

Just take a moment to imagine what it would feel like if the next time you complained to someone about how awful you felt they turned to you and said, "Of course you feel lousy! It's not you! You are hardwired to feel lousy—you have to train your own heart, mind, body, and Soul to be positive, relaxed, and at ease."

My Seven-Layer Healing Process gives you the formula to do just that. It offers you the interactive tapping™ *sequences (supercharged with the new brain science language) that target rewiring the brain activity with deliberate intent.*

LAYER ONE: Empowering Your Adult Self

Whether you are wanting to: grieve the loss of a loved one (featured in Beyond Compassion), reestablish a healthy relationship with your body (the focus of *Soul Steps*), rewire your brain and teach your inner child the laws of the universe (presented in *Share the Gift*), deal with addictions and compulsions (the content of *The Four Stages of Recovery-Living Life Beyond Addictions and Fear*), or heal a fragment of your Soul which has been addressed in *Which Lifetime Is This Anyway*), you need to be in an empowered state to do so. If you begin digging into your past pain with no fresh method to respond to that pain, you simply pull off the band-aid of an old wound while offering no hope of healing it.

In order to regain trust, and thus heal, you must establish that part of you that can respond in a nurturing and healthy manner. That part of you can orchestrate a sequential progression of tapping and meditative exercises. The healing agent for your old wounds is this very interaction between the wounded parts of you and this empowered Adult Self that can respond with compassion, love, and care. So that is where we begin. We begin by empowering your Adult Self.

A key ingredient in this empowerment is our ability to bring attention to events during which we felt confident and competent—when we indeed felt empowered. Recall of these incidents gives us a point of reference for empowerment. And if we cannot recall such experiences we invent them. Because, remember, our mind does not know the difference between what is real and what is imagined. Just as we program our future with intentions and pretend exercises, we can do the same thing by returning to the time of the wound and changing the experience of the part of us that holds onto the pain.

Again, the only reason this is possible, and I know I keep hammering on this point, but it is because it is so essential, is that you have attained the level of spiritual evolvement that enables you to intervene. You are finally, after decades, (and sometimes lifetimes) equipped to step into the original scene of the wound; and on behalf of the wounded one—protect, retrieve, and rescue him or her from the hurtful experience.

In my book, *Share the Gift*, there are a series of exercises that facilitate this process, but for the sake of this material, and so you can apply it to the focus presented here, I invite you to execute the following tapping sequence to once again clear your Adult Self for this journey. You have already worked with this sequence in the previous section, but I again include it because I strongly suggest you use this tapping sequence anytime you engage in your inner work. It enables you to get present, and when you are present your efforts are much more effective.

Exercise: Tapping Sequence to Clear the Adult Self

Begin by continuously tapping on the karate point while stating the following:

Even though there may be some things I am not totally in harmony with today, I choose, for this time, to suspend those feelings so I can now focus entirely on being present for this inner work.

So even though I may need to neutralize some general irritations, I am going to do that now because I am committed to clearing this up so I can be present for this work.

So even though I may not be in total harmony, I am willing to suspend any feelings that may distract me right now so I can be clear and open enough to be present for this work.

As before, you begin with the general neutralizing. It involves stating reminder phrases while you tap on the designated endpoints.

Neutralizing the Distraction—Reinforcing the Commitment to be Present

Eyebrow: Generally disturbed. A little bit antsy. Clear out any anger. Side of Eye: Clear out all distraction.

Under Eye: Any frustration. Upper Lip: A little bit fatigued.

Under the lip: But choose to feel empowered to do this work. Collarbone: Am excited to show up for this work.

Under Arm: Have committed to showing up to do this work.

Chest Bone: I feel empowered to respond–I am ready to be present and to begin to do this work.

Wrist: I ask my Higher Guidance to assist…

Top of Head: …so that I can move forward, clear this disturbance, and heal.

Now that you are present use the following exercise to attain a point of reference for your empowerment.

Exercise: Recalling-Inventing an Empowering Moment

Think of a recent time when you felt empowered. If you cannot recall an event, invent one. Pretend you felt empowered in a situation even if you did not. Bring in as many details of this real or, imagined event, as you can. Record your responses in your journal.

1. *See, sense, or feel, the experience.*
2. *Let yourself envision the situation. Notice as many details in your environment as you can. How does it feel?*
3. *What are your thoughts?*
4. *Embody this experience as much as you can and then try to hold it in your mind's eye for at least a minute.*

This gives your brain a chance to construct new neural pathways. The more you envision this empowering moment the more your brain will sustain it and build on it. Take a moment to record your experience. Then if you want more experience with this concept I encourage you to check out this TED TALK video presentation of Dr. Hanson. It will also inspire you to access this more empowered part of you.

Dr. Richard Hanson: Ted Talk in Marin, California

What I learned, when I studied the new Higher Brain Living model developed by Dr. Michael Cotton, is that this very exercise of concentrated recall (or invention—the mind doesn't know the difference) actually engages the Higher Brain or our prefrontal cortex—that new part of the brain recently discovered and previously discussed. It is this part of the brain that enables us, as our present-day self, to respond in a new way. It is this very discovery that is at the heart of neuro-plasticity—the new awareness that we can indeed change the way our brain processes input and experiences pain and joy! This discovery is a game-changer because it acknowledges our capacity to actually attain and sustain a new, more positive, paradigm.

Whatever experience you retrieved in this exercise you can now use as your base of empowerment. Holding the vibrational intensity and image of this empowered moment for at least 17 seconds gives your brain enough time to actually begin to build the neuro pathways needed to sustain this empowered state. Although ever-evolving, the more you can attain that vibration the more effective your ability to orchestrate the healing will be. Likewise, the more believable you are to the wounded ones the easier it will be to restore safety and trust.

Cathryn L. Taylor; MA; MFT; LADC

LAYER TWO: Externalizing the Pain—Separating From the Wounded One Within

Once the empowered Adult Self is clear you are more able to acknowledge the duality within which separates you in your empowerment from that fragile, wounded self. This ability to see these two parts of self enables you to separate from the wounded one so you can begin to respond and heal. You can be distant enough from those fight, flight, and freeze responses that kept you from taking risks and growing. But perhaps more importantly, you can also begin to appreciate how those very responses, fueled by your fear of not surviving, served a purpose. They did keep you safe until you could mature enough to develop new ways of coping. This maturity now enables you to see the relevance of the resistance and the necessary blocks. Those blocks enabled you to survive. They had value.

And once you see the relevance you cease feeling like a victim of your past. You can separate from that wounded one with appreciation and begin to very tenderly see how this very response to life, fueled by the fears of your frightened self, enabled you to survive. By acknowledging this you are better able to befriend your wounded one whose fears have been preventing you from getting what you want and deserve.

The turning point is when you can acknowledge that you are removed enough from the old issue that you can, in fact, see the value in the sabotage while simultaneously seeing there is no longer the need for it.

What is interesting is that it is this very willingness to admit to the discomfort of our fears that gives us the courage to be motivated to face those fears so we can change. That contrast and discomfort are what inspires us to do the work. It brings acknowledgment to the fact that there is something we want that we do not have. We are now inspired and feel safe enough as the Adult Self to explore the duality which blocks us from successfully achieving our goal. The courage to work with the dissonance of this duality through the process of separation is the focus of Layer Two.

To help clarify this dichotomy so you can neutralize this disparity

342

you need to give form to it. The following exercise will help you get started. You are first guided on how to write down on a piece of paper exactly what it is that you are trying to attract or allow, and then you are instructed to immediately record your knee-jerk response to what you just wrote. It is called the "weeding-out" exercise. The exercise itself was inspired by a book I read in the late seventies or early eighties, by, I believe, Sondra Ray. Unfortunately, I cannot remember which book, since that was a time of great exploration for me. But I remembered this exercise and have used it many times in my own work. It has helped me get clarity on this opposing dyad because you cannot detect what your resistance is to attracting something until you declare your desire to attract it. This very act flushes out the part of you who is put at risk because of your desire.

Exercise: The Weeding Out Process Explained

Please grab a piece of paper and pen and respond accordingly.

1. *Write a simple statement describing what you would like to manifest.*
2. *When you think about this desire what would be the most positive outcome of attaining it.*
3. *Why do you want to accomplish this goal—or attract this object or item?*
4. *How would your life be different?*
5. *Imagine how you feel once you have succeeded?*

Use the information from above to redesign what Lindsay Kenny calls your "ultimate truth statement". Include explicit feelings and concrete examples of what your life will look like once this outcome has occurred.

Example: "*I feel such joy and confidence knowing I am now employed by the Universe in this perfect job doing* _____. *I now fully enjoy the freedom to pursue my dreams, and I gleefully do so.*"

To identify your disparity take your journal or a piece of paper and write out your goal. What is it that you truly want—not how you will feel once you attain it, but just pure and simple–what is it that you want? Then record any negative statements which emerge the minute you acknowledge that desire. What is your immediate response—your inner dialogue?

This will give focus to your inner child's fears and the focus of what you will ultimately want to neutralize and release with your tapping. Use the two headings as a guide. Record your responses in the two columns.

Write your goal below: Write down any negative
                                     thoughts that follow:

1. _____
2. _____
3. _____
4. _____
5. _____
6. _____
7. _____
8. _____
9. _____
10. _____

The next tapping sequence will begin your work with these two parts of self—the wounded one and the healer within who can respond.

This is central to my approach in that it focuses on the Adult Self being strong enough to accept the feelings and doubts of the wounded one, and thus reinforces the development of self-love. You are able to put a face to the part within you who fears growth, is unable to trust, may be looking for a fight, and has most likely lost faith. You begin to separate from him or her as you "externalize" these feelings. When you externalize the disturbance, you set up a dyad between the part of you who carries the wound and the part of you who can respond to the wound.

Note: Sometimes the Adult Self has antagonistic feelings towards a fragile self and these would need to be neutralized before you can be effective. If we have not separated enough from the pain of our wound then we can detest that part of us who holds that fear. We judge him or her as "needy." We see this part of us as just standing in our way of getting what we want. The stronger our negative reaction is to this set of feelings and this part of self, the longer it will take for us to heal. If we cannot embrace this part of self by understanding the source of its fears then we perpetuate this disconnect and eclipse our own ability to manifest what we desire. We need to heal this dissonance if we are to move into a trusting and compassionate relationship with the most frightened part of self. It is the only way we can find the harmony within that allows us to move forward and create the life we desire and deserve.

To proceed, take a moment to review the discomfort you felt when you did the "weeding out" exercise. Revisit that ambivalence as you get in touch with your contrasting feelings about loving yourself enough and feeling safe enough, to allow yourself to get what you want. Again, know that this is the voice of a wounded one who needs to feel accepted and secure. Only when you can separate from this part of you, and respond, will your pursuit not threaten him or her.

The set of tapping sequences that accompany this Layer will assist you in doing just this. You will be separating from your inner child so you can "externalize" his or her feelings and be in a position to respond. This externalization of the disturbance sets up the dyad between the part of you who carries the wound and the part of you who can respond to the wound. *You will be using* the pronoun "he" or "she" to begin the separation process.

Exercise: *Separating from the Resistance*

State the setup phrase while tapping on the karate point.

Even though a part of me feels fearful of opening up and trusting again, I know this is only a part of me, and I love myself and this wounded one enough to be willing to respond to his or her pain.

Even though a part of me is really fearful of trusting, and steps in and sabotages my efforts to feel safe, I now choose to work with that part of self, to help him or her heal, I truly do love that part of self, and I understand that its efforts are in response to its fears.

So even though this part of me is trying to distract my Adult Self from achieving my ultimate goal, I am ready to respond to his or her needs because I love myself and that part of me enough to heal.

That completes the setup phrases. You are now ready to proceed with the reminder phrases.

Remember you are speaking about your inner child in the second person because it facilitates the separation process and establishes the fact that there are these two parts of you which need to interact if the healing is to occur. If you find yourself using "I" when you refer to this pain you will simply be collapsing into the younger one's feelings, and there will be no one on board who can respond.

Continue to repeat the reminder phrases until you move through any resistance to your being willing to separate from, and therefore respond to, this part of you.

NEUTRALIZING THE NEGATIVITY

Eyebrow: He or she experiences such distrust.
Side of Eye: So fearful ... and unable to feel safe.
Under Eye: Has been so abandoned ... has so much fear.
Upper Lip: He or she is afraid to open up and trust.
Under the Lip: He or she just cannot feel safe enough to trust.
Collarbone: So wounded... so afraid to reach out and trust.
Under Arm: He or she cannot imagine feeling safe.
Chest Bone: So big is this wound.
Wrist: The shame, the abandonment, the lack of trust.
Top of Head: Wonder if I will ever be able to gain his or her trust.

INTRODUCING THE POSSIBILITY OF CHANGE

Eyebrow: Maybe he or she doesn't have to feel so bad?

Side of Eye: Maybe I can help him or her to once again feel safe.
Under Eye: Maybe I can help to restore his or her faith.

Upper Lip: Maybe I can help him or her to feel enough trust to let go of the fear.

Under the Lip: Really want to help him or her let it go.

Collarbone: Maybe he or she can let it go ... maybe it doesn't have to be this bad.

Under Arm: Maybe I can forgive myself and help him or her to let it go.

Chest Bone: Maybe my faith can help him or her feel safe. Wrist: Maybe I can finally exchange this fear for faith.

Top of Head: I really do want to respond so he or she can once again feel safe.

Affirming the Conviction

Eyebrow: I am going to help ... help him or her let go of this fear. Side of Eye: I am so glad to release this lack of trust and faith.

Under Eye: Help him or her let go so he or she can feel safe. Upper Lip: I can feel compassion and help him or her release. Under the Lip: I really do feel compassion for him or her.

Collarbone: Every cell in my body feels the compassion I need.

Under Arm: The compassion to feel forgiveness for myself and him or her.

Chest Bone: Every cell vibrates with compassion and joy. Wrist: Every cell within me is willing to heal.

Top of Head: I can finally assist in replacing this fear with trust.

Continue to work with these sequences until you feel complete with this separation and can clearly experience the duality of the part of you who is in fear and the part of you who is ready to respond.

Once you are separate, you are ready to address the inner child directly. The exercises, meditations, and interactive tapping™ sequences included in Layer Three assist you in building the trust with your wounded one. They assure the inner child that you do recognize his or her pain and are willing to help him or her heal. Once done, you actually, in Layer Four, will escort the child back to the wound and use the exercises to clear it in his or her time.

LAYER THREE: Building a Relationship with the Wounded One Within

This Layer is really the heart of inner child work. Once you have separated from this part of yourself, you can truly begin to relate to him or her and respond to the fear of success. This is the true essence of building a trusting relationship between your most illuminated and nurturing self and the wounded self. It is essential to ascertain the issues this inner child has with trusting you to make him or her feel safe. Before you can clear feelings from the past it is necessary to clear issues he or she may have with you in relation to the perceived abandonment and betrayal of his or her trust.

How do you, in current time, abandon your inner child and violate his or her trust in you?

You abandon this fragile part of self every time you collapse into fear, shame, or judgment, and leave him or her unprotected with no new way of being able to cope. Every time you forget that "this is now and not then" you leave that part of you in the dust. Every time you collapse you leave that inner child to deal with the current situation with the coping mechanisms he or she had at the time of the original wound. It is the vibration of abandonment that puts your inner child at risk and leaves him or her feeling violated and abused by you.

It's difficult to entertain the reality of this self-abuse. But you have acquired new skills. Your brain has developed in such a way that you can respond differently. You are no longer dependent on others to keep you safe. When you emotionally collapse you forget who you are in present time and you regress to that time when you see the present threat through the eyes of this most fragile self. It is for this reason that Layer Two is so very, very important. That separation is the perpetual task. All of us slide back into those old coping mechanisms. But the more we can separate from the past and respond, the healthier we become, and the more successful we are, at getting what we desire and deserve.

To assist you in building this internal relationship between these two parts of you I will be introducing you to a sequence referred to as "surrogate tapping"… tapping on behalf of another. In this sequence, you will be using the pronoun "you." Addressing the inner child in this fashion reinforces the separation between you as the healer and the inner child as the wounded part within. This reinforcement creates that internal experience for the wounded aspect to finally feel that someone notices his or her vulnerability. It is honoring the fact that this part within needs to experience visibility and safety if he or she will ever again feel trust.

As was already mentioned, he or she may even feel betrayed by you. All of these feelings need to be flushed out so you can be effective and believable in your interaction. By responding to his or her pain, and operating on this little one's behalf, you enhance the experience of deservedness and nourish a sense of importance. This exemplifies the art of truly accepting yourself—accepting all the parts of you–just as you are.

Exercise: Meet your Inner Child:

Begin by taking a moment to connect with the wounded one with whom you are working at this time. You do this by first closing your eyes. Take a deep breath and then tune into the younger part of you who carries this fear. Imagine you invite him or her to sit beside you, or even to jump upon your lap. Create a "live" inner dialogue—speak to this part of self as if it were an actual child. Draw from your adult experiences of speaking to the children in your life. Engage your imagination. Remember, your mind does not know the difference between what is real and imagined. Let this interaction flow.

Record your response in your journal.

When you respond to this part of self in this way you are capitalizing on the interactive dialogue which assists you in creating a loving and nurturing relationship with your fragile one. Part of loving yourself is learning to love this part within you. If you want to be loved by others you have to begin by loving your selves ... all of your selves!

This interactive guided imagery is simply a proven way to personify the feelings of your past by giving a face to the statements you already hear in your head. Reflect for a moment on that inner dialogue that goes on every time you try to step forward to get what you want. Most often you are either barraged by the fear of the judgments of others or riddled with inner doubts—both of which are expressions of the fears of your inner child. It is this dynamic that derails the manifestation of your dreams and keeps you stuck in a state of unworthiness and self-hate.

The following interactive imagery circumvents this pattern. Tapping through this dynamic gives you a way to 1) acknowledge the fears of the fragile self, 2) assure the inner child that as an adult you have learned how to cope with the fears, and 3) affirm your intention to do so. This interactive tapping™ sequence enables you to develop a viable and trusting relationship with this part of self so you are free to dream without fear or doubt.

When you feel you have a grasp of this dynamic, close your eyes, go into your mind's eye, and simply imagine that you explain to your little one, as you would to any child, that what you are going to be doing may look a little weird. Treat your inner child in the same manner with which you would treat a biological child. Assure him or her that it is a process that will help him or her feel better and heal. It is important to include this step of explanation every time you work with this Layer because each time you do so you may be dealing with a different inner child. The link below will give you an audio example of the flow of this sequence.

Tapping Sequence: Winning the Trust of the Inner Child

When you feel ready, begin to state the following setup phrases while tapping on the karate point.

Even though you are fearful of opening up and trusting me, I love you and I love myself enough to be willing to respond to your pain.

Even though my desires and dreams illuminate your fears, I am willing

350

to work with your lack of trust so you can climb aboard and together we can heal.

So even though I want to allow myself to attract my desires, I know this puts you at risk, but I am willing to soothe these fears so together we can heal.

Reword this in whatever way works for you, but state the setup phrases so you set your psyche up to begin to do this interactive process. As you begin to envision this internal dialogue you will begin to heal.

As before, the sequences begin with the neutralization process; move into the possibility of change, and complete with the conviction to resolve this inner child's fears of not trusting or feeling safe. Use these as an example, but you may need to work with this in a little more personal manner ... so do not be shy to make up your own reminder phrases that suit your needs more specifically. To effectuate this interaction you use the pronoun, "you."

Neutralizing the Negativity

Eyebrow: Afraid, so afraid to trust...

Side of Eye: So many triggers... you carry so much fear... Under Eye: I am here to help you heal...

Upper Lip: I promise to help you feel safe...

Under the Lip: I know you are afraid to trust, but I vow to help you feel safe...

Collarbone: You witnessed so much... so much fear and mistrust...
Under Arm: So afraid to feel trust...

Chest Bone: All these years ...

Wrist: So many triggers for your fear and mistrust... Top of Head: So much fear ... so afraid to trust.

Introducing the Possibility of Change

Eyebrow: But maybe you can trust me.

Side of Eye: Maybe you will let me help you heal. Under Eye: Maybe you will learn to trust me.

Upper Lip: Just take the risk and see if this works. Under the Lip: I invite you to come along.

Collarbone: I promise you I will not let you down. Under Arm: I just invite you to work with me.

Chest Bone: Please look ... I really have healed.

Wrists: I am so ready to show up ... I do deserve your trust.

Top of Head: I am really excited to work with you on this. And if I do collapse and let you down I promise I will admit my fault, get the help I need so together we can heal.

Affirming the Conviction

Eyebrow: Trust me I really do feel a connection to you.

Side of Eye: I guarantee you I am trustworthy and can help you heal. Under Eye: I am willing to come back to your time.

Upper Lip: I WILL come to you. I can teach you how to neutralize your fears ... so together we can heal.

Under the Lip: I am so excited that you are willing to try. Collarbone: I am so excited we get to work on this together.

Under Arm: I am so excited you are willing to trust me to show up. Chest Bone: I am so excited that together we can heal.

Wrists: I love that we have been reunited.

Top of Head: I am so thankful that together you and I can heal.

While repeating your reminder phrases, do sequential rounds on the endpoints until you move through any resistance this wounded one holds. Stay with it until he or she can be responsive to your efforts to help it heal. You will sense this part moving from doubt, fear, shame, or betrayal, into perhaps anger that it took you so long, then into a willingness to believe, and finally into an eagerness to try tapping for itself.

If new feelings emerged in response to these reminder phrases, tap on them as well. Customize your sequences until you get completely clear, and when you are ready, move into the Fourth Layer of healing–the Layer where you release and let go.

LAYER FOUR: Helping Your Inner Child Heal

In the Fourth Layer of healing, you shift into a meditative state and begin to teach your inner child, or wounded one, the interactive tapping™ technique for this neutralizing process. You continue your work with this inner child by again *inviting him or her to sit beside you, or even to jump upon your lap. Once you have this fragile one's attention explain that you want to teach the tapping process so he or she can feel safe enough to participate in releasing and letting go. It is this relationship you must heal before you can truly make your life work.*

Exercise: Meditation to Escort your Inner Child Back to the Wound

Return to your mind's eye. Ask your wounded one to take you back to the time and place when he or she first developed fears and doubts and . began to feel unsafe. You will most likely be taken back to the moment of your essential wound. Even though there may be experiences which built on this, if you can get back to the core it is easier to pull the cord and orchestrate a complete healing of your past. Be prepared that this little one might even begin by taking you back to an experience in which you, as an adult, were the cause of its fear. If that occurs, neutralize that first and end the sequence with an apology. The audio recording below will give you a few more instructions on how to prepare your inner child and Adult Self for this healing.

Exercise: Connecting with the Inner Child

If you need more prompting, continue your dialogue with your inner child. Inquire about past situations where he or she felt abandoned or experienced a lack of trust and faith. Get more specifics. Who was involved? What did he or she hear or witness that resulted in so much fear, sadness, and pain? Spend time really exploring this past situation so you will be able to more effectively respond. You may want to record your exchanges in a journal so you have a record of them. Also seeing your responses on paper can bring you even more clarity which will enable you to use the worksheet found at the end of this section to design your own statements and customize your sequences in a way that will target your exact issues.

But the key to this healing is building on the understanding you acquired in Layer Three—that every time you collapse into the fear and act from this part of you, it is experienced by this inner child as abandonment or betrayal. This fragile part of self is longing for safety and has been waiting to be protected, loved, and cherished. As you progress in your work you will be able to recognize this more easily and respond more quickly. Knowing how to embrace grief, as you did in the previous sections, will help because a great deal of this healing has to do with moving through the anxiety, bargaining, anger, and despair—as you strive to attain resolution. For this reason, I recommend you refer back to the previous section on the Five Stages of Grief often-—into the way you live your life, and it will enhance, not only your recovery but your evolution as well.

Exercise: Preparation for Inviting your Inner Child to Speak the Truth–

The first task in this healing is to invite the inner child to speak his or her truth. When you are ready, close your eyes and become receptive to listen.

In your mind's eye return to the scene where the wounding took place. Pause and observe the situation for a minute. Observe what is taking place in the scene. Then freeze the scene and pull your wounded one to the side. Invite him or her to either sit on your lap or sit cross-legged in front of you. It is time for your little one to speak the truth. Build on the experience of that last sequence when this little one watched as you tapped. Explain, if necessary, how tapping works to reduce the fear and pain so he or she can feel free and secure enough to prepare to speak the truth. The first tapping sequence addresses this readiness. All he or she needs to do is to repeat what you say and tap where you tap. Speaking the truth while tapping together will help the pain to go away. Assure this little one it is safe to finally say what really happened.

When you sense the connection has been made, prepare to do the tapping sequence provided below. In the first round, you use the pronoun "I" but it is spoken from the consciousness of the inner child—not the Adult Self. If you speak it from the adult consciousness you are collapsing into the truth and there is no one present to respond to the inner child's pain. So imagine that both you and your inner child are tapping on the karate point as you use the pronoun "I" to state the setup phrase which captures the inner child's truth. Then envision him or her tapping with you and repeating after you if he or she is willing. If not, just imagine the little one tapping along to your words. Determine if these statements need to be customized to fit your inner child's specific needs. If so, give yourself the freedom to do so. You can do no wrong. Tailor these sequences to fit this specific situation. In the infinite wisdom of your psyche, no matter what words are used, the message will be delivered just as your system needs it to be.

Begin by tapping on the karate point as you state these setup phrases. Even though I am really afraid to once again trust ... I have been so badly hurt in the past... I know you love me and I love myself enough to trust you to help me heal.

Even though this is really scary for me ... and I am afraid to see the hurtful truth ... I feel safe enough with you to trust it will all be okay.

So even though moving ahead causes great fear ... I am willing to experiment with this tapping while telling my truth because I trust you enough to keep me safe.

These are only examples of your setup statements. Again, customize them to meet your needs and, when you feel complete, move into the neutralization sequences. I provide samples but, again, feel free to experiment with designing your own statements.

As you will see, the sequencing gradually helps you identify the origin of the disturbance, and then assists you in moving into the possibility of letting that go ... the possibility that something really can be different ... that this wound really can be healed. The sequences then end with the conviction that it is safe to let it go and once again feel faith and trust. Follow this to get a feel for this Layer, but, if it feels right to do so, experiment with your own words as well.

Neutralizing the Negativity

> *Eyebrow: So much pain in this scene ... just remember feeling so unsafe ... so wounded and unable to trust.*
>
> *Side of Eye: Seldom felt safe.*
>
> *Under Eye: Always feared being left ... afraid I would not be safe. Upper Lip: I remember the pain ... I am so afraid to once again open up and trust.*
>
> *Under the Lip: Seldom felt safe ... so afraid to let go and feel trust. Collarbone: I was so abandoned ... left alone to fend for myself.*
>
> *Under Arm: Wish they could just love me as I am. Chest Bone: So much fear ... will I ever be able to trust? Wrist: Wish I wasn't so afraid ...*
>
> *Top of Head: Just don't know if it is safe to trust.*

Another round...

> *Eyebrow: All that I heard was that I had too many needs.*
>
> *Side of Eye: Never felt safe ... always feared being left or abused. Under Eye: Always so afraid I would not survive.*
>
> *Upper Lip: What if I am not good enough to be loved? Under the Lip: That's how I feel ... when I look back. Collarbone: Just wish I could have felt safe.*
>
> *Under Arm: I get so afraid of being hurt. Chest Bone: So afraid to trust.*
>
> *Wrist: Don't want to be hurt or left.*
>
> *Top of Head: Just so afraid if I trust I will again be hurt.*

Introducing the Possibility of Change

> *Eyebrow: But maybe this can finally change... Side of Eye: Maybe I can finally feel safe.*
>
> *Under Eye: I have always felt so much fear. Upper Lip: But maybe it is safe to trust.*

Under the Lip: Maybe I can let this tension go.

Collarbone: Maybe my Adult Self is really here to help me heal this pain.

Under Arm: Maybe I can let go of my need for Mom and Dad's love. Chest Bone: Maybe I don't have to carry this tension that I do not deserve.

Wrist: Maybe I can let go.

Top of Head: Maybe it is safe to finally trust.

Conviction of Change

Eyebrow: I am going to let go and let my Adult Self in ...

Side of Eye: I am going to let go ... tell my story ... speak the truth about my past.

Under Eye: I am willing to let this go and trust my Adult Self.

Upper Lip: I am willing to let go and let God. Under the Lip: I know I have carried this for so long. Collarbone: But I am willing to let it go.

Under Arm: I am willing to trust my Adult Self might be different than the other adults in my life.

Chest Bone: I am willing to give it a try.

Wrist: I feel really good about joining forces with the Adult Self. Top of Head: I am ready to let it go so I can heal.

Exercise: Follow-up to the Meditation:

Follow this tapping by closing your eyes and going into a meditation in which you continue to work with this inner child. Stay present in this imagery until he or she is ready to let go and can fully begin to trust you by speaking the truth. Imagine supporting this little one, holding him or her while the story is finally revealed.

You can imagine rocking this little one back and forth, or you can continue to tap your way through the story as a way to neutralize the pain. You can also do so by simply writing out the inner child's story. Just move in and out of it as you are inspired to do so. Usually, when I use writing or journaling to process the inner child's pain, I again recommend you use your least-dominant hand to speak his or her truth. The inner child's experience tends to be purer because the rational or conscious mind is so busy focusing on the logistics of the writing itself that the inner child does not tend to get shut down by old paradigms internalized from childhood. Once done, I usually let that inner child speak its truth while tapping on my endpoints. This neutralizes the emotion of the story.

As with any issue, you will sense this little one moving through the stages of grief—the anxiety and fear, the bargaining in an attempt to feel safe and to feel trust, the anger that emerges when this did not take place, and ultimately the collapse into the total despair of abandonment and shame.

The most effective way to work with this Layer is to walk this part of you through all of these stages of grief until he or she is once again willing to trust you will keep him or her safe. This wounded one really does want to trust that you will still be mindful of his or her needs. He or she needs to believe you can set limits and keep him or her safe even when you are involved in the affairs of your day-to-day life. So in this Layer, you continue to explore what your inner child's experience is around this issue. Tap and neutralize those feelings from every angle. Eventually, you WILL win back his or her trust. Be patient. This often takes more than one sequence, and more than one day, sometimes even more than one lifetime. But this meditation will give you a start. I also recommend you refer back to the exercises on helping the inner child grieve presented in Section Six. When you feel you have healed this part enough to proceed to the next step, then do so.

But keep in mind that your healing will be progressive. Release happens in layers and expansion spirals upwards. You clear one layer. You experience a reprieve. Then another layer presents itself. That's why the process is compared to the peeling of an onion. You cannot resolve the inner layer without going through each of the subsequent layers before it. As long as you are open to growing there will always be another layer to resolve. If you are dealing with your life multidimensionally then your block may take you into past lives as it did me in my Story of Antoinette.

The point is that evolution is endless. The deep patterns do smooth out, and at some point, you find yourself more committed to the process itself instead of striving so much for a certain outcome or conclusion.

This marks the moment when you truly become a student of your pain instead of its victim.

But for now, with this Layer, once the healing has occurred, you are ready to merge back with the inner child and celebrate the reunion that has enabled you both to heal.

LAYER FIVE: Forgive, Make Peace so you can Recommit

Layer Five is when you really begin to feel the rewards of your hard work because it is with these sequences that you begin to reunite that which has been severed. The process presented below is used only for the integration of an inner child. If, as was the case in the Story of Antoinette, you have uncovered a pattern which involves a fragment of your Soul, then, once healed, you want to just envision that fragment being escorted back to the Light so that energy can be freed. But with an aspect of your personality from this lifetime (the inner child), you want to partner with him or her and build a bonding, cooperative, relationship. Layer Five assists you in accomplishing this goal.

In these sequences, you use the pronoun, "we," which enables you to begin to establish the merger and integration with your inner child. Partnering with your fragile one in this manner empowers him or her to return to your force field in a healed state. It empowers you to help your inner child reclaim the magic that was lost in the wounding experience. When you bring this magic back, the essence of trust and wonderment we all had as children returns as well.

Again, for *Layer Five, you use the pronoun "we" because you are stating the sequences as if the inner child and the Adult Self are saying them in unison. The following recording will give you a taste as to how this looks. But I have included a tapping sequence you can read as well.*

Exercise: *The Merger between Adult and Child*

When ready, state the setup phrase while tapping on the karate point. Even though we have both experienced a lot of betrayals ... have reasons to not feel trust ... have experienced a great deal of tension about not feeling safe, being left ... feeling unsure we would survive ... we are so relieved and excited that we have found each other again ... and we are so willing to love ourselves and each other enough to trust we can manifest all that we desire and deserve.

Even though we both have experienced so many disappointments, betrayals and reasons to not trust, we are so excited to have finally been reunited and are now able to feel safe enough with each other so we can begin to heal.

So even though we have so many experiences of abandonment, so many reasons to not trust ... we are so excited we have found each other ... we have come home to each other and together we are ready to heal.

The above is an example of the setup phrases you can use for this merger, but please always feel free to customize them and make them fit your particular situation. The following is an example of the reminder phrases you could use to augment this reunion. It is really not so much of a process of neutralization as it is an infusion of what you have affirmed. I have provided one round to help you come together in this fashion. The recording above will also offer guidance, but please use your imagination to embellish your meditations or your tapping sequences whenever you feel it would be useful.

Again, prepare to tap by beginning at the corner of your eyebrow.
Eyebrow: We are so excited to come together and heal.

Side of Eye: We are just buzzing with enthusiasm and trust for each other.

Under Eye: So excited we are going to finally manifest our heart's desire.

Upper Lip: Through the love for each other and the love of God, we know we deserve all we desire.

Under the Lip: We are so excited to come together to heal.

Collarbone: So excited we are together to create the relationship with each other we deserve.

Under Arm: We are so full of energy, love, and Light ... this reunion serves us as well as the world.

Chest Bone: We are so excited we have done such good work.

Top of Head: We are so proud of each other and love each other so much.

Now just keep going with that tapping, adding your own sequences as you see fit, until you are really, really buzzing with the vibration of this joy.

Again, once you have that "buzz" going, hold that vibration for at least 68 seconds. As is depicted in this YouTube video, Teachings of Abraham on-68 Seconds, *holding this emotional charge for 68 seconds gives the Universe the time it needs to begin to gather the necessary components for your intention of this merger to take form.*

When you feel ready to proceed—move on to Layer Six in which you will reprogram your DNA so the healing can be complete.

LAYER SIX: Reprogramming the DNA of the Body

No healing is complete until you clear the energy and pattern from your body. Before we move forward I want to preface this next set of tapping sequences with an interesting quote I found on the website of Carol Look (EFT Master) about your body. It substantiates this point. "Whenever we have been traumatized, hurt, betrayed or scared, our body records the feelings on an energetic and cellular level. As the well-known trauma specialist, Bessel Van der Kolk says, 'Your body keeps the score. When we have a car accident, the bruises or broken bones are evident, physical, visible to the eye and painful when touched. When we cut ourselves with a knife or burn ourselves in the kitchen, the scars can last indefinitely—proof that yes, we endured, yet, made it through a hardship of some kind. But when we've been screamed at, abandoned, or threatened, we have no visible "scars" to see or show others. Our bodies do indeed make and keep excellent records of these incidents in our electricity and our energy fields." (carollookeft.com)

The pain does not go away—the patterns do not change if we do not have the methods to clear the energy from our bodies. In Share the Gift, which fully develops each of these layers of healing, there are a series of processes you can use for this reprogramming. For the purposes of this introduction to this *Seven-Layer Healing Process,* I provide you with meditations and tapping sequences that will help you get started.

You first clear the energetic disturbance, then ask for your body's forgiveness, and finally give your body permission to release and let go. The tension and stress can be replaced with a sense of relaxation and calm. You move from what Dr. Hanson referred to as the "red or pink zone" to the "green zone". The DNA in every cell is reprogrammed. Each cell can then hold an infusion of the new energetic vibration.

I encourage you to experiment with the wording as much as your imagination will allow. Make sure, however, to proceed to this reprogramming each time you and your inner child have experienced a healing, or have done a piece of work. Only then will your body be receptive to this infusion. The reprogramming is only as effective as your energy system will allow.

When disparity does emerge (and it will because you are ever-evolving) then tap it away before you continue. I have included an example of an audio and text infusion, but please experiment. Try it on every feeling you think you have stored in your body that now eclipses your ability to attract your heart's desire.

I also encourage you to explore the benefits of EMDR and TRE which I mentioned earlier. I have found both of these practices useful in ridding the body of the tension left from unresolved traumas. Each of them, in their own unique way, assists the body in completing stress responses that got frozen in an event that could not be properly resolved.

EXERCISE: Reprogramming the DNA of the Body (Use this recording to guide you in this infusion but you have the text below as well.)

Before you begin, consider doing one round of tapping to clear any current triggers in your Adult Self and to neutralize any current disturbances that may inhibit your ability ot give your body permission to release. *State the setup phrase while tapping on the karate point. Imagine you are speaking directly to your body.*

Setup for the Clearing

Even though I have needed you, my dear body, to store my pain, I am now strong enough to process this residue myself. I am now able, with full confidence, to finally instruct you on how to release the tension and the stress. With great gratitude, I invite you to finally let it go.

So even though, my dear body, you diligently held the many feelings of tension related to my fears and my not feeling safe, I am now able to do for myself what you, for so many years, have done on my behalf. I can now, with full confidence, give you complete permission to let it all go.

And even though I know I had little choice back then ... I really did not know what else to do ... but for this I now choose to forgive myself ... and in turn, ask you to forgive me as well. I do humbly apologize for needing you to hold this disturbance for me for so long ... but I now give you total permission to release it and let it go. I firmly commit to you that I will now neutralize and dissolve all disturbances related to my lack of trust and my inability to feel safe. I am so appreciative of all you did on my behalf.

Repeat these setup phrases until you feel you have moved through all the resistance your body is storing for you. Really sincerely give your body permission to release what it has held. Reassure it that you are now completely willing to use the tools you have acquired to deal with whatever comes your way.

As with all of these processes, the release is progressive. Each time you engage in this healing another block in your body will let go. Once you have cleared what can be cleared in this round you are ready to tap in a new program. When replenishing your body with a new vibration you are, in essence, reprogramming the DNA of every cell by infusing it with your new intention. To do this I suggest you gently tap on what is called your "sore spots". They are located on your chest, several inches from your collarbone, and can be found by slowly tapping and putting pressure on this area of your body. You will know when you have hit the right spots for they will be a little tender.

As you tap on this two sore spots begin to tell the story of your new intention. Continue to tap again for at least those 68 seconds while you feel the "buzz" (emotional charge) of your infusion. As I suggested earlier, it is this emotional "buzz" that energetically reprograms each cell. And again, according to the Teachings of Abraham, holding that "buzz" for these 68 seconds gives the Universe enough time to start to gather the necessary components to solidify what you intend and the process of manifestation can begin. The following is an example of how your affirmation might flow.

Meditation: The Affirmation for the Infusion

While tapping in a narrative fashion on the sore spots state something like this:

I now envision compassion and safety radiating from every cell of my body to every area of my life. All my needs and wants are fully realized in the presence of the Light. I am so fortunate to experience such acceptance and unconditional love. I feel so safe and am willing to respond with respect and love. Every area of my life is enriched with this sense of acceptance. Every cell is vibrating with the pure essence of joy.

This new vibration radiates out to all I attract. I absolutely love the rewards my actions bring back. I radiate unconditional love, and this vibration attracts the perfect people into my life; the perfect job, ample abundance, and harmony in all my endeavors. I am safe to be present in my body. I trust I can cope so my body does not have to take on my pain.

I am rich with experiences of love and Light. I see the magic of the Universe everywhere I look. I am truly a worthwhile being, and I exude that worthiness in every act! I am perfect in mind, body, heart, and Soul! I deserve to be loved. I trust enough to allow all that I want to be created in my life.

Then complete this infusion by tapping on the endpoints while stating reminder phrases such as those included below which anchor this into your body, mind, heart, and Soul.

Eyebrow: My body has held onto all of this fear and mistrust.
Eyebrow: This fear of abandonment ... betrayal, and mistrust

that my body has stored because I didn't know how to process the emotions and feel safe.

Under Eye: My body has held onto this fear and mistrust ... this lack of safety and fear to love.

Nose: But I now give my body permission to let go.

Chin: I release all of this mistrust, fear of abandonment, and inability to feel safe.

Collarbone: My body is now reprogrammed with faith and trust.

Chest Bone: Every cell now holds this new DNA vibration of compassion and love.

Wrist: My body forgives me ...

Under Arm: ... and vibrates with unconditional love.

Top of Head: I am so glad my body can finally let go and vibrate with safety and trust.

Repeat these sequences and modify according to your need until you feel a release in your body.

Exercise: "Meditation on Reconfiguring your Electromagnetic Field around You"

In your mind's eye see, sense, or feel this vibration you have just tapped in ... imagine the healing Light all around you. Make the command that the electromagnetic field around you is now recalibrated to hold this new intention and vibration. The recalibration enables you to better connect with your Divine Self, Inner Being, Higher Self. Breathe this experience in. Feel every cell in your body in its aliveness. Know that the neuropathways in your brain have been reconstructed to hold this new paradigm. For now, the healing is done!

LAYER SEVEN: Giving Back to the World

The final Layer of the *Seven-Layer Healing Process* invites you to share your healing with the world. Mother Earth also needs an infusion of compassionate, unconditional regard. Use the recording and the text below to take all you have neutralized and realigned and send this energy into the Universe as an offering for planetary healing. When you do this it *dissolves isolation and contributes not only to the increasing of the Light on the planet but also to the healing of Mother Earth.* It reinforces the fact that you are part of something bigger than yourself and a valuable agent of change for mankind. *You have shared the gift with your inner child and the fragments of your Soul. You now have an opportunity to share it with the world.*

Again, I encourage you to experiment with the wording as much as your imagination will allow. Just keep tapping and saying affirming statements. I have included a written example, as well as the audio version above, but please experiment, and try it on everything. Make sure, however, you use this only after you have experienced the reunion between your Adult Self and inner child, and the release in your body because you want the energy you send out into the world to be as pure as possible.

Exercise: Meditation on Giving Back

Enter into a meditative state. When you feel ready, begin again to tap on your sore spots while you say something like:

I feel so fortunate to have done this work. I now envision the cylinder of Light running from the center of Mother Earth to the grid of unconditional love about 60 feet above my head. This cylinder is filled with Healing Light.

I am so full of this Light and illuminated energy. From this highest place within myself, I now offer 10% of this healing back to heal the planet. I gift it to Mother Earth to use in her healing the energy wherever it is needed on the planet. I then contribute 10% of this healing to the mandala of transformation that cloaks the planet, making it available to all who choose to tap into this healing energy and use it for their own expansion and growth.

I feel so fortunate I have been able to complete this work and am so grateful I am now in a position to share this gift. I love feeling safe. I love contributing this sense of safety to the world. Thank you, God, Goddess, Higher Power, Angels, Masters, and all above, for your support and direction. Thank you for your support in my feeling safe. Thank you, fragments of my Soul, for having the courage and fortitude to call me back to you in all dimensions of time and consciousness. And thank you my dear little ones for having the patience to await my return.

I love that we are healed and have methods to continue the ever-evolving healing within and without. I can now hold the Light which allows all within me to attract all that we choose. I so appreciate that we can now contribute to the expansion of this world in a supportive and safe way. Thank you, Thank you. Thank you.

This is, again, but an example. As you work in this fashion, the inspiration will come to you ... the words will come to you. But always keep in mind, as you go forward, that when you, as the Adult Self, are secure in knowing that no matter what happens you will not abandon this inner child, he or she will trust you ... will not feel at risk ... and will not need to sabotage your efforts to attract all that you desire and deserve. *The sequence you just stated simply augments your willingness to allow yourself to receive because you are able to accept who you are and have learned how to share this gift with the children within you.*

Whether it is harmony and peace, resolution of your grief, a renewed relationship with your body, the attraction of that intimate relationship, abundance, or right livelihood, when you are no longer being sabotaged by your inner child's fears, or high-jacked by the unresolved bleed-throughs from your Soul's past, you are free to **observe** the abundance, love, grace, and beauty of the world. Then, based on the simple law of attraction, what you observe, you attract— what you conceive, you achieve. You naturally begin to manifest grace, beauty, success, and abundance in ALL areas of your life.

But this can only happen when the fragments of your Soul have been healed and returned to the Light and when you and your inner child are one. My *Seven-Layer Healing Process* provides a map for you to confidently chart the course for your continuing journey of expansion, evolution, and growth.

The last worksheet I want to give you is a formula for designing your own tapping sequences. You can do no wrong with tapping, but having a formula with which you can work empowers you even more with this process.

APPENDIX

Designing Your Own
Unique Sequences:

THIS WORKSHEET IS provided so you can begin to design the sequences that will more effectively target your specific concerns. Play with it until you can make the process of tapping your own. Always begin by getting a sense of where you are at and where you want to go. What is your concern? How do you feel about that concern? And how do you want to feel about this concern? That way, you design statements that reflect the challenge, the goal and the conviction of a new response. Once you get comfortable with creating your own sequences this tool will become one of your mostimportant remedies for distress.

Focus for the Tapping Setup: When you are designing the setup phrases for this tapping sequence you may want to revisit or redo to the weeding-out exercise you did in the previous section. This will give you an idea of what your goal is in this tapping. Then use the reminder phrases to address all of the aspects of your concern.

When you you're your issues determine what the intensity level of feeling is regarding this concern. Rate: 1 (being low) –10 (being high) intensity level: _____

What I want to feel:

Setup Statements–State each of these while tapping on the karate chop point:

Even though a part of me _____, *I accept all aspects of me completely and fully or* _____.

Even though that part of me _____, *I accept all aspects of me completely and fully or* _____.

Even though that part of me won't _____, *I choose to try something new on its behalf or* _____.

Now refer to your responses above and use the worksheet on the next page to design your own unique reminder phrases. Remember, you are moving first through your negative feelings, then to the possibility of change, then to a conviction for change. Come up with a reminder phrase for each endpoint. Then tap on this point 5–7 times while repeating your phrase.

Neutralizing the Negative
Possibility of Change

Eyebrow: _____

Side of the Eye: _____

Under the Eye: _____

Upper Lip: _____

Under the Lip: _____

Collarbone: _____

Under the Arm: _____

ChestBone: _____

Wrist: _____

Head: _____

Repeat sequences, altering words accordingly, until, on a scale from 1–10, you feel at least a 2 or 3. Then proceed. When you are ready to move into the possibility that something different can occur, come up with a reminder phrase for each of the endpoints below, then tap on this point 5–7 times while repeating your phrase.

Possibility of Change
Eyebrow: _____
Side of the Eye: _____
Under the Eye: _____
Upper Lip: _____
Under the Lip: _____
Collarbone: _____
Under the Arm: _____
ChestBone: _____
Wrist: _____
Head: _____

To complete this series, come up with phrases which capture your true conviction to feel or do something new. When you are ready to move into strengthening that conviction, tap on each of the endpoints on the EFT graph 5–7 times while repeating your phrase.

Conviction of Sequences
Possibility of Change
Eyebrow: _____
Side of the Eye: _____
Under the Eye: _____
Upper Lip: _____
Under the Lip: _____
Collarbone: _____
Under the Arm: _____
ChestBone: _____
Wrist: _____
Head: _____

Again, if you are interested in pursuing your inner child work please check out the mother book of all of my publications, *The Inner Child Workbook*, or my *Share the Gift* book, which includes the 4-part module application on attracting intimate relationships, abundance, right livelihood, and reciprocal partnerships.

If you are suffering a personal loss of a loved one then I invite you to read *Beyond Compassion*. If that loved one is a pet then you might also enjoy reading my shamanic tale called, *Maximized.*

Soul Steps takes this work into integrating your body, mind, heart, and Soul through "conscious aerobic exercise™".

Which Lifetime Is This Anyway? Which guides you through the multiple dimensions of your personality and Soul; and Life Beyond Confusion and Fear gives you a Four Stage model for multidimensionally dealing your addictions, compulsions, manifestations. Each of these can be found at www.EFTForYourInnerChild.com or purchased through Amazon.com in printed form or as a Kindle book.

Sample Daily Check-In Sheets For Day # Date:

Use this sheet as a guide to set your intentions for each day of the week. Make a note regarding what you would like to focus on today during your workout:

_____

_____

Exercise Intention for the day: _____

Spiritual Connection for the day: _____

Angel Card for the day: _____

Thoughts: _____

Food Plan for the day: _____

General Feelings for the day: _____

SAMPLE 7-DAY REVIEW

Date: _____

Take a few moments to review your work from this past week-then reflect on how these discoveries weave into your relationship to your body, mind, heart, and Soul. How can this new information be used in the ever-evolving development of your future self? What new behaviors, thoughts and actions would you like to try this next month; how might those efforts contribute to your new self? Always remember, reinventing yourself and becoming who you want to be occurs one step at a time. This review will support that evolvement. Record your thoughts and feelings in your journal.

Daily Workouts—Nutritional Replacement And Enhancement Belief Systems Which Relate To This Week's Focus:

Keeping In Mind That Your Heart Is Also An Emotional Muscle, What Is Your Heart Response To This Week's Work:

Connection To Your Angels or Spiritual Source:

Impact On The Development Of Your Future Self:

Based on the above reflection—what new behaviors would you like to experiment with in this upcoming week? Envision how this will contribute to who you want to be as you establish the next step in the evolution of the new you.

ABOUT THE AUTHOR

ATHRYN TAYLOR IS the author of, *The Inner Child Workbook-What To Do With Your Past When It Just Won't Go Away*, which was published by Jeremy P. Tarcher, Inc. in 1991. Since that time it has been translated into Dutch, Spanish, Czech, Romanian, and Korean, is in its 40th printing and can still be found on the bookshelves of Barnes and Noble and through Amazon.com.

Cathryn was licensed in the state of California in 1979 as a Marriage and Family Therapist was certified in Chemical Dependency in 1985 and is now licensed in the state of Minnesota as an Alcohol and Drug Counselor and as a Marriage and Family Therapist. She is also trained as a Personal Life Coach, an EMDR practitioner; a practitioner of Gary Craig's Emotional Freedom Techniques and is a certified EFT practitioner by EFT Master Lindsay Kenny. EFT is a self-administered form of acupressure that shows great promise in resolving stress-related issues and biochemical imbalances. These challenges originate in childhood. They, however, emerge n adulthood–not only as compulsions, addictions, and spiritual and mental challenges, but also, and perhaps more profoundly, as severe emotional traumas (such as post-traumatic-stress-disorder–PTSD, depression, anxiety, or unresolved grief). Cathryn has recently obtained certification in David Bercelli's Tension and Trauma Release Exercises, commonly referred to as TRE®. This technique completes Cathryn's healing modality. She weaves each of these additional methods of healing with her expertise of the inner child work in a very dynamic and expansive way. Her approach incorporates consultation and facilitation—assisting individuals in building the relationship between their Higher Self, their Adult Self, and their Children Within.

Cathryn's signature brand of tapping referred to as Interactive Tapping™ assists individuals in arresting addictive behaviors and in addressing all concerns of the psyche. The muscular release experienced with the Trauma Release Exercises (TRE®) supports the body's ultimate health. To obtain insight regarding the spiritual aspect of childhood traumas Cathryn acquired additional training as an Akashic Records Consultant which provides the soul's perspective on issues needing resolution. She is one of the first practitioners to merge the psychological, addictive, and spiritual perspectives with the energy therapies of EFT and TRE® to offer one of the most comprehensive modalities available.

Cathryn is well-known in the mental health community as an integrationist. She has an uncanny ability to weave all the above methods of healing together and continues to offer on-going assistance and direction through interviews, guest appearances on summits and seminars, and her 100+ YouTube educational videos which have established Cathryn as a leading inner child and soul expert throughout the world.

To visit her YouTube channel, click here:

https://www.youtube.com/user/ctinnerchildwork

To view a video illustrating her most recent work, click here:

From Therapist to Medium

Her website: www.EFTForYourInnerChild.com

To contact Cathryn directly please call her at 1.612.710.7720.

Made in the USA
Middletown, DE
13 November 2023

42611966R00223